To Geral,

In light

Jennifer

ARTHUR
of
BRITAIN

*Universal Archetype for Healthy
Chakra Development*

JENNIFER SAULT

BALBOA.
PRESS

A DIVISION OF HAY HOUSE

Balboa Press books may be ordered through booksellers or by contacting:

Balboa Press
A Division of Hay House
1663 Liberty Drive
Bloomington, IN 47403
www.balboapress.com
1 (877) 407-4847

Print information available on the last page.

ISBN: 978-1-9822-0949-0 (sc)
ISBN: 978-1-9822-0950-6 (hc)
ISBN: 978-1-9822-0951-3 (e)

Library of Congress Control Number: 2018909915

Balboa Press rev. date: 08/27/2018

For my precious Izabella

Contents

Preface

We shall not cease from exploration
and the end of all our exploring
Will be to arrive where we started
And know the place for the first time.

From *Little Gidding* by T. S. Eliot

That is how it was for me when I came home to King Arthur: I knew him for the first time. I had loved the stories as a child; not for their spiritual wisdom—at least not consciously: I grew up in Yorkshire in the north of England and whatever I had of spiritual teaching was in the tradition of John Wesley and the Methodist Church—but simply because they are wonderful stories. Later on, after my exploration of other spiritual teachings of the west and east had led me to the chakra system of Kundalini yoga, I rediscovered the Arthurian legends and found that they were saying the same thing, wrapped in a different package.

Since earliest times our species has transmitted its collective wisdom through songs and stories. And since earliest times an important part of that collective wisdom was devoted to the search for Transcendent Truth, the truth that informs and animates and gives meaning to all that is. It is something that most of us can perceive only briefly, perhaps during moments in deep meditation when we experience a kind of all-encompassing knowing, or when we watch the sun set or rise and we know, fleetingly, that all is right with the world. Those moments transcend the boundaries of space and time and cannot be communicated through reasoned argument, and so mystics over the ages, in trying to share their spiritual insights with the rest of us, have used the figurative language of myth, metaphor, allegory, and parable.

This is the tradition to which the Arthurian stories belong. They are more than legend, or stories told for entertainment; they are myths in the original meaning of that term, a story that conveys a spiritual truth.

Too often, though, we have taken the figurative language of our sacred stories literally, and instead of viewing stories from diverse cultures and traditions as different ways of communicating the same Truth, we have developed many and varied spiritual traditions that seem to be very different, when in fact, in their essence, they are all the same. A disastrous consequence of confusing the two kinds of truth and of taking a symbolic truth literally is that we have to say that everybody else is wrong. When her creation myth says that god is male and created the world in seven days through the power of his word, and his creation myth says that god is a female spider who wove the world into being out of her own body, the literal left brain has to make a choice. It cannot accept that both stories are true. When each of us becomes locked into the belief that our sacred story is the one and only truth it is only a short step to the belief that we have to fight to defend it, hence the religious wars, the crusades, the inquisitions, the genocides, the jihads of our collective past.

In recent decades numerous Western authors and thinkers have begun to seek a common truth underlying various spiritual traditions instead of focusing on the differences between them, and they have identified similarities between Eastern and Western spiritual traditions, between Eastern spiritual concepts and Western psychological theory, and between Eastern philosophy and quantum physics. Thanks to these discoveries we have realized that the spiritual map is not a single authority but myriad individual maps that each of us designs specifically for our own spiritual journey, taking from many religious and spiritual traditions those parts that resonate as Truth within our own souls. And we are finding those truths not only within the major religious traditions of East and West, but also within pagan earth-based religions, in shamanic teachings, and in myths.

King Arthur and his Companions of the Round Table is one of our most beloved myths. It has captured the hearts and minds of much of the world for some fifteen hundred years, and there has been more written about King Arthur than about any other topic in human history, including the Bible. There are the historical sources based on archeology, and those based on written sources such as epics, annals, and chronicles; there is a vast body of research and commentary on the medieval literary sources; there are historical sources based on oral tradition; there are psychological interpretations; there are fictional adaptations: novels, movies, and TV series; there are Tarot cards; and there is probably much more.

This book makes no claim to expertise in any of these areas. It is my interpretation of the aspect of the Arthurian myth that speaks most intimately to me, and I offer it as an invitation to consider a common truth underlying a western myth and an eastern philosophy. And, like everyone else, in retelling the stories I have taken great liberties of the imagination while remaining true, I believe, to the symbolic truth. My hope is that you will find here at least some pieces that will fit into your own spiritual map. This book approaches the legend of King Arthur from four perspectives: an historical context; a retelling of some of the legends; a spiritual interpretation that correlates the legends with chakra development; and personal experience through guided imagery meditations that use the archetypal symbols of the myth to awaken and bring into consciousness the resources and knowledge that we all carry within.

Guided imagery is a tool that allows us to communicate with the deepest aspects of our being. Imagery is the natural language of the subconscious mind; it is the language in which we store our memories, and it is the language in which the deeper levels of our mind communicate with us through dreams and reveries. We all use the language of imagery all the time. It is a very powerful language, but it is one in which most of us are not well educated. Our education system is based on verbal language, the left-brain, logical, analytical, sequential way of thinking. We are taught to dismiss the imagination as somehow not real and to give credence only to the logical and analytical and the empirically proven. We use imagery, therefore, largely unconsciously and often in negative ways, most often when we worry. Worrying is nothing more than creating an image of something negative or frightening that may happen, and as we know that image can have the power to give us tension headaches, insomnia or digestive problems. Stress is largely the creation of scary images, and stress is a factor in all illness because it depresses the immune system.

When we follow a guided meditation we use the language of imagery in a positive way to lead us into the deeper levels of our mind and being to discover the wisdom and guidance that we all carry within. When we are following a guided meditation our minds are functioning on many levels at the same time; the conscious mind may be listening to the surface meaning while the unconscious mind is understanding the symbolic significance. The unconscious takes what is relevant, what is most meaningful to us at any given time, and makes the connections that are most helpful to us.

The guided meditations in this book use the mythological elements—the archetypal patterns and symbols—of the Arthurian legends in order to reawaken the inner knowing of those truths that we seek. In the guided meditations we can journey through the myths of King Arthur and explore the symbolic significance for each of us of the characters and the symbols in the myth. The Arthurian myth can be one part of the map we create for our individual spiritual journey as we gather pieces of many different teachings that together work uniquely for us.

Introduction

At the dawn of humankind the islands of Britain on the remote western fringes of the European continent were lands of lush forests and fertile lowlands. To the east, low-lying marshland and numerous estuaries offered easy access to raiders and invaders from various parts of the European continent. The Gulf Stream gentles the climate of Britain and the mild winters in a land so far to the north must have seemed miraculous to tribesmen from the central and northern areas of the continent. Spurred by overpopulation and hunger and the promise of plunder successive waves of invaders descended on to the shores of the fairest isles. They raped and pillaged and carried off slaves and, in time, decided to stay.

Invasion. Resistance. Assimilation. Invasion. For thousands of years the cycle repeated itself, until in the centuries before the Roman conquest the tribes collectively known as Celts dominated the Isles of Britain. They shared a common culture—similarities of language, spiritual beliefs under the guidance of the Druids, metalworking, art, social structure and a love of fighting—but politically the land was divided into several Celtic kingdoms that continued to fight each other. One such kingdom was Rheged, whose ruler Coel was immortalized as Old King Cole, the merry old soul, in a nursery rhyme still sung by children in Britain today. Another was the land of the Iceni whose queen, Boudicca, led the most famous revolt against Roman domination. Sometimes there were loose confederations of tribes against a common enemy—such as that organized by Boudicca—but the Celts were fiercely independent and these never lasted for long.

When the Romans first came to Britain it was under the leadership of Julius Caesar, but he penetrated barely ten miles inland before more pressing conquests drew his attention elsewhere. It was to be almost a hundred years before Claudius led the definitive invasion force that conquered what is now England and Wales.

To the west and north Britain is mountainous, more of a challenge to invaders than the lowlands of the east, and it was to the mountains that the inhabitants fled when faced with superior numbers or superior technology. The Romans never did conquer what is now Scotland in the north. There Celtic culture survives, behind what is left of the wall that the Emperor Hadrian built from coast to coast to try and keep the blue-painted barbarians at bay.

For some four centuries Rome defended the coasts of Britain, exploited its mineral and human resources, and maintained the *Pax Romana*. Many Celts accepted Roman domination, particularly in the south where Briton and Roman were assimilated into a common culture, but Roman might had to contend with continuing rebellions by some Celtic tribes, and then invasions by Germanic tribes that were nibbling at the fringes of the Empire in Britain as elsewhere. After Rome fell early in the fifth century and the legions withdrew from Britain the old Celtic tribes reclaimed their lands and took up their ancient pastime of fighting each other. They were again overrun by invaders who eradicated Roman culture, destroyed the Roman cities, burned the libraries and plunged the country into the Dark Ages.

In that darkness, legend tells us, was a brief flash of light: King Arthur.

By the time of the Roman withdrawal the Celts were probably divided. Some no doubt still followed the old ways under the guidance of the Druids, who honored the land as sacred and continued to venerate feminine forms of divinity and to share power equally with women, but after four centuries of Roman rule much of the Celtic population in the south had assimilated Roman civilization, which had a patriarchal structure and was by that time officially Christian.

The story of the spread of Christianity to Britain in the early centuries after Christ is scarce in evidence. There are the stories of Joseph of Arimathea, a wealthy tin merchant with probable ties to the tin mines of Cornwall, who is said not only to have visited Britain after the crucifixion, bearing the cup of the last supper and the blood of Christ, but also to have taken the young Jesus— who may have been his nephew—to Britain to study the ancient wisdom of the Druids. Christianity may have spread to Britain along the trade routes from the Middle East in the first and second centuries CE. Christianity became the official religion of the Roman Empire in the fourth century, some say as a deal of mutual benefit between the tottering Empire and a Christianity split by schism that then became the monolithic Church of Rome. But Roman Christianity was centered on Constantinople in the east and was slow to predominate over all other religions in the west. Of the close to 300 bishops at the Council of Nicaea none came from Britain.

Christians—like many before them—sought to encourage the acceptance of their doctrine by taking over existing sacred places and symbols. Churches were often built on existing sacred sites, and sacred places—like the sacred stories, like the deities themselves— were adapted to fit different belief systems. Just as the Celtic Sula, Goddess of water, had become the Roman Minerva, the Celtic goddess Brigantia or Bride became St Brigid. But people are slow to change all levels of their spiritual beliefs and we cannot say, at this remove, how deeply the conversion to Christianity had impacted the belief systems of the people by the fifth and sixth centuries, the time of King Arthur. The well-documented spread of Christianity to Britain and its dominance over all other religions did not take place until Saxon times, a couple of centuries after Arthur.

Many versions of the Arthurian legends, certainly the medieval ones—most notably *Le Morte d'Arthur* by Thomas Malory—portray Arthur as a Christian king. More recent interpretations, such as

The Mists of Avalon, describe the time of King Arthur as a time of conflict between the ancient ways of the Druids and the new Christian religion. Arthur's religion—like Arthur's military skill, like Arthur's very existence—has been long debated, and barring the discovery of some definitive contemporary evidence the truth of it will never be known. Mary Stewart, author of the *Merlin Trilogy*, opines that when Gildas the monk, writing in about 540 AD, mentions the victory of Mount Badon without mentioning Arthur, he may have been indicating disapproval of a leader who had shown himself no friend to the Church.

Notwithstanding the medieval versions of the story, it is probable that Christianity in Arthur's Britain was a relatively minor phenomenon. Stewart Perowne believes that the tone of Roman society remained predominantly pagan throughout the fourth century and well into the fifth, and if that was the situation in Rome, how much more so is it likely to have been the situation in the furthest western outpost of the Empire, in Britain?

King Arthur was probably a Romanized Celt. Everything about the historical Arthur is only probable or possible. Any contemporary written evidence has long since disappeared; perhaps the Saxons or the Vikings destroyed it, perhaps it never existed. There is doubt, in academic circles, as to whether there was an historical Arthur at all, or if there was, when and where he lived. (The movie *King Arthur*, which claims to be historically based, posits that the historical figure who inspired the legends of King Arthur was a Roman soldier, Arturius Castus, who was stationed on Hadrian's Wall. Castus lived in the second century, and his enemies were the Celtic Britons. The movie transposes him into the fifth century, where he becomes the champion of the Celtic Britons in their fight against the Saxons. Such liberties characterize much of the search for an historical Arthur.)

Whatever their origin, the legends of King Arthur—a large and diverse collection of tales, sometimes only loosely associated with King Arthur—persisted in poetry, song and folk tale for several hundred years. They were not collected and organized into a coherent narrative until the Middle Ages, and the Arthurian legends most familiar to us now have been overlaid with the ideals and values of the medieval period, the age of crusades, chivalry and romance.

The Middle Ages were times of chaos—perpetual warfare, the Black Death—when life was indeed "nasty, brutish and short." It was a time that cried out for a belief in something greater, something noble and good. And it was a time that embraced the stories of King Arthur, as have many ages since, as an ideal, a reminder of the best that we can be when all around us we see the worst. Successive ages have continued to interpret the legends according to the needs of the time. Twain, Longfellow and Wagner in the nineteenth century reflected the mores of their time and place in their versions of the legend. For T. H. White, writing *The Once and Future King* in the nineteen thirties, the legends were a vehicle for his pessimistic view of the human species and the dangers of totalitarianism in Nazi Germany and Soviet Russia. Marion Zimmer Bradley in *The Mists of Avalon* in the nineteen sixties reclaimed the divine feminine through a new interpretation of Morgan le Fey, while Mary Stewart in her brilliant life of Merlin explored a pagan spirituality that is now witnessing a rebirth. Like the novels, each of the other contemporary sources—films, musicals, and TV series—has a particular interpretation, each has been highly selective in its choice of source material, and each has invented new material to bridge awkward gaps and inconsistencies.

The archeological evidence, too, is controversial. It is based on probability and more or less intelligent guesswork. You read the sources and you make your own choice, and whichever choice you make there are going to be myriad unanswered questions, and archeologists, historians and medievalists who will "prove" the opposite. Some historians cite political reasons why the myth endured. The myth of Arthur became the defining myth of Britain as a political unit, and it was adopted and tailored, some say, to legitimize the Tudors after the Wars of the Roses in the fifteenth century, as the myth of Charlemagne legitimized France.

Though tradition locates the myth of Arthur in the south of England, recent scholarship makes a compelling case for his having lived in Scotland, and for all his twelve battles having being fought in the area that is now the border between Scotland and England. In many ways that makes more sense, both geographically and historically. It would explain, for example, why King Lot of the Orkneys—a remote group of islands off the northern coast of Scotland, practically in the Arctic Circle—manages to play a prominent role in the legends, and why King Arthur is not mentioned in the Saxon chronicles, since the Saxons never conquered Scotland. In that case, the medievalist Norma Goodrich's argument goes, Avalon would have been the Isle of Man, not Glastonbury, and Camelot would have been the Roman city of Carlisle in northern England, not Castle Cadbury.

Whether or not they are the "true" Arthurian sites, the places that are most commonly associated with Arthur—Tintagel in Cornwall, said to be the site of Arthur's conception and birth; Castle Cadbury in Wiltshire, considered by some the most likely site of Camelot; and Glastonbury in Somerset, that claims to be the mystical Isle of Avalon—are places of power that would have been sacred in pagan times. The hill fort of Castle Cadbury would have been a sacred site to the Celts because it is a natural hill that rises high above the surrounding area. High ground was sacred to the Celts because it was believed that there the veil between the worlds was thin. For the same reason, Tintagel in Cornwall was no doubt a sacred site long before the monastery and the castle that have been discovered through archeological excavation. At Glastonbury there are two sites, side by side, that would have been sacred to ancient peoples: the Tor, on which are remnants of terraces, or possibly an ancient ritual maze; and the spring now known as Chalice Well.

In any case, whether or not Tintagel, Castle Cadbury and Glastonbury were the "genuine" Arthurian sites, 1500 years of belief that they were have created their own magick.

These stories of a brave and noble king and his devoted companions have enduring relevance because the symbols and characters are archetypal; they answer some call of our souls beyond the specifics of time and place. They do take place in a particular place and at a particular time in British history, and at the same time their symbolism transcends those specifics of time and place to convey Truths valid for all times and places. Arthur, for example, was the High King of Britain, so much a part of his kingdom that he came to be identified with the land; he became the symbol of Britain itself. Arthur's bond with Britain represents the bond between each of us and the land, between us and the planet that we live on, the sacred bond between heaven and earth, between spirit and the physical plane; it symbolizes our first chakra connection to the earth.

Claude Levi Strauss, the French anthropologist who pioneered the study of myth, taught that myths are the collective dreams of a culture, and he suggested that just as an analysis of our dreams can help us to understand ourselves, so can an understanding of a culture's myths help us to understand that culture. We can take that idea further, and say that an understanding of the elements common to myths throughout the world can help us to understand life, reality, and our reason for being. We know from the work of Joseph Campbell that myths all over the world have similar themes and similar symbols, as if they were all drawing their inspiration from the same source. Which indeed they are. They draw their inspiration from the collective unconscious, from that level of spiritual reality where we are all connected, and which is the realm of archetypes, or universal energy patterns.

The term "collective unconscious" comes from the work of Carl Jung, who began his career as a student of Sigmund Freud but broke away from his mentor over their differing understanding of the nature of the unconscious. For Freud, the unconscious was a maelstrom of primitive and repressed sexual urges that holds us at its mercy. For Jung, the unconscious was a reservoir of unlimited potential.

Jung conceptualized the unconscious as separated into a personal unconscious and a collective unconscious. Imagine a series of waves on the surface of the ocean: the tops of the waves correspond to our individual conscious minds, and at this level of consciousness we have the perception of being separate beings. The body of the wave is the individual unconscious, again reflecting individual experience, and is where we hold all our memories, attitudes, beliefs and fears. The ocean is the collective unconscious where we are all one, and is the realm of archetypes, or universal energy patterns. And it is from this level of consciousness that we draw the symbols that inspire our myths, the stories that inform and shape our cultures, and whose elements are remarkably similar all over the world.

Archetypal symbols, deep in our tribal memory, have been mythologized in the stories of King Arthur, which is why these myths and legends continue to hold fascination for us. They embody archetypes that link us through the collective unconscious with myths and archetypes common to cultures all over our planet. They are the archetypes that we all share, at the level of the collective unconscious in Jungian terms, or at the level of the Great Sacred Mystery in Native American terms, at the level of the World of Emanation in the Kabbalistic tradition, or at the level of the shamanic journey. Though we may respond viscerally to one path more than another they are all leading us in the same direction.

The Arthurian myth is the universal story of the human drive towards self-realization. It is the quest for justice, for wisdom and truth and meaning, for enlightenment, and we can use the legends as a map in our own individual spiritual journeys. The myth of King Arthur and his Companions of the Round Table is one particular culture's way of communicating the same eternal truth that is expressed in different ways in all religious traditions and cultural myths; different, and yet all the same. In the tradition of Yoga, the chakra system teaches the same truth.

So the intricate, painstaking and ingenious investigations into the historical reality of Arthur, Merlin and the Holy Grail—by medievalists such as Norma Goodrich, for example, whose linguistic detective work is spellbinding, or the historian Geoffrey Ashe, or the archeologist Leslie Alcock—are not necessary to a spiritual and archetypal approach to the legends. The deeper truth of myth is not tied to any specific time or place. In the search for the timeless spiritual truths of the Arthurian myth it is irrelevant where and when exactly an historical Arthur was born, lived, or fought his battles, or in fact whether he lived at all. Or if he did, whether he was in fact the courageous, just, charismatic, honest, kind, brilliant military strategist of legend.

What is relevant is the way in which our collective wisdom over the centuries has molded and crafted these stories so that they emerge as a coherent spiritual truth. Myths create their own reality, and what is meaningful to a spiritual interpretation of the legends is the archetype that Arthur represents, and the developmental stages that he passes through in order to become the best a person can be, regardless of the specific circumstances of time and place in which a particular life on the physical plane takes place. We might compare the myth of King Arthur to the Bhagavad-Gita, an ancient sacred text of the Hindu tradition, in which Arjuna is asking the god Krishna for advice on how, or indeed whether, to fight a battle, because those whom he has to fight are his relatives. It is within the context of that particularity—a fratricidal war—that timeless truths are articulated.

The Chakra System

We are, Yogi Bhajan reminds us, spiritual beings having a human experience. The human experience provides the opportunity for our souls to heal and for our spirits to develop. Our bodies, minds and emotions are our teachers in this process, and the chakra system offers us a tool for understanding physical, mental and emotional development within a spiritual framework.

Our knowledge of chakras comes from the eastern tradition of Kundalini yoga, though in recent years many westerners sensitive to the subtle energy bodies have also perceived the chakras, for example Caroline Myss in *Anatomy of the Spirit* and other works,

Barbara Brennan in *Hands of Light*, and W. Brugh Joy in *Joy's Way*, to name but a very few. The chakras are seven energy centers within the body that govern stages of development. Kundalini Shakti, the divine within, is symbolized as a serpent coiled at the base of the spine. As we develop—physically, emotionally, mentally and spiritually—the serpent gradually uncoils herself and reaches up the spine, energizing each of the chakras in turn. When the serpent reaches the seventh chakra at the crown of the head she joins with the masculine Shiva and we experience what in the Hindu tradition is called Samadhi, the ecstasy of the spiritual connection: enlightenment, or what in Western psychological terminology has been called self-realization.

At each chakra there are certain developmental tasks, or life lessons, to be confronted and resolved. When we successfully resolve those challenges we are empowered, our consciousness expands, and we create another stable rung on our ladder to enlightenment. When we do not understand or recognize the spiritual lesson of the challenge a part of the psyche can become blocked and fail to develop. We may lose energy in blaming or feeling victimized. We can, over time, develop physical illness in the part of the body associated with the chakra where the energy block occurred.

The life of King Arthur is a blueprint for the regular and sequential opening, nourishment and balancing of the chakras. Arthur shows us how create a strong and stable foundation in the first three chakras through his example of how to live within the world, doing the best we can to live honorably and honestly, accepting responsibility for our mistakes and learning from them. The Arthurian myth shows us how to balance our masculine and feminine energies, how to open the heart that is the doorway to the inner planes as we develop the upper chakras, growing towards the full realization of our potential. Always, like Arthur, we have the guidance of Merlin, archetype of the inner spiritual teacher and counselor.

Most of us do not proceed smoothly along this path. We have wounds or gaps in our development, traumas that keep parts of the psyche stuck in emotional pain, parts of us that fail to develop. We can also use the legends as a kind of diagnostic tool, to identify those wounds and recruit the inner resources to help us heal.

We will begin the inner journey with the Triple Shield of Light meditation. Find a comfortable place, turn off the phone and ask anybody sharing your living space not to disturb you for twenty minutes or so. As you proceed you may choose to record the meditations in your own voice, or perhaps take turns reading them to each other in a group. You may want to keep a Quest Journal of your meditative experiences. Perhaps you would like to create a sacred place for your meditations: a quiet corner of your home, perhaps, with an altar. You can light a candle or burn incense if you like, and perhaps as time goes on collect for your altar objects and symbols that are meaningful to you. Ritual is not a necessary part of meditation, but it can be helpful in creating a peaceful and focused state of mind because it signals all levels of the mind that you are about to engage in something of great importance and meaning.

Begin by taking some deep abdominal breaths, and hold the intention of opening your mind and your heart to the protective and relaxing imagery that will underlie all phases of your journey though the Arthurian myth. It would be best to practice this meditation daily. In time, the protective imagery will become second nature and will provide a safe environment for self-exploration, as well as a protective shield that you can carry with you always. Remember that an image is not necessarily a picture; it can be a thought form, a sensing, or inner knowing.

Triple Shield of Light meditation

Sit comfortably in a place where you can be free of interruptions for twenty minutes or so. Sit with your spine erect, either in a chair or cross legged on the floor. If you are on the floor, sitting on the edge of a cushion or a folded blanket will tilt your pelvis and lower your knees which will allow you to maintain an erect spine without effort. Begin with three complete breaths, consciously drawing the breath all the way down into your lower lungs so that your abdomen expands on the inbreath, and deflates on the outbreath. Deep breath in now to the count of four ... 1, 2, 3, 4 ... and out to the count of 4, drawing the abdomen back towards the spine and expelling all the used air. Inhaling ... 1, 2, 3, 4 ... and exhaling ... 1, 2 3 4. One more deep, complete breath in ... and out. Relax your breathing now, breathing normally, just allowing your body to breathe itself.

Imagine that in the ground beneath you there is a glowing sphere of light. The upper surface of this sphere touches the soles of your feet, or your thighs, buttocks and ankles if you're sitting cross legged, and from its lower surface a strand of light reaches deep into the heart of the planet, down to the very molten core of the earth, symbolizing your connection with the earth, keeping you grounded, stable and safe. With the breath now, begin to raise this sphere of light, up into your feet and your legs, to the top of your thighs, so that your legs and feet are contained within it.

This part of your body corresponds to the element earth. Think of mountains and valleys, forests, grasslands, deserts, and fields of grain. The blessings of earth are stability and strength, nourishment and support. Your sense of being grounded, of being solidly and strongly connected to earth, gives you a stable foundation on which to construct the rest of your personality. You can perhaps offer thanks to this precious element that nourishes and supports you, and accept with gratitude the blessings of earth as you affirm to yourself: I am grounded. I am stable and safe. I am strong. I am nourished and supported.

Repeat this to yourself and experience the truth of it: I am grounded. I am stable and safe. I am strong. I am nourished and supported. I am grounded. I am stable and safe. I am strong. I am nourished and supported.

With the breath now, raise the ball of light to the level of your waist. The pelvic area is the part of your body that corresponds to the element water. While earth represents your physical body, water represents the energy of emotion. Where earth is solid and stable, water is fluid and changeable; it conforms to the shape of its container. Think of the many ways that water can manifest. Take yourself in your imagination to a mountain lake; the surface is calm and still and reflects the surrounding mountains and overhead clouds. Allow yourself to feel the silence and the deep peace of the waters. And then take yourself to a stream high in the mountains. Here the water flows swiftly, imagine that you can hear the happy bubbling sound the water makes as it falls over rocks on its way down the mountain. Go in your mind to visit a mature river, where the movement is slow, barely perceptible in fact, and then visit Niagara Falls where millions of gallons of water fall every second from a great height, creating a roar that drowns out all other sound. Imagine being on a mountain top in the early morning, watching the mist in the valley below slowly evaporate as the sun rises, and then take yourself to the north or south pole, where water is locked in the ice of the polar caps.

Water corresponds to emotional energy. Like water, our emotions are changeable. In the course of the day, or sometimes within hours or minutes, we can feel happy and sad, anxious and calm, angry and relaxed. It is the firm grounding in the earth that creates the container for the flowing energy of emotion. If there is no container, if we are not grounded, emotional energy can feel out of control. Or at the other end of the continuum, if the container is too small or too rigid, emotional energy cannot flow. When these two feminine elements of earth and water are in balance, emotional energy can flow freely within appropriate boundaries.

Raise the sphere of light to the level of your shoulders now, and think of the element fire. Fire too can wear many faces. Fire can be the gentle glow of a candle flame, the comfort and security of a camp fire, or the raging energy of a forest fire that is part of the natural cycle of death and rebirth. There are certain plant species that can germinate only after a fire, which cleanses the debris and opens the forest to the light. Fire is purifying and transformative. We refer to our life challenges as tests of fire, and is through our tests of fire that the soul is tempered and strengthened, and recognizes its true purpose. Experience tempers and tests us just as a sword master tempers and tests the steel of a great sword. The steel is heated and beaten over and over again, and through this process all the impurities and weaknesses are removed and the sword reaches towards perfection, flexible and strong. Think of the sacred sword Excalibur, its blade so perfect that it sings; it is the sword of truth that will serve you in your journey through the myths of King Arthur.

Raise the sphere of light now above your head, the part of the being that corresponds to the element air. The blessings of air are inspiration, and life. When we are born, our first breath signals our emergence into physical reality as a separate being, it is our first action within physical form, the beginning of a new life. We are told that God breathed life into the first human created. We are inspired by the sacred breath. And just as we seek to create balance between the feminine elements of earth and water, so do we need balance between the masculine elements of fire and air. Without air, fire cannot burn. Without fire, air would be too cold to sustain life.

The entire body is now filled and surrounded by this glowing sphere of light, connected to the heart of the planet by a strand of light from its lower surface. Within the feminine elements of earth and water, we balance and harmonize the strength, stability and solidity of the physical body with the flowing energy of the emotions. And within the masculine elements of air and fire we integrate the power of mind with the energy of fire that brings ideas and inspirations into physical form.

This is the first shield of light, and as you probably know, what you imagine, and where you put your focus, creates your reality. So imagine that this shield of light is protective, and that all negative energy simply bounces off it: negative words, negative thoughts, feelings or actions *bounce off the shield of light and you are safe inside. You can perhaps give that energy a symbolic form, little colored balls perhaps, that bounce off the shield of light, or little arrows that bend and break as they come into contact with it. Only energy that is loving, empowering, and positive can penetrate the shield of light and reach you on the inside.*

Imagine now a second glowing sphere of light above your head. The lower surface touches your crown, and from the upper surface a strand of light reaches high into the heavens, symbolizing your connection with the spiritual source, however you conceive that to be. As you bring this sphere of light down over your body, you are going to breathe light into each of your chakras, the energy centers in your body that are places of interchange between spiritual, mental, emotional and physical energy. As you use the breath to bring the sphere of light down over your body, open and energize each chakra by breathing light into it, and imagine the chakra clear and in balance. At the crown, you can imagine a cone of light, the point touching the top of the head and opening upwards. And at the base of the spine the root chakra opens towards the ground. All the other chakras open both in the front and the back of the body, like two cones of light whose points meet at the chakra.

So breathe light now into Sahasrara, the crown center at the top of your head; into Ajna chakra, the third eye center in the middle of your skull; into Vissudha chakra at your throat center; Anahata chakra at your heart center; Manipura chakra at your solar plexus; Svadhisthana chakra just below your navel; and Muladhara chakra, the root center at the base of your spine. And now breathing the light down your legs and beneath your feet. The glowing sphere of light from above, the second shield of light, now becomes integrated with the sphere of light from below. From the lower surface a strand of light reaches deep into the earth, keeping you grounded and safe, and from the upper surface a strand of light reaches high into the heavens, your open and clear connection to the Source.

And you can perhaps see now, or sense, or feel, that the strand of light that reaches down into the earth, and the strand of light that reaches up to the Source, form a continuous column of light through your chakras, so that you are the bridge, the place of integration and balance and harmony, between heaven and earth, spirit and matter. And where those two strands of light meet, at your heart center, here—at the core of your being, the essence of who you are—is a third source of light, your inner light. Breathing into that light now, expanding it with each breath to fill your heart, to fill your torso, expanding into your limbs and your head and beyond your physical body to fill your energy field and create the third shield of light.

Filled and surrounded now by the triple shield of light, from below, from above and from within, you can allow yourself to sink deeply down, to deeper and deeper levels of mind, deeper levels of awareness and understanding, deeper and deeper levels of knowing. Safe within the triple shield of light you can take some time to simply be.

And when you are ready, you can begin to bring yourself back to full conscious awareness, bringing with you a sense of peace and safety, and bringing with you the image of the triple shield of light that you can keep with you always, a gentle reminder that you are safe, firmly grounded in the earth, with an open and clear connection to Spirit, honoring your own inner light. If you like you can take some time to record your experience in your Quest Journal.

PART I

Winter
Tintagel

Early in the fifth century the Romans abandoned Britain; Saxon raiders settled on the east and south coasts, what came to be called the Saxon Shore, and were constantly pressing to expand inland as well as giving welcome to their compatriots from across the seas. We read in the legends of three high kings of Britain—Ambrosius, Uther Pendragon, and Arthur—all trying to maintain a coalition of Celtic tribes to fight their common enemy, when Celtic tribes were often more interested in fighting each other.

We begin our story with the second of these high kings of Britain, Uther Pendragon. He was by all accounts a skilled warrior, though not so skilled as his brother Ambrosius in the art of politics; a man of great appetites and passion who fought and womanized with gusto. His sexual prowess was legendary, and fathers learned to guard their daughters and husbands their wives, because it was the thrill of pursuit and conquest that excited Uther. Until he saw Igraine.

Igraine and Uther

Igraine stands on the battlements staring into blackness. She cannot see the sea but she can hear it, an angry roar that would make conversation impossible even if there were anyone for her to talk to. And she can feel it; the wind is peppering her face with needles of ice-cold salt water from the waves that crash against the cliff wall beneath the castle walls. She closes her eyes and turns her face into the wind, almost enjoying the harshness of it after a day of being cooped up in the dark indoors and breathing stale smoky air. All day the spring storm has howled around the drafty old castle, as if some demon from the deep were trying to pluck it from its perch high on the cliff tops, but the castle—as Igraine knows to her cost— is as sturdy as the rock itself and can hold its own against any aggressor, even the angry sea.

Igraine wraps her cloak tightly around her. She is cold, and wet, but she cannot bear the thought of returning within the castle walls. As she thinks of her life with Gorlois, the old Duke of Cornwall, it seems as bleak and as empty as the castle itself, stretching before her into a future of unchanging lonely days. She almost despairs at the thought of squandering her youth and beauty locked away from the world in this desolate stronghold.

She thinks of Londinium with hopeless longing: the colors, the textures, the sounds of teeming life. Her brief time there was hardly a moment in the span of her life yet it feels more real to her than all the rest together. Igraine tries to wish she had never seen it, had never left this stark outpost where she had lived ever since her arranged marriage and where she had reached an acceptance of sorts of the life she had been given, but in spite of her present despair she cannot regret those moments that make all the other moments of her life seem wan and lifeless in comparison.

She had not wanted to go when her husband the Duke had first commanded that she accompany him to the capital. High King Ambrosius had died, some said by Saxon poison, and the nobles were gathering to celebrate the crowning of the new High King, Ambrosius's brother.

Uther Pendragon. "Uther Pendragon," she whispers to the wind. It is both delicious and heartbreaking to think of him. His image is as clear as if he were standing before her, his bright curly hair with its circle of gold, his fair skin and reddish beard, his tall muscular warrior's frame. In her mind's eye she sees him seated at the high table in the great hall, surrounded by light and color, music and laughter.

Gorlois had sweetened his command with promises of shopping in the Londinium market and she had indeed spent some happy hours there, buying fabrics and spices that were not to be found in the local markets of Cornwall. Their journey had taken several days and once on her way she had relished her brief freedom, disdaining her litter whenever the weather permitted and riding beside her husband. Gorlois, too, had been more relaxed and happy than she was used to seeing him. Though he had little idea of how to speak to a young woman—he had spent most of his life fighting—it pleased his vanity to ride with his young and beautiful wife beside him and he was kind to her in his own way.

She had dressed in her finest for the great banquet, decorated her hair with ribbons and fairings, and had sat—dutiful and bored— beside her husband as the men offered their oath of allegiance to the new High King. She had not been much interested in the ceremonies, or the new High King for that matter. She had heard tales of Uther's military prowess, and of his sexual exploits, and had indeed been advised by her husband to beware of him, but her interest had been focused elsewhere. She had never before seen such splendor, and her attention had wandered over the rich hangings on the walls and the sumptuous clothes of the people around her.

Then, during the banquet, as she turned to accept a morsel of lark's tongue offered to her by Gorlois, she had caught the High King looking at her, and as their eyes met it had seemed to Igraine as if she had known Uther from the beginning of time. In the noise and bustle of the great hall they had shared a moment of intimacy such as she had never felt before. The people and the activity around her faded away and she saw only Uther's eyes, full—like her own, she knew—of hopeless longing.

For the rest of the evening Uther had barely taken his eyes off her. He had sent delicacies on golden plates down to her, and repeatedly sent to inquire if she were content and needed for nothing. She remembered her husband's warnings but she saw that Uther was a young man unsophisticated in the art of dissembling. His heart was open and his thoughts and desires written on his face and it was clear to everyone—including the Duke—that he was smitten with Igraine.

Gorlois had abruptly stood, holding tightly to Igraine's arm, and with a stiff bow and a curt, "By your leave, my lord," he had practically dragged Igraine from the hall. They had walked back to their lodgings in silence; he had immediately given orders to pack their belongings and they had left Londinium before first light, without the consent of the High King.

Igraine shakes her head in despair. Uther and his army have followed them to Cornwall and Gorlois now stands accused of treason. He has left Igraine with a small contingent of soldiers in his castle at Tintagel, and despite the storm has ridden forth to challenge the High King. At this very moment the two armies are camped facing each other a few miles to the north at Dimilioc, and Igraine is here, locked in this dreary castle at the edge of the world. The wind, howling through the cave beneath the headland, sounds like a soul in torment, and Igraine shivers. She looks up at the night sky. The heavy clouds have been blown away and there are patches of stars. She searches the sky, but in the stars she can see no happy ending—for her, for Gorlois, or even for Uther.

Igraine had never seen Ambrosius but she knew he had been well loved by the people, and esteemed by most of the tribal kings as he led them in repelling the barbarians who raided and plundered incessantly now that the Roman legions had withdrawn from Britain. Igraine had heard the stories told of him in the market place, stories of his military might and the charisma that inspired the devotion of his followers. No such tales were told of his brother Uther. That Uther was a great warrior there was no doubt—he had been Ambrosius' battle chief—but as yet he had shown none of his brother's magnetism. There had already been strains in the fabric of Ambrosius' coalition before it had been rent by Gorlois' defection.

Igraine sighs in despair, turns her back to the wind and goes back inside to sit beside the hearth. The fire has died but she does not call a servant to rebuild it. The cold, empty hearth matches her mood. How can she bear to live here for the rest of her life, a prisoner of her husband's jealousy and with only little Morgan for company? She shivers and wraps her cloak more tightly around her, but it is soaking wet and offers little relief from the cold.

There is suddenly the sound of disturbance in the courtyard below. She can hear raised voices and running feet, and one of the men her husband left to guard her—keep her prisoner more like—bursts into the room. "My lady," he says, "my lord Gorlois has returned!" Immediately on his heels a tall man strides into the room. Igraine is confused. This man is obviously not Gorlois, but the servants are bowing to him and welcoming him home. She looks in confusion at the face beneath the hood, the face that has been haunting her sleeping and waking dreams.

"Come, Igraine," Uther says, with a warning look, and she leads him into her chamber.

"What is happening? Why do they call you Gorlois?"

"For that I have to thank Merlin. It is a glamour he conjured up out of the mists. But they will not be deceived for long, my beloved."

Tintagel

Tintagel, Cornwall

Cornwall, the peninsula on the southwest corner of England that juts out into the Atlantic, has a beautiful and dramatic northern coastline of high cliffs that continues to be sculpted by the ocean waves. Tintagel is a headland on this northern coast that is connected to the mainland by only a narrow spit of rock. Beneath the headland is a cave that runs clear through from one side to the other. At high tide the cave is flooded but at low tide it is possible to walk through it.

There are, sometimes, strange sounds within the cave. According to local legend the sounds are the laments of Merlin who was imprisoned in the cave by Nimue after she had tricked him into sharing the secrets of his magical power. (There is a cave on the west coast of Scotland that carries the same tradition.) At times, the mist that in legend is called the Dragon's Breath swirls through the cave. Continued erosion by the ocean will in time enlarge the cave even further and the rock above it will collapse, converting the headland into an island. Even that in all probability will at some point be swallowed by the ocean.

You can access the headland today by climbing steps cut into the rock and you can explore the remnants of a thirteenth century castle. Excavation has revealed evidence of an earlier structure from the fifth or sixth century, the time of King Arthur, possibly a monastery, possibly a castle, and pottery from the Mediterranean that indicates a site of some size and wealth. But long before any of these buildings the Celts would have revered the headland as a sacred place because it is high ground, where the veil between the worlds is thin.

At the highest point on the Tintagel headland a natural platform juts out over the Atlantic. Beneath it is a sheer drop down to the ocean. The roar of the waves is constant, even when the sea is relatively calm, and when the sea is rough it hurls itself against the cliff face with such force that the salt spray is flung several hundred feet into the air. The village of Tintagel is about a mile from the headland. Cornishmen did not build their villages on the coast but inland, because they were not fishermen; they were miners. There was a flourishing industry of copper and tin mining in Cornwall in biblical times, and vigorous trade with the countries of the Middle East.

From the village, a steep track leads down to the cove beneath the headland. The track ends abruptly at the edge of the cliff that falls sheer down to the cove's narrow and rocky shore, and on either side are towering cliffs, honeycombed with caves. Tintagel Castle is on the one to the left, and according to legend it was here, on the night of the spring equinox, that Arthur was conceived.

When Uther collected an army and followed Gorlois to Cornwall, Gorlois left Igraine in his castle and rode out with his army to challenge Uther. He believed Igraine to be safe and Tintagel to be impregnable. Indeed, if any castle were impregnable it would be Tintagel. The narrow spit of rock that connected the headland to the mainland could be easily defended (it has since collapsed; today the headland at high tide can be reached only by a bridge), and on all other sides the sheer rock face falls precipitously to the sea. Only by magic could Uther gain entry into the castle, and for magic he turned to Merlin.

Merlin is the archetype of the spiritual teacher, a self-realized being who returns to the physical world and offers his guidance in time of need. In the Buddhist tradition he would be called a *Bodhisattva*. His "magic" is the divine connection of the seventh chakra, and the psychic sensitivity—known in centuries past as the Sight—that comes with the wisdom of the sixth chakra. These are not powers to be used lightly, even to satisfy the lust of a High King. Merlin used his power to help Uther reach Igraine only because he knew that from their union on that particular night would come the king that would save Britain, the king who would provide a guiding light in the dark centuries to follow.

Merlin invoked the magical mists known as the Dragon's Breath and disguised Uther as Gorlois, Duke of Cornwall and rightful husband of Igraine; himself and two others he disguised as companions of the Duke. They all were readily admitted to the castle where Uther made love to Igraine and Arthur was conceived. As it happened, Gorlois was killed in battle that very night. It could be said that if Uther had only contained his passion for one more night he could have been with Igraine legitimately without the need for intrigue and deception. But then the child who would have been conceived would not have been Arthur. He would have been some other configuration of genes and chromosomes.

Clearly, the moral values of a specific culture are irrelevant to the divine plan. Uther used magic and manipulation to bed another man's wife. His actions should—by the standards of the day—have cast a shadow over his reign and rendered impossible the recognition of his son as rightful heir. But it was destined that the product of the union of a specific man and a specific woman at a specific time would create the light of Britain. All the rest is immaterial.

The divine plan often has to work its way through less than perfect human material. In *Sacred Contracts*, her groundbreaking work on the role of archetypal energies, Caroline Myss reminds us of the all-too-human faces of the great masters. Abraham offered his wife to Pharaoh in exchange for his own safety, and yet it was he who was chosen to found a nation and father a people and introduce a new religious paradigm. Siddhartha Gautama abandoned his wife and infant son in his own quest for enlightenment. We do not judge these spiritual leaders because we recognize that what are important are the symbolic and mythological elements of their stories.

Arthur's conception and birth, as pivotal elements of myth, had to take place at times of power and significance. Only on the night of the spring equinox could Arthur be conceived so that his birth would coincide with the midwinter solstice. He represents the beginning of new life in the depths of winter, the rebirth of light on the shortest day of the year. He is the Mabon, the child of light, the great hope of Britain—and by extension of humanity—in the dark winter of chaos and peril.

The symbolic meaning of the solstices has been etched for all time on the landscape of Western Europe in the great megalithic monuments, of which the most well-known is Stonehenge. Stonehenge is oriented towards the summer solstice. In Ireland, not too far to the north of Dublin, is another famous megalithic monument, Newgrange, which is oriented towards the winter solstice. Newgrange has been recently restored, and from a distance it looks like a pimple on the top of a low hill.

Newgrange is called a "passage tomb" because cremated remains have been found inside. The "tomb" is a circular chamber on top of the hill, lined with massive upright stones. A passage, also lined with upright stones, leads from the entrance into this central chamber. This structure was covered with 750,000 tons of rock and topped with turf. The face surrounding the entrance was decorated with chunks of marble, and it is this white facade that the traveler sees from afar. If you were to take off the top, and look down on the structure from a helicopter, it would look like a vagina and uterus.

Newgrange, Ireland

As the sun appears over the horizon on the shortest day of the year, the rays of light shine through a small opening above the entrance and begin to creep along the passage as the sun rises. They fall upon an upright slab of limestone at the far side of the inner chamber, on which are carved sacred symbols. The rays of father sun penetrate into the womb of mother earth after the longest night of the year, symbolizing the fertilization of the earth and the rebirth of a new year. From that time on the days begin to grow longer, the life that has been dormant within the earth begins to stir, ready to sprout forth in a new cycle of growth celebrated at the spring equinox.

Archeology can tell us only what has been proven by physical evidence. All that is known of the culture that created the megalithic monuments is that they were Bronze Age farmers. The creation of Newgrange, we are told, would have taken some twenty years: five to observe the cycles of the seasons and plot the position of the rising sun, and perhaps fifteen more years of actual construction during the idle months of winter when little could be done in the way of farming. With the information thus far available that is all that can be said, but it seems unlikely that a simple farming culture would have had the advanced knowledge of both astronomy and engineering that it took to construct these monuments that were precisely engineered and have stood for some five thousand years. There is probably an important piece of the puzzle missing, an even older culture perhaps that has left no physical evidence, or at least the evidence has not yet been found.

Arthur, then, was born at midwinter solstice. He was the physical manifestation of the symbolic fertilization of mother earth by father sun that happens each year at Newgrange.

Birth of Arthur

It was time. Merlin could feel the ripples in the energy of the Source. It was time to confront Uther the Pendragon and hold him to his promise. "Ask me anything," he had said. "If you bring me to Igraine I will give you anything, half my kingdom if you want it."

Merlin had smiled; Uther knew he was safe in making such an extravagant promise because he knew that Merlin had no ambitions for earthly power. "There is one thing I will ask of you," Merlin had replied. "You will conceive a child this night, you and Igraine. When he is born, I want you to give him to me."

Uther had stared at him, his thoughts clearly written on his face. He would never understand Merlin. Why on earth would he want to burden himself with a newborn child? But in the fever of his passion he had readily agreed. Not, Merlin now thought with an inward sigh, giving any thought to Igraine's feelings about giving up her first-born son. It would be Merlin's task to persuade her. He would not take her child away from her without her consent, no matter Uther's promise.

He had spent the months of waiting in his cave on the shore of the northern kingdom of Strathclyde. If he left immediately, by the time he reached Tintagel Igraine would be near her time. As he watched the sun setting into the Irish Sea he thought of how he would speak to her, what he might say to convince her to give up her newborn son. He had never met Igraine, only heard of her great beauty and devotion to Uther. And Uther, it seemed, continued to honor her, treating her as his equal in the old style of the Celtic kings. The king and queen were still living at Tintagel, though much of Uther's time was spent far from his hearth in the continuing wars with the Saxons.

It was several days before the midwinter solstice when Merlin arrived in the village of Tintagel. The winter sky was overcast, the clouds dark and heavy. He thought of seeking shelter at the tavern, but since it was only midafternoon he decided to press on to the castle. He did ask at the tavern if the king were in residence and learned that Uther was fighting to the south, near the Saxon Shore. He was not to have Uther's support, then, in his coming interview with the queen. And he very much doubted that Uther had told her of his promise to Merlin.

His pony picked its way delicately down the steep rocky path towards the cove below Tintagel castle. A little over half way down he took the path that branched to the left, climbing towards the headland. He was kept waiting at the gate while a messenger was sent to the queen, blowing on his half-frozen hands as he looked across the narrow spit that was the castle's only connection to the mainland.

Queen Igraine received him in the main hall by a roaring fire. The walls were hung with tapestries, and the rushes in the wall sconces were already lit against the fading light.

"Please forgive my appearance, my lady. It has been a long journey."

"There is no need of forgiveness, Lord Merlin. You are indeed welcome." She invited him to sit by the fire, and sent for warm spiced wine and someone to bathe his feet. Only when he was comfortably settled and the servants had withdrawn did she sit herself and look at him with polite inquiry, her hands folded over her swollen belly in the classic pose of the expectant mother. She was a queen indeed, Merlin realized, even dressed simply in a soft gray gown. Her skin was like alabaster, fair and translucent, and her long dark hair shone with *golden highlights. She was not the young and unsophisticated girl he had expected but a self-assured woman, and her deep gray eyes, fringed with impossibly thick long lashes, were not afraid of holding his own. He began by inquiring after her health.*

"I am well, thank you." She patted her swollen belly, and smiled. "We are both well."

"And the king?"

They spoke for a while of generalities, while Merlin attempted to take her measure. He had little experience of women, except for the priestesses of Avalon; his life had not included much interaction with other kinds of women, especially those of Igraine's station.

There was a disturbance behind him and a small child ran to Igraine's skirts. Igraine's face softened.

"This is my daughter, Morgan. And this is the great Lord Merlin, Morgan."

The child's eyes widened. "Lord Merlin? Is it true that you can be in three places at once and you can make the sun rise in the west and you can disappear in a cloud of mist?"

She looked no more than three or four but spoke with ease and composure. Igraine made as if to hush her but Merlin smiled. "I wish indeed that I could do half the things people say of me, child. But no; I am simply human, like you. Though I have been schooled in the mysteries that can seem magical to those who do not understand them."

"Mysteries? Can I learn about them some day?"

"Perhaps. If you are called."

"But ..."

"That is enough, Morgan," her mother interrupted her. "Run along now, go to the kitchen and see how the preparations for supper are coming along. Perhaps there is a treat for you there."

"But I would rather talk with Lord Merlin ..."

At the look in her mother's eye she dropped a polite curtsy to Merlin and skipped away. Igraine turned her straightforward gaze on Merlin. He was used to inspiring awe, even fear, but Igraine's eyes were disconcertingly acute.

"I know you did not come all this way to exchange pleasantries with me, Lord Merlin. I can almost believe, in fact, in some of those magical powers. I feel as if you knew I wanted to see you. I am in need of guidance and I do believe you are the wisest man in the kingdom."

"I am at your service, madam."

And he found, as he listened to her, that it came as no great surprise to him that she had herself thought of the same arguments he had prepared to use on her. She too must be sensitive to the flow of the Source, he thought, perhaps unconsciously. She had, after all, trusted in the depth of her feeling for Uther in the face of accepted propriety. She told him of her fear that her child, if a son, would not be safe at Uther's court; he would be at risk from petty kings who had their eye on the throne of the High King. And the land itself was unsafe. It was under constant attack in the east from Saxons, Angles and Jutes, in the north from Picts and Scots, and in the west from the Irish.

Igraine fell silent, and gazed into the fire. There was more, Merlin knew, and he knew what it was, but he could not help her to express it. At length she took a deep breath and faced him directly.

"My husband, the king ... I know, and Uther knows, that this child is his, but there will always be those who whisper. If the child is another girl there will be no problem, but if it is a son ... Uther says he cannot recognize him, that we must have other sons." She stroked her belly, as if the child within could hear and she wanted to comfort him. "What am I to do, Merlin? How can I keep my babe safe and offer him a meaningful life?"

Merlin exhaled. All he had to do, he realized, was surrender, and all would unfold without his direction.

"With your permission, madam, I will take the child. I will keep him safe, and teach him, and see that he is fostered in a secret place where he will learn what he needs to know, so that he will be ready when the time comes to take his rightful place."

"You know then that my child is a boy?" She hesitated. "What do you mean by his rightful place?"

He shook his head. "I know that there is a plan, but the unfolding of it is not shown to me all at once. Only as much as I need to know to take the next step."

"'His rightful place,'" she repeated, softly. The implications of it seemed to penetrate slowly. He saw the moment when she understood, and a shadow crossed her face. "I will bear other sons, will I not, Merlin?" He looked with compassion into the lovely eyes. Though her face was composed her eyes were brimming, and he wished he could lie to her but he could not. "I can only tell you what I know, Igraine," he said gently. "Whether Uther wills it or no, this child will be king."

For his own safety, therefore, Arthur's whereabouts were kept secret. Merlin provided for his physical safety—the prime requisite of the first chakra—by taking him away from the dangers at Uther's court and hiding him at the court of Count Ector and his wife Flavilla, loyal followers of Uther. There Arthur would be trained in the arts of war necessary to any leader of the time, and educated in the art of living an honorable life by Merlin. Arthur spent his childhood and early adolescence—the developmental stages of the first and second chakras—ignorant of his true parentage, playing second string to his foster brother Cai.

Take a break from reading now to experience the Mabon Birth Meditation. King Arthur was the Mabon, the child of light, born in the depths of winter. He symbolizes the inner light that is the true essence of all of us, a light that can become hidden by the trials of our daily lives on the physical plane and that is reborn when we "remember" who we are: source energy, having a human experience.

So turn off the phone, ask anyone sharing your living space not to disturb you for a half hour or so, and begin by taking some deep abdominal breaths.

Jennifer Sault

Mabon birth meditation

In your safe place, free of interruptions, take a few moments to settle yourself comfortably, perhaps moving your body until you find the position that feels best for you, keeping your head, neck and trunk in a straight line to allow the energy to flow freely. Breathing deeply now, feel the gentle rise and fall of your abdomen as you breathe in ... and out. Again, deep deep breath in ... and out. And one more deep breath in ... and out.

And now relax your breathing, allow your body to breathe itself. Raise the shield of light from below, filling and surrounding your body with light, creating a protected space. Bring down the shield of light from above, balancing and blessing each of your chakras, Sahasrara at the crown, Ajna chakra at the third eye, Vissudha chakra at the throat, Anahata chakra at the heart, Manipura chakra at the solar plexus, Svadhisthana chakra just below the navel, and Muladhara chakra at the base of the spine. And now breathing into your inner light at the heart center, expanding your inner light to fill your body and your energy field, so that you are now filled and surrounded by the triple shield of light, from below, from above and from within, grounded in physical reality, with an open and clear connection to Source, honoring the light within.

You are an extension of Beingness, the Great Is, the energy of the Source that experiences itself beyond time and space. Out of itself, and within itself, Beingness creates the physical dimension of time and space. Imagine that you can watch that creation from its beginning as a tiny speck of matter, indescribably dense. There is a flash of light, unimaginably bright. Time begins, the tiny speck expands in a swirling maelstrom of light, and particles combine to form atoms that are drawn together to form the first generation of stars.

Development, in the physical realm, is measured in time, and as you watch the development of this physical dimension you can measure time. A billion years to create the first generation of stars. Within the furnace of those stars are created the heavier atoms that are flung out across space as the stars explode and there is a second cycle of particles of matter being drawn together into a new generation of stars, and the stars become organized into galaxies, some spherical, some spiral, some elliptical. Orbiting the new stars are planets, some with orbiting moons of their own. Some are gaseous, some are solid. Some are fiery hot, some are indescribably cold.

Within these myriad environments, aspects of Beingness experience themselves in different ways. Imagine now that you decide to enter the physical dimension of space and time. You are at the leading edge of a filament of light, traveling through the darkness of space. You are a part of the whole that seeks to individuate, to grow within a physical form, to create a bridge between spirit and matter. You seek the experience of creating balance on all levels of being, to grow individually and to offer the higher vibrational energy of your development to Spirit, the One, the All that expresses itself in myriad forms and in myriad dimensions.

As you travel through the physical dimension of stars, planets and space dust you can see spiral galaxies, exploding supernovas, nebulae of radiant colors. You are mystically drawn towards a distant spiral galaxy of billions of stars. On the outer edge of one of the spiral arms of this galaxy there is one particular star, not the biggest nor the brightest, but it is the one that seems to beckon you. You float closer, and you see that this star has planets in its orbit. You pass by a dark and cold planet on the outer reaches of the star's light, and a Catherine wheel of a planet, with encircling rings of rocks and stones and dust, and its own moons. You pass a giant gas planet, in stripes of yellow, orange and red, with several moons. You float through a wide field of orbiting asteroids, and past a red planet.

The third planet from the sun is a blue and white jewel against the backdrop of black space. It has one moon, glowing silver. It is enveloped in a membrane of shimmering light, an oxygen-bearing atmosphere that supports the development of physical life. You sense that you are home. You are drawn towards the northern hemisphere of this planet that is still enfolded in winter. Life is dormant; the nights are long, the days cold and short. You are the Mabon, the child of light, come to serve in a period of transition and chaos, to hold your center of peace and wholeness. You have chosen, with ancient mystical wisdom, the precise and perfect place of your entry into physical reality. As you grow, within the safe, warm, fluid environment of your mother's womb, you are nourished by her, and soothed by the beat of her heart. Your cells divide and specialize, you grow limbs and organs, until that moment when the wisdom of life pushes you forth, out into the world.

Imagine yourself now at the moment of your birth. You are both the child being born and the adult who witnesses the birth. And as you the baby emerge into the world, you the adult take this precious baby in your arms, and you welcome him or her. Holding the baby close to your heart you look into his or her eyes and tell the baby he or she is beautiful, intelligent, resourceful, capable, perfect, born at the perfect moment in time, the right sex, the right ethnic group, whatever loving and empowering message you want to give, that you perhaps wish you had heard. ...

Take the baby in your arms now and walk through a forest to a sacred circle of standing stones. Waiting for you within the circle is an image of the Lady of the Lake, who represents the feminine aspect of divinity, and Merlin, who represents the masculine. Each of them blesses the baby, and you take the child into your heart where he or she will remain, safe and loved, for the rest of this lifetime.

If you would like, take a few moments now to communicate with the Lady and Merlin. Ask any question you want to ask ... ask if they have any message for you. Or you can simply enjoy the experience of their radiant energy.

Then, in your own time, and only when you are ready, begin to bring your focus back into the outer world. Open your eyes whenever you're ready, and take some time to write or draw about your experience in your quest journal. And from time to time, you can lay your hands gently over your heart, and think with love of the child that dwells in there, innocent, creative, playful, eager to experience and enjoy life, *courageous, inventive, learning and growing, there with you in every moment*

First chakra: Muladhara

When we are born the dominant energy is that of the first chakra at the base of the spine. We are all first chakra energy; we do not yet know that we are separate beings. The challenges of the first chakra are to establish a firm foundation on which to build the personality, to create a sense of safety in physical form, and learn to form emotional bonds with another. It is at the first chakra that we begin our conditioning and lay the foundation for our basic beliefs and attitudes about the world and our place in it: whether it is safe or not, whether we feel we belong, whether we believe that we have the capacity to take care of ourselves and provide for our basic needs.

If we are born into an environment and a family that are stable and secure, and we are loved and our needs are met, we have a sound foundation and a fundamental belief that we are safe in the world. If we are born into an environment that is not safe, where there is violence perhaps, or our caretakers are themselves insecure or immature or lack adequate parenting skills, we may have a weakness at the foundation of our being, a belief that the world is not a safe place, or that we do not belong on this planet, or even that we do not have the right to take up space.

At this stage of our development there is no separation between the self and the environment; whatever happens in the environment is perceived as happening to us, so if we are surrounded by violent sound and violent action, even violent thoughts, we perceive it as if the violence were directed towards us. We can decide that the world is a violent and dangerous place and live with constant but undefined anxiety. It becomes our challenge later in life to create a sense of safety for ourselves.

If, on the other hand, we are enveloped in love and acceptance, nurtured by people who themselves feel safe in the world, we are likely to develop a core belief that we are safe and that we belong on the physical plane. A strong, healthy and balanced first chakra helps us to weather the vicissitudes of life with equanimity because we are confident that we can take care of our needs.

Imagine two friends, Joseph and Anthony, who both lose their homes to the sudden devastation of a tornado. Joseph contemplates the wreckage—the loss of the home he has worked and saved for, the destruction of all his personal memorabilia, his letters, photographs, souvenirs of his travels—with a profound sense of loss. He confronts the reality of that loss and works his way through the stages of grieving: he denies, he rages, he cries, and then he takes a deep breath and sets about rebuilding.

Unspoken and unreasoned, at the foundation of Joseph's sense of himself is a belief in his ability to provide for his needs. He rebuilds his home and gets on with his life. The experience of the tornado— that dominated his thoughts and conversation during the first weeks or months—in time becomes just another memory.

Anthony, on the other hand, contemplates the wreckage with a sense of despair. When he thinks about all the work and planning that went into building his home, all the treasured memories of his life that are lost, he feels hopeless and cannot summon the energy to deal with anything. He remembers all the other times that life dealt him unfair blows and is strengthened in his conviction that life is a bitch. He develops a phobia for loud sudden noises. The tornado dominates his thoughts and his conversation and becomes the defining experience of his life.

Joseph has a healthy and balanced first chakra; Anthony has not. Fears connected with survival and safety can drain the energy of this center and leave us tired and depleted, unable to function adequately in providing for our basic needs of shelter, nourishment and a sense of belonging. We may continue to believe we have to depend on others to provide for us—parents, spouses, friends—and not claim our right to be independent and self-sufficient. We may live with myriad vague fears and a sense of unease. And our feelings and beliefs about the world attract the kind of experiences that reinforce the belief, so that insecurity, anxiety, and instability become our reality. A wounded or weak first chakra can also manifest in physical illnesses, such as a weakened immune system, or problems with the legs and lower back.

Wounds to the first chakra can also be discerned through evidence of blocked or excessive energy. One of the ways this can manifest physically is excess weight, and it is a common consequence of sexual abuse. Incest is not only a physical and psychological invasion; it is a betrayal of the most sacred trust. The child is abused, manipulated and frightened by the very person who above all others should provide support, love, and safety. And it is a violation of the place that above all others should be a haven and a sanctuary: the child's home. It is a small wonder then that the incest survivor often cannot trust anyone and does not feel safe anywhere. Those who have a wounded first chakra because of early sexual abuse can hold on to fat as an unconscious protective device, to "cushion" them or to make them undesirable and therefore safe from molestation.

It is appropriate, here, to mention a caveat. Until relatively recently books such as this one would not have been possible. Traditionally this knowledge has been available only to those in secret mystery schools or monasteries. And until recently we had the luxury of spending lifetimes learning a particular lesson. But no more. Caroline Myss suggests that on August 6, 1945, when the atom bomb was dropped on Hiroshima, our spiritual development was put on fast forward. We have developed the technological means to destroy ourselves and we have to develop the wisdom to manage that capability. If we are to survive, our spiritual and moral development has to catch up with our technological development.

What was once secret mystical information is widely available to us now as individuals—in books, on the Internet, through spiritual channels, in workshops—to help in that development, to help us to grow in wisdom. It is for our own knowledge and understanding of ourselves. It is not for us to diagnose other people. There are many reasons for excess weight, as there are many reasons for illness: some choose illness as a service, for example. Blocked energy or loss of energy at a particular chakra is one possible cause of illness or dysfunction to be considered and tested against your own inner knowing.

We can check out the health of the first chakra by examining how well we take care of our physical needs for food, shelter and physical safety; to what extent we honor the physical environment that we live in: our home, car, workspace; and the priority we assign to our own health. This is not, of course, to say that illness or physical disability is necessarily a sign of a wounded first chakra. It is more a matter of the attitude we take towards our physical health, whether or not we believe we are worthy of time and care.

There are clues to that attitude all around us. A tendency to hoard things may signal a fear of loss or lack of safety; a messy house may indicate a lack of respect for the self, or a sense of unworthiness; a diet of junk food and no time or energy for exercise likewise. If we assume that what is reflected back to us from the outer conditions of our life is our inner belief about ourselves and our place in the world, we can gain insight into that often-subconscious belief pattern by paying attention to those conditions.

Healing the first chakra can be through counseling that explores the conditions of very early life and relationships to primary caretakers; reconnecting with the body through exercise and Hatha Yoga, particularly grounding postures such the Mountain, or Tree, or any standing postures; or through touch—from a loved one, or a massage. Or through meditations that emphasize grounding, connection with the earth, being an integral and necessary part of the natural world.

Arthur, as we have seen, was born into an environment of national and personal threat. Had he remained at the court of

King Uther his life would have been uncertain, and his first chakra connection to the physical world weak. If Arthur was to become the saving light of Britain he had first of all to survive, the basic need of the first chakra. It was Merlin, as we have seen, who provided for Arthur's safety and who created a space where he could grow up safe and secure, with a solid connection to the land.

Merlin was probably a Druid. Generally speaking the Druids are believed to have been the priestly cult of the Celts, though some traditions claim they are much older. "Priest," in any case, is not an accurate term. Druids were thinkers, advisors and philosophers. They were leaders who enjoyed prestige and respect within the tribe equal to that accorded the king. The ancient Mesopotamians, Greeks, and Egyptians knew of the Druids and respected their wisdom. Druid training in the mystery schools took some twenty years and included the bardic arts of poetry and music; the Ovate level of divination and healing; and the Druid level of training in the deeper mysteries. Druids believed that life was a journey of learning, and that the soul was reborn many times in its journey towards reunion with the divine source.

The Druids have been misunderstood and maligned because of the accounts about them by Roman historians that tell of human sacrifice. Roman sources are the only written sources that we have about the ancient Druids, because the Druids themselves did not keep written records; their wisdom and traditions were transmitted orally in song and stories and poetry. History is written by the conquerors who tend to color their interpretations to flatter themselves. The Romans, who were more tolerant than many conquerors of various religious traditions—provided due respect was paid to the deities of Rome—were decidedly intolerant of the Druids, in whom they perceived a threat to the monolithic power of Rome and whom they systematically destroyed.

It would be prudent, therefore, to take Roman accounts of druid practices with a healthy dose of skepticism. In Gaul, the Romans killed the Druids and burned the sacred oak groves. The final Roman assault on the British Druids was on the island of Mona (off the north-western coast of Wales, now called Anglesey). Roman sources tell of priestesses shrieking curses upon the heads of the attacking Romans, who slaughtered them nevertheless. The surviving Druids were driven underground, but no doubt still enjoyed prestige among the people during the time of Arthur.

(It is interesting to note, however, that while Suetonius Paulinus was completing his massacre of the Druids on Mona, news arrived of trouble in the east. Upon the death of the king of the Iceni, Roman officials had robbed Queen Boudicca of her lands, beaten her and raped her daughters. Joined by many other tribes she led her people in rebellion, and was to destroy Londinium and take over large areas of the country before she was defeated.)

Merlin comes to us via the twelfth century Geoffrey of Monmouth, and many historians believe that Geoffrey of Monmouth invented him. Geoffrey claimed to have based his life of Merlin on a little book that has since disappeared, though Norma Goodrich makes a case for its existence. In any case, in legend it was Merlin who created Arthur—by engineering his conception on the night of the Spring Equinox—and who protected him as a child and educated him in the art of living an honorable life and in being a just and righteous king.

It is immaterial, from the perspective of the spiritual quest, whether Merlin was an invention of Geoffrey of Monmouth, or a composite of several Celtic poets and mystics, or a title held by a succession of Druids. As myths and legends develop they create their own reality as they reflect the deeper truth of the realm of archetypes and symbols that is the collective unconscious, universal consciousness, spirit, or God/Goddess. Merlin represents the spiritual teacher, the inner guide, who is always available to each of us once we take the step of asking.

The "magic" of Merlin is what we would call psychic power, and there are two levels of this power. The first is "sight," or what we might call intuitive knowing, part of the power of the sixth chakra. The other is a kind of prophesy, when Merlin feels himself flooded with spiritual power and speaks with absolute authority, the times when his intervention is vital and pivotal to Arthur's safety or success. This we would call the opening of the seventh chakra, the power of the divine connection.

Merlin as he appears in epics and folklore is a wise man, highly educated, trained in druidic lore and at one with nature. He is very different from the Merlin of the medieval versions of the legends. The medieval writers' treatment of Merlin had to somehow fit into the world-view of the time. If Arthur was to be a Christian king, the *sine qua non* of medieval treatments of the stories, what was to be done with a wizard? Christian dogma had no place for a teacher with direct access to the divine, unless that teacher were a priest and part of the church hierarchy. The Church frowned on psychic power as the work of the devil, and only through the mediation of the priesthood could one come to know God. In the older versions of the legends Merlin is a spiritual teacher and healer. In medieval sources he becomes something of a comic figure, his magic sometimes childish and funny. In more recent interpretations, such as Mary Stewart's masterful *Life of Merlin*, Merlin becomes a spiritual renaissance man: prophet, poet, healer, engineer, historian.

As the story of Merlin became myth, as the historical facts—whatever they were—were molded into a coherent spiritual truth, the archetypal aspects of Merlin took center stage. As the bearer of eternal rather than temporal truth, Merlin becomes the guide, the teacher, the revealer of Truth. He is a self-realized being, open at the sixth and seventh chakras.

It was Merlin, therefore, who took the infant Arthur and gave him into the safekeeping of Count Ector. Arthur was raised as the foster son of Ector, his identity and his whereabouts kept secret until such time as he was needed to take his place as High King of Britain. King Arthur's first chakra development was in an environment where he was nurtured physically, emotionally, mentally and spiritually, where his growth during the early, pivotal years of his life could proceed free of threats to his survival.

Many of us are not so fortunate; we may have wounds to the first chakra that continue to impact our lives, not necessarily from overt abuse; even the best of parents at times make mistakes, and our needs are not met. When these wounds are not recognized and addressed they constitute a weakness at the foundation of our personality, and they continue to affect how we think, feel and act in the world. The good news is that it is never too late to heal them, and we now have multiple resources to help us to do that.

Take a break from reading now, find a quiet and comfortable space, and open your mind and your heart to the imagery of the first chakra meditation; you will explore the wellbeing of your own first chakra, and discover any weak places at your foundation. And then, through the symbolism of the oak tree, sacred to druidic lore, you can reconnect with your deep inner knowing that you have within you all you will ever need to create a sense of safety, stability, and inner strength.

First chakra: Red Cube and Oak Tree Meditation

In a safe place, free of interruptions, take a few moments to settle yourself comfortably, perhaps moving your body until you find the position that feels best for you, keeping your head, neck and trunk in a straight line to allow the energy to flow freely. Breathing deeply now, feel the gentle rise and fall of your abdomen as you breathe in ... and out. Again, deep deep breath in ... and out. And one more deep breath in ... and out. And now relax your breathing, just allowing your body to breathe itself.

Raise the shield of light from below, filling and surrounding your body with light, creating a protected space. Bring down the shield of light from above, balancing and blessing each of your chakras, Sahasrara at the crown, Ajna chakra at the third eye, Vissudha chakra at the throat,

Anahata chakra at the heart, Manipura chakra at the solar plexus, Svadhisthana chakra just below the navel, and Muladhara chakra at the base of the spine. And now breathing into your inner light at the heart center, expanding your inner light to fill your body and your energy field, so that you are now filled and surrounded by the triple shield of light, from below, from above and from within, grounded in physical reality, with an open and clear connection to Source, honoring the light within.

Imagine now that you are walking through an ancient forest. It is springtime, and the signs of new growth and reawakened life are all around you. Each step takes you deeper and deeper within, and as you walk on the carpet of last year's fallen leaves you can perhaps imagine hearing the swishing sound that your feet make. The trees are haloed in fresh, yellowish green, and here and there fresh green shoots are peeking through, a fiddlehead fern perhaps, and splashes of color, wild irises, crocuses and forget-me-nots.

You walk, each step taking you deeper and deeper into relaxation, surrounded by huge, ancient trees, listening to the breeze as it rustles through the treetops, the sound of birds singing, perhaps in the distance there is a stream and you can hear the sound of the water as it gurgles and flows over rocks. The trees all around you have been here for hundreds, perhaps thousands of years, and they carry the wisdom of the ages. Their roots reach deep into the earth beneath your feet, an intricate, intertwining web that reaches deep into the earth. Above you the branches reach high into the sky, and they too intertwine.

As you walk, notice whether your feet make any sound. Notice how the sunlight shining down through the branches makes patterns of light on the forest floor. The air smells fresh and clean, and you breathe deeply, easily, grateful for the life-giving oxygen that is the gift of the plant life all around you.

As you walk through this ancient forest, you find yourself drawn to one particular tree, an ancient oak tree. It is immense, its trunk perhaps nine or ten feet in diameter. As you get closer, the details of its bark, and its root structure, become clearer. Notice the pattern of its roots, the texture of its bark, whether the oak is straight and tall, or weathered and crooked. Perhaps lightning has damaged it, and you can see where the bark has grown over and around the wound. Perhaps some of its branches have fallen in winter storms, and yet the tree itself is healthy, strong and whole. Notice the pattern of its leaves.

Ask the tree if you can touch it, and if you sense its agreement, touch the bark with both palms and feel the rough texture. Run your palms over the exposed roots. Perhaps there is soft velvety moss growing in the spaces between them. Perhaps you would like to sit in the hollow of the roots and lean against the tree.

After birth, before the developing soul has any sense of time or awareness of physical separation, we receive the imprint of the surrounding environment and form beliefs and opinions about the nature of physical reality. We have as yet no mechanism for selection or defense. We take in all the stimuli that come within our range and form preverbal, precognitive conclusions about the dimension we have entered: whether it is safe or not; whether we belong or not; whether we have the right to be here, or not.

The fundamental challenge of the first chakra is survival. The instinct to survive is rooted in the oldest part of the brain. When this instinct is satisfied we are not even aware of it. But when survival is threatened, it dominates our consciousness.

Muladhara means root, and the root chakra at the base of the spine roots us to the earth, to physical reality. Earth is the element that corresponds to this chakra, and its blessings are stability, and strength, and a sense of safety.

When the first chakra is healthy and whole we can feel safe and secure, we have a strong foundation and the stability to know that we have the resources to face and survive whatever confronts us. When there are wounds at the first chakra, we may be plagued with issues connected with survival: health, money, shelter, job problems. We may find that our basic right to feel safe in the world eludes us, even when there are no real threats to our survival.

Focus your attention now on the Muladhara chakra at the base of the spine. The symbol of the root chakra is a cube, and its color is red. Imagine yourself within a cube of red light. With the intention of exploring the health and balance of your first chakra, begin to explore this cube. You may experience flashes of memory. If these become uncomfortable, you can move your consciousness outside the cube and examine it from a distance that is comfortable for you.

When our survival is threatened, fear protects us by heightening our awareness and focusing our attention on the here and now. Fear stimulates the fight or flight response that prepares us for action. When the first chakra is wounded, fear can work against us by making us hypervigilant, restless, and anxious. We may lose energy to this fear and be unable to evaluate a threat realistically.

If as you explore the red cube of the first chakra you should find fear, take a moment to breathe, and to detach your consciousness from the fear. If your fear had a shape, what shape would it be? If it had a color, what color would it be? What size is it? Examine it from all angles, with no judgment or blame, from a place of detachment. Allow yourself to be curious about this fear, and now imagine that this fear image has a voice. Tell it that you want to understand it, and ask if it is willing to communicate with you. It may take a while for the image to trust you enough to be willing to communicate. Be patient. As you demonstrate your consistent and sincere desire to get to know this fear image it will communicate. And when it does, simply listen, with detachment, with curiosity.

We heal and strengthen the first chakra, not by learning to live with fear, but by working through it. And to do that it can help to understand it. You can ask the fear, Where did it come from? How did it serve you? Consider how you feel in its presence. Consider whether the origin of the fear is still a factor in your life, or if it can now be released. File away the answers to these questions so that you can consider them again at some future time, and explore how this information can change your behavioral and emotional responses.

Consider the mighty oak tree that is supporting you. Its roots reach deep into the earth, giving it stability and strength, and drawing nourishment to feed its trunk and branches and leaves. In the same way, our connection to the earth through the root chakra keeps us grounded, stable and safe. Without grounding, like a tree with no roots, we are unstable and vulnerable to extremes of emotion.

As you continue to explore the cube of red light, allow your intention to be focused on the here and now, and the ways in which the condition of the first chakra is manifesting in your life; in your physical health, for example; or in the way in which you nourish your body and take care of yourself physically. The health of the first chakra can be apparent in the conditions of your living space, or your car. How well are you meeting your needs for food and shelter, and for the freedom to grow beyond survival?

The oak is deeply connected to the heritage of King Arthur. It represented the very essence of the earth, and the ancient spiritual link between the High King and the land. Old oaks were venerated by the Druids, and indeed the term "druid" is believed to come from the Gaelic word for oak. The ancient Druids held their sacred ceremonies in mighty oak groves. In the Celtic tree alphabet, the Oak is given the word Duir, which comes from the Gaelic word meaning "door": it is the symbolic door to inner strength and spiritual power. The Oak leads the way to Truth, to vision and understanding.

For generations upon generations, people have gone to sit beneath the mighty Oak to gain strength and spiritual renewal. Within the energy field of the oak the outside world can be forgotten and the inner world come back into perspective. The Oak can help us to gain new understanding and vision from our experiences, which brings the strength and courage to face whatever life offers. The presence of the oak helps to restore our faith in ourselves.

If it feels right to you, ask the tree if it will allow you to experience what it feels like to be a tree. And allow yourself to be enveloped into the tree. Imagine that you can feel, reaching down from your toes, strong roots reaching deep into the earth. And branching off the main roots, ever smaller and smaller roots, reaching into the crevices of the earth, around rocks and stones, seeking out moisture and nutrients. Each filament of root is covered with microscopic root hairs, sensitive, of brilliant design, and sure of their purpose. Your roots provide a strong and stable foundation for your trunk and branches, spreading and interlocking with the roots of other trees, so that it is impossible to tell from down here which roots belong to you and which to other trees.

The roots symbolize the wisdom of the past; the wisdom of the ancestors passed down to us in song and story; the wisdom of the world's cultures available to us in libraries and on the Internet; your own wisdom patiently and sometimes painfully learned. All the knowledge of the ages; that too is part of your foundation.

Take your attention now to your trunk, tall and strong, firmly planted in the ground yet able to move and bend in the wind. Be aware of the sap flowing through your intricate circulatory system, bringing nourishment to every cell. Be aware of the hard, rugged bark that protects you from harm and keeps you stable, upright and proud. The trunk symbolizes the present, the life you are living now from moment to moment, your place in the world.

Imagine now, that within the tree you raise your arms up high above your head and reach for the sky. And imagine that from your fingertips sprout branches, in progressively smaller sizes. And from each branch and twig sprout leaves that turn their face to the sun, absorbing sunlight, and through the mystical process of photosynthesis converting sunlight into nourishment, to feed every part of your being. Your leaves inhale sunlight, and exhale the oxygen that supports the animal life of the planet.

A similar process in the subtle bodies takes the power of spirit, and through the mystical processes of the energy centers called chakras converts the vibration of that energy into the appropriate rate for physical growth and healing, for movement, for emotional expression, for thought.

Imagine that you can feel the warmth of the sun on your leaves, and a tingling perhaps as this conversion takes place. Imagine that you can feel the intimate yet gentle touch of leaves belonging to other trees.

The branches symbolize your future, the life yet to come, pregnant with promise.

Imagine now, the strand of light connecting the root chakra with the center of the earth. And just as you are rooted to the earth, you are also connected to Spirit, to the Source, and you can access unlimited resources to help you heal any wounds you may have found at the first chakra. You can ask for guidance and direction, that is in truth already there within you. Relax now into the knowing that you have within you all the resources you need to meet any challenge, and to deal successfully with whatever your daily life presents to you.

You can choose, now, to explore any part of the tree. You may choose to spend more time among the roots, or in the trunk, or high in the branches. And when you are ready, thank the tree for sharing its experience and wisdom with you, and bring your consciousness gently back into the outer world, bringing with you any insights or wisdom that you have gained. Spend some time writing about your experience in your Quest Journal.

PART II

Spring
Court of Count Ector

Within days of his birth, the infant Arthur was collected by Merlin, according to his agreement with Uther Pendragon. Merlin entrusted the baby to Count Ector and his wife Flavilla, loyal followers of Uther Pendragon, who were sworn to secrecy and who raised Arthur during the early years of his life. It was not at all unusual in those times for the sons of the powerful and well-born to be fostered at a different court, though it was probably unusual for the foster child's origins to be kept secret. The fosterlings would be trained in the martial arts and in the social conventions that would govern their behavior, in preparation for the life of a warrior. By all accounts Ector and Flavilla were very fond of Arthur and raised him as their own.

Arthur and Merlin

Under the leather tunic the sweat was running down between Arthur's shoulder blades, and the dark hair escaping from underneath his leather helmet was plastered to his forehead. He was beginning to feel the weight of the sword in his right hand and it took all his strength and concentration to hold it steady. In his left he held a small round leather shield.

His deep gray eyes, legacy of his mother Igraine, were fixed on his foster brother Cai, who was smiling mockingly at him as they circled each other in the dust of the courtyard. Cai was three years older, a head taller than Arthur, and Arthur had never yet succeeded in besting him. Arthur was only vaguely aware of the sword master and the other trainees forming a circle around him. His whole world was Cai; he watched his foster brother's expression, trying to anticipate his next move, determined that today he, Arthur, would be the winner.

But it was not to be. He found himself flat on his back in the dust, Cai's sword at his throat. "You did well, lad," the sword master said, and Cai helped him up with a laugh. Arthur laughed with him, as he brushed the dust from his britches. "One day," he said to Cai, "you're going to be surprised." "I'm sure I will," Cai replied good-naturedly, as he slapped him on the back, "but not today."

The mornings Arthur spent in warrior training with Cai and the other boys and girls who were fostered at Count Ector's court. The afternoons were spent in hunting and hawking, or playing games of chance, but whenever possible Arthur spent his afternoons with Merlin. Today, after cleaning and storing his equipment, he ran to the stables, jumped on his pony and galloped across the clearing and into the forest, ducking under branches and laughing aloud with the joy of freedom.

The path began to climb and there were rocks and roots in his path, but Arthur and his pony flew over them, sure-footed and secure, until they came to a small clearing within a grove of ancient oak trees. To one side of it was a bothy, a small hut built by hunters or perhaps woodsmen in days gone by, but for now the dwelling of the Druid Merlin.

Arthur erupted into the peace of the clearing, the explosive energy of youth creating waves of vibration that alerted Merlin to his arrival long before his actual appearance. Sometimes Merlin pretended not to know that Arthur was there and continued to stir his medicinal herbs or read his Greek manuscripts or play his harp. Arthur would wait respectfully at the door, using every ounce of discipline to curb his impatience to know what adventure his teacher had ready for him today, and in his own good time Merlin would turn his head with a slow smile of welcome.

This day, Merlin sent Arthur on a quest. There had been a landslide, and Arthur was to search within the rubble for … something. Merlin was not specific. Arthur followed Merlin's directions through the forest and at length arrived at the place where a part of the mountain had broken away, leaving a jagged wound in the rock face. He poked around in the rubble looking for whatever might catch his eye but all he saw was a heap of broken rock. He caught himself muttering that he wished just for once Merlin would be explicit, and immediately stopped and looked over his shoulder, a little guiltily, as if he half expected his teacher to materialize.

He began to walk across the pile of rock, carefully testing the loose rubble to be sure it would bear his weight. After fruitless minutes he became careless, stepped on an unstable chunk of rock and created a new small landslide that swept him a few yards downhill. After slithering to a stop he looked back up at the mound of unstable rock behind him, said a brief prayer of thanks under his breath, and began to explore his cuts and scrapes.

While examining his left knee he noticed a flat rock that had split in half along its length. He picked up the top half, thinking to take it back to Merlin's bothy to put in front of the door where it was sometimes muddy, and noticed some strange markings on the exposed surface of the lower half. He bent closer and saw the delicate tracing of what appeared to be a fern, but not one he had ever seen in all his studies with Merlin of the natural world. He turned over the rock he was holding and saw a mirror image of the design.

A small knot of excitement began to bubble just below his breastbone. This was it, he was sure; this was what Merlin had sent him to find. He balanced the two split halves of the rock together again and managed to get to his feet. Crossing the shaky surface of the landslide while carrying a fair sized rock took all his powers of concentration, and by the time he arrived back at the bothy with his treasure he was as sweaty and tired *as after a morning of fighting with Cai. But he was too pleased with himself to care as he displayed his treasure at Merlin's feet.*

"Why did you drag a big old rock all the way back here?" Merlin demanded, but there was a crease at the corner of his eyes and the hint of a smile in the depths of his beard.

As always, he took his own sweet time before explaining anything. First he had to dress Arthur's cuts; then he and Arthur had to prepare a simple meal. Merlin never lacked for provisions because although the villagers held him in awe they took regular advantage of his healing arts. There were many in the village alive and well who would not have survived without the aid of Merlin, and they showed their gratitude by sharing with him the products of their farms and their hunting. Merlin munched contentedly at his bread and cheese, and Arthur did his best to do likewise while squirming with impatience.

At last, Merlin set his plate aside, laid the two halves of the rock side by side and traced the design of the fern with his fingertip. "Imagine, Arthur," he said, "a world of green. There are no flowers, only a great variety of ferns and mosses that grow alongside the waters of lakes and streams and rivers." His voice fell silent as he contemplated the design on the rock. "At some point during those vast ages long ago, this fern was trapped in sediment. It has been preserved for millions of years so that we, now, can see the shape and form of plants that no longer exist."

Arthur reached out a finger and delicately touched the rock. "Millions of years," he said in wonder. "And why does it no longer grow?"

"It is part of the natural cycle," Merlin answered. "Plant and animal species develop slowly over long periods of time, adapting themselves to a particular type of environment. Then, perhaps, the environment changes, and some plants and animals can no longer survive in the new conditions. New ones develop to take their place."

"Why does the environment change?" Arthur asked.

"There can be many reasons. Our world as you know revolves around the sun. In space, there are countless other bodies, sometimes they collide and debris is cast out into space." Night had fallen and a full moon had risen over the treetops. Merlin pointed out the dark patches

where the moon had been hit by asteroids and meteorites. "Our world, too, has collided with other heavenly bodies. Perhaps some of them were big enough to change the climate. Perhaps changes in climate are part of the natural cycle. Not so very long ago, in geological time, there was a great sheet of ice that covered the top of the world and extended all the way down to where we are now, in the northern half of Britain. Imagine it, Arthur, a great wall of ice, taller than these trees around us, and trapped within it there were strange and wonderful creatures that died out many years ago."

"How do you know?" Arthur asked. "They must have disappeared when the ice melted."

"Because there is other evidence of their existence. Tomorrow I will show you. It's very late. Too dark for you to ride home. Put your pony in the shelter and you can sleep here."

Arthur grinned with glee and ran to do Merlin's bidding. Then he snuggled down among furs and fell asleep to the sound of Merlin's harp and the flickering shadows cast by the dying fire. He dreamed of lost worlds, of fantastic tree-like ferns as tall as oak trees, of creeping sheets of ice, and of heavenly bodies hurtling through space. And the following day, as promised, Merlin took him into the mountains and showed him an indentation in the rock where the enormous foot of an unimaginably huge animal had stepped in mud eons ago. And Merlin drew a design in the ground of what the animal might have looked like, and had Arthur pace the probable length of its tail.

"Not only plant and animal species flourish and die," Merlin said, as they walked back to the bothy. "Civilizations, too, rise and fall." He stopped suddenly. "Look around you. What do you notice about the forest here?"

Arthur pondered. "Well," he finally said, "the trees in front of us and behind us are smaller than those on either side."

"Why do you think that is?"

Arthur looked at the trees, and at the undergrowth, and walked around for a while studying the ground. Then something caught his attention and he began to sweep away the detritus around his feet.

Beneath it was a flat stone, and another alongside it. "There was once a road here!" he said excitedly, looking up at Merlin.

"Indeed there was. As you know, not so very long ago the Roman civilization was the most powerful in the world. They conquered almost all the known world, and for almost four hundred years they ruled here in Britain. They forced our people to work in the mines, and they shipped many thousands of us back to Rome as slaves." He sat on a fallen log and stretched his legs out in front of him. His sandals looked new, Arthur noticed. Probably a gift from the cobbler whose child Merlin had healed of a nasty burn a couple of weeks ago.

"The Romans have gone now, Arthur, but the Britain you see around you is a Britain conditioned by their presence here for such a long time. There were some among us who had adopted Roman ways even before they came, through trade with our Celtic cousins in Romanized Gaul, but for the most part when Claudius came we still lived as we had lived for centuries, in small round huts such as those still to be seen in the remote hills and marshlands. Local chieftains built their halls on the highest ground and protected themselves with ditches and earthworks topped with wooden palisades, where all the inhabitants of a settlement would take shelter with their animals when under attack. We fought the Romans and suffered many massacres ..."

His voice faded away, and his eyes as they gazed into the distance seemed to gaze back through time. "At Maiden Castle we fought almost to the last man woman and child. The legionaries massacred us and then set fire to the huts. The few survivors offered beakers and food-vessels to the souls of the slaughtered to help them on their way in the other world. The offerings are still there, under the ground, but all that you would see, if you were to look with the eye of the hawk, would be faded indentations in the land in the shape of the stronghold." He spoke as if he had been there himself, and perhaps—Arthur thought, because nothing about Merlin seemed impossible—he had.

"The Romans were uncompromising, Arthur. Submission or destruction, those were the only choices. In the south and east we submitted, we became Roman. In the north we continued to resist and suffered devastation. The Caledonians preferred war to submission, and in the end the Romans stopped trying to subdue them. The Emperor Hadrian built a wall from coast to coast and settled for trying to keep them behind it."

He drew a rough map in the dust. "Here, off the west coast of Wales, is the sacred island of Mona, where for eons Druids were trained in the mysteries. The Roman assault on Mona was a scene of carnage and destruction such as the world had never seen. Since then, the Druids have gone underground, and pass on their wisdom and sacred teachings to carefully selected apprentices. Just as I am teaching you," he said to Arthur.

"Am I to become a Druid, then?" Arthur asked, and Merlin smiled gently, but did not reply.

Merlin then spoke about the other island within the summer country to the south, an island often hidden by the mists that hung over the surrounding lake, the island known as Avalon. Here, too, was a mystery school, for the training of priestesses.

"For you see, Arthur, there is balance in all things: light and dark, sun and moon, masculine and feminine, Mona and Avalon. Each brings to the mystery of life its own gifts. Just as you are cultivating the gifts within you."

Merlin was quiet for a time. "They are all gone now, the high civilizations of Mesopotamia and Egypt and Greece, and very soon Rome, just as you and I and our culture are about to pass into history. But before we do…" Merlin did not finish. It was not the first time that he had hinted vaguely at some great deed, a destiny, something important. Arthur was silent. He knew Merlin would elaborate only when he was ready.

Merlin took a deep breath and smiled. "But the Truth will remain," he said. "And it will surface again when the time is right."

Second chakra: Svadhisthana

> *Our birth is but a sleep and a forgetting:*
> *The Soul that rises with us, our life's Star,*
> *Hath had elsewhere its setting,*
> *And cometh from afar:*
> *Not in entire forgetfulness,*
> *And not in utter nakedness,*
> *But trailing clouds of glory do we come*
> *From God who is our home:*
> *Heaven lies about us in our infancy!*
> *Shades of the prison-house begin to close*
> *Upon the growing Boy,*
> *But He beholds the light, and whence it flows,*
> *He sees it in his joy;*
> *The Youth, who daily farther from the east*
> *Must travel, still is Nature's Priest,*
> *And by the vision splendid*
> *Is on his way attended:*
> *At length the Man perceives it die away,*
> *And fade into the light of common day.*
> William Wordsworth (1770-1850)
> from "Intimations of Immortality"
> in *Recollections of Early Childhood*

Arthur, therefore, spent the years of his childhood not knowing who he was. And so do we. In the early years of life, when the first chakra is dominant, the psychic membranes that separate the individual spirit from universal spirit are porous and there is free flow of energy back and forth. Then, as the second chakra becomes dominant at about age seven, we fortify those membranes and shut off memory of the spiritual dimension that we come from.

Healthy psychological development requires that we focus our attention inward as we meet the challenges of the second and third chakras, the development of a sense of self and of our individual will. In order to do that we forget, in a sense, who we are. We forget that we are individual expressions of the great Oneness of Spirit. The Wordsworth quotation that introduces this chapter is the poet's perception of the second chakra stage of development. The "shades of the prison-house" are the psychic membranes that we begin to fortify at the second chakra. We create a kind of prison around us as we build up our ego boundaries, as we build walls around the psyche and shut out awareness of the dimension of Spirit so that we can learn what we need to learn to function safely and effectively in the physical world.

This is the time, typically, when we begin to go to school. We discover a whole new world outside of the family structure, with new authority figures who are not our parents and grandparents, new companions who are not our brothers and sisters and cousins. School teaches us how to develop the intellect, and also how to relate to people outside the family sphere. We learn the foundations of how to be in the world of matter, we learn the building blocks of the physical, emotional and intellectual bodies that will allow us safely to reopen our psychic membranes in full consciousness to the infinite dimension of Spirit.

In every lifetime it is necessary to learn basic skills—how to walk, talk, read and eat peas—to create a stable foundation within the physical world regardless of the level of evolution of the spirit. In each lifetime we have to mold and purify and develop the raw clay of material existence in order to create the foundation and the vessel for taking the spirit one step closer to enlightenment. Each lifetime, though the spirit carries its power and spiritual development from one physical body to another, the physical, emotional and intellectual discipline of the personality must begin at the beginning. This is one aspect of the paradox of physical existence. We are, at the same time, eternal spirit *and* finite matter, all-knowing *and* constantly learning and developing.

Though the energy of the second chakra becomes distinct at around the age of seven, the shift in focus does not happen all of a sudden. Second chakra energy has been developing along with the child's physical development: in the dawning comprehension that the child is a separate being; in the first tentative steps on the journey towards individuation as the child explores the expanding parameters of his world and the giddying sensation of personal power. The terrible twos are so-named because that is when children first realize that they can say no, and they say it all the time.

Having a 2-year-old is like having a blender without a lid.

Jerry Seinfeld

As the child realizes that he or she and the mother are not the same person he may stomp his feet and refuse to each his spinach, or she may run away and hide in another room. But she will come right back to make sure her mother is still there, as she explores the truth of what developmental psychologists call "object permanence," the awareness that people and things continue to exist even when they are out of sight. This is why the game of "peek-a-boo" is a favorite of children this age, and they can play it for hours.

If we have wise and secure parents who allow us to run away and come back and test our independence, we reach the age of seven feeling safe and confident about stepping out into the world, out of the family environment. This is the age when children begin to interact with other children and adults more independently of their parents and outside the home environment. They begin to individuate, to form relationships, and explore their power of choice.

The first chakra is our relationship with the earth and with group energy, when we learn how to bond with another, to develop a sense of safety and belonging, and to establish the foundation in physical reality that will support the rest of our development. The second is the center of our relationships with other individuals; with emotional energy; with sensuality and pleasure; with physical creativity.

Building relationships and exploring emotional energy is a process often fraught with disillusionment and betrayal, as we discover that those in whom we have invested our trust fall short of our expectations and desires of them. We can lose energy from this center if we hold on to feelings of "you owe me, you hurt me, you done me wrong," (we could call this the country music chakra.) If we feel insecure in our relationships and have a need to control others in order to feel safe, the damage will be manifest here at the second chakra.

The first chakra corresponds to the element earth, or physical energy. The second corresponds to the element water, which symbolizes emotional energy. Emotional energy, like water, is changeable. Water can take solid, liquid, or gaseous form; it responds to the conditions of the environment and conforms to the shape of its container. Emotions, too, are volatile. In the course of several hours, or minutes in some cases, we can feel elated, despondent, calm, anxious, full of hope or tumbling towards despair. It is the solid grounding in earth, the first chakra, that creates the container for the flowing and changeable energy of emotion. If there is no container, if we are not grounded or if the first chakra connection is weak, emotional energy can feel out of control. At the other end of the continuum, if the container is small and rigid, if we keep a tight hold on our emotions, then emotional energy cannot flow. Stuck energy stunts growth and can lead to physical illness in the part of the body governed by the second chakra.

Think of a fountain: perhaps a large fountain, like the famous Trevi Fountain in Rome.

Rome, Fontana di Trevi

The water flows freely, yet it is contained within the structure of the fountain. Without the structure, the water would simply flow down the street, become dirty, evaporate, disappear down the drains. On the other hand, if the plumbing within the fountain were composed of quarter-inch pipes the water would merely trickle; if there were a block in the plumbing the water would not flow at all. When everything works as it is supposed to do, when the fountain is well designed, the plumbing adequate and well-maintained, the water flows freely within appropriate containment. The Fontana di Trevi continues to offer its beauty and healing energy to millions of tourists who toss coins over their shoulders so that the fountain will bring them back to Rome, someday.

In the same way, by creating balance between earth and water, our first and second chakras, we can create a stable container for the fluid energy of emotion; we can allow emotional energy to flow freely within acceptable parameters.

Emotional health means that we are able to feel and express the full spectrum of emotions, from grief and sadness to ecstasy.

When we try to avoid painful or uncomfortable emotions we freeze the water in our emotional fountain. We may shield ourselves from grief, for example, by turning to anti-depressants. Someone once told me she was taking an anti-depressant that had been prescribed for her when her mother died. She had tried to get off the medication several times, she said, but every time "it feels like my mother died yesterday." It had been ten years since her mother's death, ten years of avoiding the pain of confronting that painful loss. Sadness is an appropriate response to the loss of a loved one, but rather than allow herself to experience her grief she had spent a decade dampening her emotional energy, with deleterious consequences to her relationships, her sense of self, and her ability to enjoy her life.

This is not to say anti-depressants are always a bad idea, far from it. They can be wondrous lifesavers. In the acute stages of depression they can stabilize the emotions and give us breathing space in which to deal with the causes. However, except for the small percentage of people who have a congenital chemical imbalance, anti-depressants do not fix the cause of depression. They are a crutch, not a solution. Sadness at the death of a loved one is an appropriate emotion. When it is experienced it can be released, and we can move on. Sadness becomes an emotional wound when we get stuck in it, or when it is repressed.

Many of us stuff pain, because whatever the consequences we believe it is better than feeling. Women often say they are afraid to cry because they think if they start to cry they will never stop. Their perception of the well of pain inside is that it is bottomless, and that the tide of emotion—if once released—will sweep them away. The metaphorical container for the fountain, here, is broken, or non-existent, and grounding strategies are helpful: grounding meditations, gardening, physical exercise, massage, Hatha Yoga, especially the tree and the mountain poses.

Anger, too, is an uncomfortable emotion for many of us. Men often say they are afraid of their anger, afraid of what they might do if they relax their tight control on emotional expression, but perhaps they are most afraid of being out of control. The fountain here is

45

switched off, or frozen, and strategies that help the flow of emotional energy are appropriate: talking, writing in a journal, parking under an overpass and yelling or screaming, exercising with the conscious intent to release blocked energy. Anodea Judith's *Eastern Body Western Mind* is an excellent source for healing strategies.

Many of us have been taught from our earliest days that certain emotions are unacceptable, and that expressing emotion is a sign of weakness. Little girls are told it is unfeminine to be angry, little boys that it is unmanly to cry. Many men repress fear or pain, or learn to channel those "unmanly" emotions into anger. As a culture we have created a fear of the energy of emotion rather than healthy learning and development through honoring emotions and allowing them appropriate expression.

Emotional difficulties may manifest at one or the other of several extremes, depending on whether the wound to this energy center creates a weakness that allows emotional energy to be out of control, when the boundaries are fragile or non-existent, or whether the energy is blocked and held rigidly under control. So at one extreme there might be outbursts of anger or uncontrollable crying, and at the other a flat affect and inability to feel pleasure or pain; poor boundaries that are often invaded because of an inability to say no, or excessive boundaries that do not allow another person to come close; obsessive attachment and emotional dependency, or manipulation and inability to empathize; sexual acting out, or impotence or frigidity and fear of sex, or indeed a denial of pleasure in any form.

Emotions are the language of the deeper levels of the mind. They are the way in which our inner wisdom lets us know that something deserves attention. We were not created to be sad, depressed, angry, irritable, or despairing all the time; we were created as joyful individualized expressions of source energy. Any uncomfortable emotion is a signal that we are out of alignment, that something is interfering with our natural flow.

We empower the second chakra when we find the balance that allows our emotional energy to flow while maintaining appropriate containment, and when we take steps to heal the emotional wounds we have suffered as a result of inappropriate treatment of emotional energy. It is a fallacy that emotional healing has to be painful and take a very long time. We have been conditioned perhaps by the procedures adopted by Sigmund Freud, the father of psychology, who saw his patients for an hour at a time, four or five times a week, for several years. (It has been suggested that there is nothing magical or imperative about the therapeutic hour; it was simply the amount of time it took Freud to smoke a cigar.) We have made great progress in research and understanding since Freud's time. There are many psychological and emotional tools available now for rapid emotional healing. Hypnosis, Interactive Guided Imagery*sm*, EMDR, the Emotional Freedom Technique, and a host of other procedures facilitate and support emotional healing in a time frame that is comparable to or even faster than physical healing.

Beyond healing emotional wounds caused by repression or denial of emotional energy, we can learn to nurture the emotional body and keep it in balance with the physical, mental and spiritual aspects of being. Just as our physical bodies need nourishment, movement and exercise in order to be healthy and strong, so does our emotional body need nourishment and the full exercise of its power. Emotional nourishment can come from the self, when we take the time to honor ourselves and our emotional needs: for relaxation, for occasional pampering, for putting ourselves first once in a while; it can come from nourishing and supportive relationships; and it can come from professional guidance, from a counselor, psychologist, or minister.

Arthur's flute

Arthur arrived at the bothy breathless and out of sorts. Cai had beaten him yet again. He was feeling all the unfairness of the world, and was still smarting at the comment of one of his companions about his lack of parents. He wanted to kick something, or shout at somebody, or ride his horse into the sunset and never come back. He wanted Merlin to sympathize, but all Merlin did was hand him his flute.

"Come."

Arthur followed him to the top of a hill, above the tree line, where Merlin told Arthur to sit down and play his flute. It was the last thing Arthur wanted to do, but Merlin had already turned with a cheery wave and was on his way back down the hill. "See you around sunset," he called back over his shoulder, making it clear that he expected Arthur to stay there for several hours.

Had Arthur not been a warrior he might well have cried. He sat in the grass and looked at the flute. He wanted to break it over his knee. He threw it on the grass, sighed and looked around him.

It was a perfect summer day, he noticed grudgingly. The sky was a clear, shimmering blue, the sun high overhead. All around him the flowers of summer were blooming merrily, unconscious of the weight on his heart. Their perfume drifted on the wind, and in spite of himself Arthur began to feel infinitesimally better. He closed his eyes and swayed a little with the wind, enjoying the warm sun on his face. Insects were humming, and far off he heard a bird cry and the sound of falling water. Almost unconsciously he reached for the flute and began to play.

Merlin heard the distant music as he sat at the entrance to his bothy, his feet on the stone slab Arthur had brought from the landslide. He bent and traced with his finger the outlines of the ancient fern etched into its surface. He nodded in homage to the ancient trees enclosing the clearing as his mind wandered over the paradox of eternal truth and constant change.

There had been great changes in Britain during the four hundred years of Roman occupation, but not here. These trees, the lustrous mosses covering their massive roots, the feathery ferns: they formed a natural cathedral with an air of eternal peace and balance—earth, water, fire, air.

And yet he knew that even here peace had not always reigned. In a far corner of his mind he could hear distant sounds of battle, the epic Battle of the Trees passed down in druidic lore. And at the same time he heard the clashing steel of a different kind of battle, this one in the future, a battle that Arthur would fight among these trees.

As he allowed his mind to reach out to Arthur, sitting alone on the hilltop, it seemed to Merlin that his love for the boy would explode his heart. For all his machinations to keep the whereabouts of Arthur secret he thought sometimes that the natural sterling qualities of the child must broadcast a beacon the length and breadth of the land. Arthur was a natural leader among his companions, they deferred to his opinion and followed him without question, but Arthur himself was oblivious to the effect he had on those around him. He had never spoken to Merlin of his status in Count Ector's household but Merlin knew from the shadow that crossed Arthur's face at times that his uncertain parentage was a burden and an embarrassment, but he did not complain.

Merlin himself was already a legend. He had been advisor to the great Ambrosius; he had raised the ancient circle of standing stones on Salisbury Plain where Ambrosius was buried; and he had seen to it that the magical conception of Arthur had passed into legend, preparing the ground for Arthur's return to take his place as High King. The people told stories of the prince who was being raised in some foreign court and who would come home to lead them, many hoped sooner rather than later because it was clear that King Uther was failing. Merlin had told Arthur the story of the prince's conception and Arthur too commented from time to time on the prince who would succeed Uther. But it had never occurred to him that the prince might be he.

As the distant sounds of the flute drifted on the wind, Merlin allowed his mind to sink deeper into the great Oneness. Time and space resolved. It was as if he lived in all times and all places yet still the land of Britain held a special place in his heart. He saw the arrival of Claudius, the march of the legions, the desperate resistance and ultimate acceptance. In Britain the Romans had done their best to recreate Italy—villas, baths, amphitheaters for chariot racing and gladiatorial shows—and in time the governing stratum of most Celtic tribes in the south had adopted the ways of the conqueror. The educated among them spoke Latin, lived in Roman villas and dressed in togas. They bathed in Roman termae *and were entertained in Roman amphitheaters and traveled on Roman roads. After a hundred years or so all freemen in the empire had become Roman citizens.*

Many Britons had come to depend on the legions to protect them and contemplated with horror rather than relief their abandonment by Rome. The Irish raiders from the west and the Saxons from the east became more bold, but when Britain appealed to Rome the bleak response was that Britain must see to her own defense. The grandeur of Britain's Roman past was crumbling and soon it would be as if the Roman Empire in Britain had never been.

Yet Merlin knew there was to be one last great flowering in Britain before waves of invaders swamped the country, a great light that would ignite the inner light of all Britons and maintain its glow for centuries to come. Arthur. He would inspire Britons to dig deeply into themselves and their past, to take the best of both their Celtic and Roman heritage and forge a new Britain.

Arthur was playing a tune of his own creation, the notes meandering up and down the scale in a haunting melody that carried the pain of his wounded heart away on the wind. He played on as the sun sank lower in the sky, and his music seemed to be part of a great natural symphony, in harmony with the sound of falling water, the rustling grasses, bird songs and the drone of insects. He finally opened his eyes when he became aware of the chill evening breeze. The sun had disappeared, and in the crepuscular light he could see that the animals of the forest had gathered around him.

He was to remember that day. In the carnage of his battles with the Saxons and in the dark nights of self-doubt he would close his eyes, and remember.

The first chakra at the base of the spine is associated with the element earth. It gives us solidity and strength, keeps us stable and safe, it gives us nourishment and a sense of belonging. It is dominant at birth and during the first years of life. When the first chakra is dominant we have no sense of separation.

The development of the second chakra is the beginning of the creation of a sense of self, and we begin to fortify the psychic boundaries that differentiate our individual spirit from universal spirit, and from those around us, so that we can focus our attention inward on the creation of our individual will.

The second chakra is associated with the element water. Think for a moment on the many ways that water manifests itself: the deep peace of a still mountain lake; the bubbling of a mountain brook; the slow meandering progress of a mature river; the immense power of a waterfall; ice and snow; the steam from a pot of pasta; the many faces of ocean waves, the energy of the tides. The cells of our body are mostly composed of water, and calcium is the building block of our skeletal system because we evolved from creatures of the sea.

Within the body, the element water corresponds to emotional energy. In the West, we have been acculturated in a society that holds little respect for emotions. Feeling in our culture is considered inferior to thought, and historically has been associated with the inferior status of women and feminine qualities in general. We believe that emotions are to be controlled by our will.

But emotion provides the power that drives creativity. John Bradshaw has said that emotions, E-motions, are energy in motion. If we do not express our emotions that energy is repressed. According to Carl Jung, emotion is the chief source of becoming conscious. There can be no transforming of darkness into light and of apathy into movement without emotion.

Emotions have a spiritual function as the language of the soul. Our emotional responses are the language through which our inner wisdom communicates with us and teaches us about ourselves. Emotion is the language that gives meaning to our experiences and is the key to buried memories, to events that that we may have banished to the deep levels of the subconscious but that continue to make their presence known, and to demand our attention, through our emotional responses. They continue to have an impact, even though our conscious mind may have denied them.

Imagine an iceberg, floating in the ocean. What we can see of the iceberg, from the deck of the Titanic for example, is only a small part of it. Most of the iceberg is submerged. In the same way, most of our mind is submerged. The conscious mind, the part of the mind that we are aware of, that receives all the sensory input, the part that we like to think is in control, is only a small part of the mind. The greater part of the mind is beneath the level of conscious awareness, it is subconscious.

Everything we see, hear, smell, taste, touch, and experience enters our mind at the conscious level, the part of the iceberg visible above the water line. And then the mind encodes it somehow and stores it in the subconscious, the part of the iceberg hidden in the water. Much, in fact most, of our life experience is forgotten by the conscious mind but at the subconscious level it is faithfully stored.

We often do not know how the subconscious has interpreted a particular experience. Imagine that you are three years old. You are walking through the mall, holding your mom's hand, and you see a tall man with a beard coming towards you. In that same moment, something makes a loud and scary noise behind you. Your three year old mind, that is soaking up experience like a sponge and trying to make sense of the world, might decide that those two events, because they happened at the same time, have a cause and effect relationship. It might connect fear with tall bearded men so that you continue to feel uncomfortable around them, because the sight of a tall bearded man continues to trigger the emotion of fear.

In the language of your soul, the emotion of fear is a message from the deeper levels of your mind that something requires attention; that old memory must be brought into consciousness, to be evaluated in the light of your greater experience and wisdom, so that it can be understood for what it is and released. Otherwise that fear response will continue to condition your reactions. What if your soulmate happens to be tall and bearded? You won't give him a chance.

Once during hypnosis training one of the participants volunteered to explore her phobia of turtles. Her fear of turtles was such that not only did she avoid any place where she might see a live turtle, she was even afraid of watching nature programs on television, or reading books about the natural world in case she should come across a picture of a turtle. Under hypnosis she was asked to return to the origin of her fear, and she remembered camping by a lake with her family when she was around two. She walked down to the water's edge and saw a turtle emerging from the water. It was almost as big as she was and it terrified her.

Frightening experiences sometimes remain in the conscious mind, we continue to be aware of them, and sooner or later may decide to work through the fear that they evoke in us. And sometimes we forget about them at the conscious level and they are stored in the subconscious, and when they are they are buried with all the emotion that we experienced at the time. The sight of a turtle, or even a picture of a turtle, triggered the terror of the two year old confronted with a huge unknown animal emerging from the water. Bringing that memory into consciousness robbed it of its emotional power.

It is one of the tasks of the second chakra to bring repressed energies into consciousness so that they can be released. Another is to reclaim the shadow, the aspects of consciousness that are undeveloped. Again to quote Jung, one does not become enlightened by imagining figures of light, but by making the darkness conscious. So take a break from reading, now. Find a comfortable place, turn off the phone and ask anybody sharing your living space not to disturb you for twenty minutes or so. Perhaps you would like to go to a sacred place you have created in your mind. Begin by taking some deep abdominal breaths, and hold the intention of opening your mind and your heart to the meaning relevant to your spiritual journey of the symbolism of the second chakra.

Jennifer Sault

Second chakra: orange pyramid meditation

In a safe place, free of interruptions, take a few moments to settle yourself comfortably, moving your body until you find the position that feels best for you, supporting your spine if necessary to keep your head, neck and trunk in a straight line to allow the energy to flow freely. Begin by taking some deep, complete breaths, consciously bringing the breath all the way down into the lower part of your lungs, so that your abdomen inflates on the inbreath, and deflates on the outbreath. Breathing deeply now, feel the gentle rise and fall of your abdomen as you breathe in ... and out. Again, deep deep breath in ... and out. And one more deep breath in ... and out. And now relax your breathing, just allowing your body to breathe itself.

Raise the shield of light from below, filling and surrounding your body with light, creating a protected space. Bring down the shield of light from above, balancing and blessing each of your chakras, Sahasrara at the crown, Ajna chakra at the third eye, Vissudha chakra at the throat, Anahata chakra at the heart, Manipura chakra at the solar plexus, Svadhisthana chakra just below the navel, and Muladhara chakra at the base of the spine. And now breathing into your inner light at the heart center, expanding your inner light to fill your body and your energy field, so that you are now filled and surrounded by the triple shield of light, from below, from above and from within, grounded in physical reality, with an open and clear connection to Source, honoring the light within.

Focus your attention now on the second chakra located just below the navel. The color of the second chakra is orange, and its symbol is a pyramid. As you breathe into the second chakra, imagine that the orange pyramid grows and expands, so that you can imagine stepping inside it.

Imagine yourself within the pyramid of orange light. Allow the orange light to permeate your being, orange like the fruit, like the robes of a Buddhist monk, like the leaves in the fall. With the intention of exploring the health and balance of your second chakra, begin to explore the pyramid, and notice any changes in the quality of color, or texture, or light. If you find places of shadow, explore more deeply, and open your consciousness to the awareness of what is contained within the shadow. You can ask what needs to happen for you to bring light into the area of shadow. You may experience flashes of memory. If these become uncomfortable, you can move your consciousness outside the pyramid and examine it from a distance that is comfortable for you.

One of the most pervasive and corrosive emotions that all of us feel is guilt; it is an uncomfortable emotion that we often banish to hidden and fortified regions of the psyche but that continues to influence our thoughts, feelings and behaviors. If in your explorations of the second chakra you should discover guilt, you can think about what you were trying to satisfy or accomplish at the time. ... Is it possible that you were copying that behavior from one of the authority figures in your life?

And now think of ways in which your needs can be, or could have been, met more appropriately. If you have caused harm, look for ways to make amends, to the one you harmed, or if that is no longer possible to "pay it forward" through generous and loving actions towards others. Decide how you will respond more positively to similar situations in the future, and then forgive yourself so that you can move on with your life free of this burden.

Often we feel guilty about innocent behaviors such as pleasure or time to ourselves. If you should find such guilt, ask yourself where you learned it? Whose voice is it that tells you pleasure is a waste of time, or even a sin? When you identify the source of a belief, you are empowered to decide if it is one you choose to keep.

The name of the second chakra is Svadhisthana, which means Sweetness. Consider now the sweetness of Svadhisthana. We live on a planet of ineffable beauty, of infinite gifts, within bodies that are designed to express joy. Consider now the sources of pleasure in your life; what is it that gives you the joy that Arthur found in his flute and in galloping through the forest? Perhaps it is watching the sun set or rise; walking through a forest or on the beach; listening to music; time with loved ones; a massage or a long lazy bath ... And now consider how often you allow yourself to experience those things. An important aspect of spiritual growth, as well as physical, mental and emotional health, is creating balance. Time for pleasure is just as important as time for work, and for duty. Consider how you can increase the pleasure time in your life.

You may find the answers now, in which case you can store them on a mental shelf for retrieval and consideration later. Or you may find the answers arising in the days and weeks ahead as you keep your heart and mind open to new and creative ways of creating balance and harmony. The secret of happiness, says the Dalai Lama, is very simple: identify what makes you unhappy and do less of it; identify what makes you happy and do more of it. It is an exquisitely simple concept; and all the resources and energy of the universe are there to help you to implement it. All you have to do is ask, and pay attention to what is going on around you.

The second chakra is our center of sensuality and pleasure. It is free flowing energy here that allows us to enjoy a beautiful sunset, the sound of music, the laughter of a child, as well as physical intimacy.

Many of us have been acculturated with distorted messages from religious and social sources that for untold generations have created guilt around physical intimacy; that guilt has often restricted the free flow of energy at the second chakra, and spilled over to impede a full and free enjoyment of pleasure from any other source. A legacy of the Victorian era was a lingering cultural belief that it is somehow sinful to experience pleasure; that our lot in life is to work hard and suffer and sacrifice, and that pleasure will be our reward in some other dimension of existence; that sex is for the procreation of children and that recreational sex for pleasure alone is not part of God's intention.

For untold generations women were taught that it was their wifely duty—and indeed their legal obligation—to fulfill their husband's sexual needs regardless of their own inclinations, and many suffered through a kind of nightly rape. If by some miracle a woman did find pleasure in the sexual act she was likely to be labeled a whore. We can only speculate about the state of mind of the Victorian male, who often satisfied his sexual needs in brothels but kept that part of his life secret from his betrothed or his wife.

Though our current practices belie these old-fashioned beliefs they are often accompanied by deep-seated, often unconscious guilt, resulting from longstanding misconceptions about sensuality and pleasure. And the tension, or contradiction, between belief and practice take their toll: in physical illness, in emotional distress, and in quality of life.

As we contemplate the second chakra it is perhaps one of our greatest challenges to question the ideas about sex with which western societies have been acculturated for two thousand years or so. "Truths" about sex that are taught to us from an early age have become so embedded in the fabric of our belief system that we rarely question the right and wrong labels that we assign to certain behaviors. The idea that sex can be at all spiritual, or that spirituality can include sex, is one that challenges our deepest and most cherished ideas of morality. We in the Western world are entrenched in religious traditions that separate spirit from matter; that look upon sex as a necessary but spiritually distasteful act that should be legitimately performed for procreation only.

God made us in his image, we are taught, but the matter of sex is the defining feature of our difference from God. The icons of our dominant religion are a virgin mother and a bachelor. It is the act of sex that denies that we could ever be of the same essential spiritual stuff as Jesus, or God, and that labels anathema the idea that God is within us all. The suggestion that Jesus was married or even contemplated marriage was blasphemy to the debunkers of Dan Brown's *The Da Vinci Code* and the groups that protested, picketed and boycotted Martin Scorsese's 1988 film *The Last Temptation of Christ*.

In the ancient ritual of Hieros Gamos, or Sacred Marriage, a country's leader and a priestess of the dominant religion engaged in sexual union to provide symbolic and literal fertility for the land and the people. Such religious ceremonies often included sex in groups. The original meaning of the term "orgy" was "secret worship," but in today's parlance there is no differentiation between these sacred rituals and the drunken "orgies" of the declining Roman Empire.

In *A Passage to India*, E. M. Forster juxtaposes the upright uptight straight-laced British of the Victorian era against the sensuality of India and the frank sexuality of its religious art, an aspect of Indian culture that was probably no small contributor to the British sense of moral superiority. Yet the ecstasy of sexual union is perhaps the closest we can come to finding a physical corollary for the spiritual ecstasy that mystics throughout the ages have tried to communicate to us. St Teresa of Avila, a medieval mystic, describes her experience of divine ecstasy in terms that we can recognize as sexual:

> It pleased the Lord that I should sometimes see the following vision. I would see beside me ... an angel in bodily form. He was not tall ... very beautiful, his face so aflame that he appeared to be one of the highest types of angel who seem to be all afire. ... In his hands I saw a long golden spear and at the end of the iron tip I seemed to see a point of fire. With this he seemed to pierce my heart several times so that it penetrated to my entrails ... and he left me completely afire with a great love for God. The pain was so sharp that it made me utter several moans; and so excessive was the sweetness caused me by this intense pain that one can never wish to lose it, nor will one's soul be content with anything less than God. It is not bodily pain, but spiritual, though the body has a share in it – indeed, a great share.

St Teresa of Avila, *Autobiography, Chapter XXIX*

St Teresa was canonized in 1622, and in 1970 was declared a Doctor of the Church for her writing and teaching on prayer, one of only two women to be so honored. She is the patron saint of, among other things, headaches and opposition of Church authorities.

St Teresa's description of her experience of ecstasy, in terms not only spiritual and emotional but also physical, brought her to the attention of the Inquisition. Some of her confessors told her that such experiences must come from the devil. When Gian Lorenzo Bernini created a statue of St Teresa for the Cornaro Chapel in the Santa Maria della Vittoria church in Rome he was inspired by this description of her mystical experience, and created a statue that very clearly communicates the "great share" of the physical aspect of the spiritual ecstasy of St Teresa, so much so that, predictably, his statue earned the censure of the church.

Gian Lorenzo Bernini, The Ecstasy of Saint Teresa

As in so many areas of our lives, when it comes to sex we are plagued by the either/or duality of our thinking. There is legitimate sex—within marriage, or at least within a committed relationship, with or without the intention to procreate—that is enmeshed with a historical sense of duty and entitlement; and at the other extreme there is indiscriminate promiscuity and license. In neither case do we approach sexuality with a sense of the sacred. The character of Robert Langdon in Dan Brown's *The Da Vinci Code* challenges his students to seek the sacred and the mystical in sex:

> "The next time you find yourself with a woman, look in your heart and see if you cannot approach sex as a mystical, spiritual act. Challenge yourself to find that spark of divinity that man can only achieve through union with the sacred feminine."
> The women smiled knowingly, nodding.
> The men exchanged dubious giggles and off-color jokes.

In ancient cultures the union of the male and female principles that creates life was sacred. This sacred union is honored in the Great Rite of Wicca, the western version of the Tantric tradition, where the union is enacted either symbolically—when a small dagger, symbol of the masculine, is plunged into a cup, bowl or chalice, symbol of the feminine—or actually as the high priest and high priestess unite in the sexual embrace. Druidry too regards sexuality as sacred. It is the force that conveys life. The union of the masculine and feminine principles at a spiritual and psychological level, says Philip Carr-Gomm, gives birth to, or reveals, the divine child within.

It is one of the challenges of the second chakra, as indeed of all the chakras, to reintegrate the sense of the sacred: into relationships; into sexuality; and into the recognition of the spiritual communications encoded in our emotions.

So while the first chakra embodies our right to exist, to belong, to be stable, safe and nourished, the second chakra is our right to feel. The sweetness of *Svadhisthana* is our right to feel pleasure, and to know intimacy with another. Feeling is the flow of dynamic energy that is essential for growth, change, and transformation. It is through our emotions that we learn. As we honor and respect and seek to understand our emotional reactions we progress in our knowledge of self. So take a break from reading now; ensure your privacy for a half hour or so and repair to your sacred place for the Lake Meditation that will help you to reclaim and honor your right to know sensuality and pleasure.

Lake meditation

In a safe place, free of interruptions, take a few moments to settle yourself comfortably, perhaps moving your body until you find the position that feels best for you, keeping your head, neck and trunk in a straight line to allow the energy to flow freely.

Breathing deeply now, feel the gentle rise and fall of your abdomen as you breathe in … and out. Again, deep deep breath in … and out. And one more deep breath in … and out. And now relax your breathing, and allow your body to breathe itself. Raise the shield of light from below, filling and surrounding your body with light, creating a protected space. Bring down the shield of light from above, balancing and blessing each of your chakras, Sahasrara chakra at the crown, Ajna chakra at the third eye, Vissudha chakra at the throat, Anahata chakra at the heart, Manipura chakra at the solar plexus, Svadhisthana chakra just below the navel, and Muladhara chakra at the base of the spine. And now breathing into your inner light at the heart center, expanding your inner light, so that you are now filled and surrounded by the triple shield of light, from below, from above and from within, grounded in physical reality, with an open and clear connection to the Source, honoring the light within.

Imagine that you are walking along the shore of a lake. Perhaps you are barefoot and the mud at the water's edge feels soft and moist. Perhaps there is a heron standing motionless on one leg in the shallows, waiting patiently for breakfast to swim by. The sun is low in the eastern sky and you cast a long shadow in front of you as you walk.

You look out over the water and you see an ethereal image of a woman, hovering over the surface of the water. She beckons, inviting you to slip into the water. You feel totally safe; you step into the water and walk towards the Lady of the Lake, and when the water reaches your waist you lift your feet and lie back on the surface of the water. Floating now in the deep, clean water that supports you, and caresses you: the sun is now warm on your face, the water cool and refreshing as you float, safely, comfortably, the Lady of the Lake at your side.

You become aware now of a current within the water that is tugging gently at your feet. You surrender to the movement of the water, and find you are being drawn out of the lake and into a river. You may want to notice the vegetation on either side of this river, weeping willows perhaps, trailing the tendrils of their branches in the water, brightly colored flowers, soft feathery ferns. You let the river carry you safely, gently, and comfortably downstream. The river here flows quite swiftly and you know it is safe to allow the river to carry you.

As you float along with the current, allow yourself to notice all the different sensations you are feeling: the warm sun on your face; the cool caress of the water; the movement of the current; the sounds within the water and in the environment around you. We as human beings have a deep affinity with water. Water is the fundamental component of our cells. And calcium is the building block of our bones because we evolved from creatures of the sea. We carry that history within us, an awareness in the deepest levels of our being that water is home; water is life.

The river widens, the flow is more gentle. As you allow your limbs to float freely, surrendering completely to the energy of the river, you find that you can reach out with your consciousness, back behind you to the swiftly flowing river, to the lake, to the falling rain, to the clouds. And forward, ahead of you, to the mature, slowly moving river, and to where the river meets the sea. Imagine that you can hear the beat of the surf that echoes the beat of your heart. You are the sea, you are the river, you are the lake, you are the condensation and the clouds and the drops of rain. You are the ice of winter storms, and the gentle spring rain, you are the hail and the snow and the dew and the soft mist of a summer morning. You are the waterfalls and the pounding surf; you are the deep peace of the lake and the vast energy of the tides. As you float down the river, you can contemplate the richness of your being, your vast resources, your limitless potential.

The second chakra, then, is the seat of sensuality and sexuality, and it is also the center of our physical creativity, not only in the reproduction of the species—our reproductive organs are here—but also it is the energy of this center that allows us to manifest our ideas. A creative idea comes from the universal source, it can arrive like a thunderbolt or a flash of light and we are full of enthusiasm and we talk about it and think about it and we are full of excitement until … until it comes to doing something concrete about it.

It takes second chakra energy to bring that idea into physical form, and it is at the second chakra that we confront what it will cost us to actualize that idea: in time, energy, effort; in the ridicule perhaps of people in our lives who think it is too different or too weird. Many wonderful creative concepts bite the dust at the second chakra; they are what Caroline Myss calls "energy abortions," and can be a factor in disorders of the pelvic area. The blockage of creative energy at the second chakra, like the blockage of emotional energy, can over time create physical illness such as fibroids or menstrual difficulties, sexual dysfunction, chronic constipation, pelvic or lower back pain or problems with the urinary tract or prostate. A healthy second chakra manifests in mutually respectful, loving and supportive relationships, and in the free and frank enjoyment of sensual pleasure, not only through physical intimacy but also in play, in art, in movement, in touch.

King Arthur spent the years of his second chakra dominance learning the skills he would need to survive and rule. Neither Geoffrey of Monmouth nor Thomas Malory has much to say about this period of his life. Modern writers, perhaps influenced by psychology's appreciation of the importance of this stage of development, have devoted greater attention to Arthur's education and to the development of the relationship between the young Arthur and Merlin.

T. H. White opens *The Once and Future King* with Arthur's daily schedule: mornings spent with a governess, afternoons spent on tilting, horsemanship, hawking, fencing and archery. White perceived that in his own time the world of man and the world of nature were in opposition; his Merlin, therefore, comes from the opposite direction and teaches Arthur the morality of the natural world. He uses his magical arts to change Arthur into various kinds of creatures in order to teach him theories of government through direct experience. Arthur learns the dangers of totalitarianism when he is transformed into an ant, in a world where there is no individual freedom of thought and "Everything Not Forbidden is Compulsory." He learns about dictatorship in the moat where he becomes a small fish at the mercy of the powerful carp. And he learns about respect and loyalty when he is transformed into a goose, one of the rare animals that bond for life.

Because White has invented the ingenious literary device of having Merlin live backwards in time, Merlin becomes the mouthpiece for White's commentary on twentieth century politics. (That is not the only liberty that White takes with time. White's source was the medieval Malory and he evidently decided that since Arthur was to embody the values of the medieval period he might as well be medieval. He transports Arthur from the sixth to the twelfth century, transforming Celts into Saxons and Saxons into Normans; Uther Pendragon becomes William the Conqueror and reigns from 1066 to the twelfth century, and White is able to include the medieval myths of Robin Hood and his Merrie Men.)

Mary Stewart devotes the second book of her magnificent trilogy of the life of Merlin to the period of Arthur's youth and Merlin's role as his teacher; Douglas Monroe's *The 21 Lessons of Merlyn* describes Arthur's mystical training as an apprentice of Merlin.

Merlin therefore supervised the period of Arthur's second chakra dominance. In a perfect world we would all have spiritually enlightened beings guiding our development. In a less than perfect developmental environment it becomes our challenge in later life to seek the Merlin within and discover the psychological and spiritual tools that will allow us to heal our developmental wounds and nurture our inner light. Merlin was Arthur's mentor and protector, and then, when the time was right, he was at Arthur's side as he stepped forward to meet his destiny.

Many sources that attest to the existence of an historical King Arthur call him a "War Duke." Certainly any leader of the time had to be first and foremost an able warrior, and Arthur's training in the martial arts and his talent for military tactics was the foundation of his right to rule. The later, mythical, dimensions of the legend are grafted on to this foundation of a brilliant tactician and leader of great courage and charisma. Arthur came to his kingship as a teenager, and if it was a mythical sword that marked him as God's chosen one he was also, like all noble young men of his time, well-trained in the arts of war.

The Sword in the Stone

Arthur watched his foster brother Cai as he tied the leather thongs around his calves, and helped him fasten the leather breastplate and helmet in place. He looked wistfully at the sword his brother carried, and wondered when he would bear his own sword into battle. His foster father Count Ector strode into the room. "Ready, lads?" He put an arm around each of his sons' shoulders. "Come, the horses are ready," he said, and led them out into the castle courtyard.

The journey to Londinium took three days. They arrived tired and covered in dust, ravenously hungry, yet the inconveniences of travel had not dampened the boys' high spirits nor their excitement at the coming ceremonies. The body of the High King, Uther Pendragon, lay in state in the center of the great hall surrounded by his warriors. But before the ceremonies could begin there was a great shout from outside and a messenger burst into the hall. "The Saxons, my lords, the Saxons have landed!"

Arthur watched as the warriors streamed out of the hall calling for their horses, swords and armor. Cai was among them, a look of disbelief and frustration mixed with acute embarrassment on his face. He started to run in the direction opposite from the other warriors, and Arthur ran after him.

"What's going on?" he said.

"I'm an idiot," Cai called over his shoulder. "I've forgotten my sword!"

"Let me get it for you," Arthur said, "I can run faster." And he took off like the wind, dodging through the crowds at the gate and down the street. There was a church at the end of the street, and he took a short cut through the churchyard to save himself valuable time.

As he ran full tilt through the churchyard Arthur was brought up short by a strange sight, a large stone, with a kind of anvil on top of it, and stuck in the anvil was a sword. Arthur had no time to wonder why. He looked hastily around, but there was no one of whom to ask permission, and besides, in a time of great peril such as this who would question putting such a sword to good use? He grasped the handle and pulled the sword out of the anvil, and ran back to Cai. "Here," he said, handing him the sword, "use this one." The look Cai gave him was strange indeed, but he took the sword and ran off to join the battle.

The Saxons had chosen their time unwisely. The best warriors in the kingdom were gathered in this one place and their victory was swift and brutal. In little more than an hour they were congratulating each other. They were laughing and knocking back tankards of mead and ale when an old grizzled warrior noticed the sword in Cai's belt.

"Where did you get that sword, boy?"

There was something in his tone that drew the attention of the other warriors, and a sudden hush fell over the company. They encircled Cai and the old warrior asked again: "Where did you get that sword?"

Cai was confused. He looked towards his father, and then at Arthur, questioning. Arthur knelt before Count Ector. "Forgive me, foster father. I was going back to our lodgings to get Cai's sword when I saw this one stuck into an anvil in a churchyard. I thought the owner would not mind its being used to defend the kingdom."

The warriors gathered around him. "Are you saying, boy," the old one said, "that you took the sword out of the stone?"

"Yes," Arthur replied. "If I did wrong I ask your pardon."

"It's not possible," the warriors said to one another. They took Arthur back to the churchyard, and the old warrior stuck the sword back into the anvil. It slid easily down into the stone, and when he tried to pull it out again it was stuck as if it had become part of the stone itself. One by one the other warriors tried, each one unsuccessfully. The old warrior grinned at them, crossed his arms in front of his chest and nodded to Arthur.

"Go on, lad," he said. "Show us how you pulled the sword out of the stone."

Arthur was bewildered, and embarrassed to be the focus of so much attention, but at an encouraging nod from Count Ector he stepped up to the stone and grasped the handle of the sword. He gave a gentle tug and the sword slid out of the stone. Arthur raised it above his head and looked around the circle of warriors. He did not know whether they would be pleased or angry, but the last thing he expected was that all of them would bow the knee before him. Even his foster father and Cai knelt and called him "My Lord."

"Please, father," he said, pulling Count Ector to his feet. "What is going on?" Count Ector was looking over Arthur's shoulder. Arthur turned and saw Merlin waiting in the shadows. He came slowly forward, his deep-set eyes and their timeless wisdom looking deeply into Arthur's. He pointed to wording carved into the side of the stone:

> Whoso pulleth out this sword of this stone and
> anvil, is rightwise king born of all Britain.

Arthur grew up not knowing of his royal blood and unaware of
the great plan of which he was the pivotal part. At the court of Count
Ector and Flavilla he was loved and nurtured and taught the skills
he would need to survive and rule. He learned the value of trust in
relationships and formed the bonds that would be the foundation
of his Round Table. Merlin nurtured his intellect and guided his
moral development, so that he entered his adolescence with all the
resources he needed to flower as himself. And, when the time was
right, he "remembered" who he really was. He was, Geoffrey of
Monmouth tells us, "a young man only fifteen years old; but he was
of outstanding courage and generosity, and his inborn goodness gave
him such grace that he was loved by almost all the people."

Arthur was the son of Uther Pendragon and his queen. Even
if the circumstances of his conception were unusual he was the
legitimate heir to the throne. But because he had been raised by
foster parents in obscurity there needed to be some supernatural
sign for him to be accepted as king. In the fifteenth century *Le
Morte d'Arthur*, Sir Thomas Malory tells us that a rock appeared in
a churchyard:

> [A] great stone four square, like unto a marble stone;
> and in midst thereof was like an anvil of steel a
> foot on high, and therein stuck a fair sword naked
> by the point, and letters there were written in gold
> about the sword that said thus: Whoso pulleth out
> this sword of this stone and anvil, is rightwise king
> born of all England.

(England did not exist in the sixth century. The name comes
from the Angles, one of the Germanic tribes collectively referred
to herein as Saxons, who conquered Britain in the centuries after

Arthur and who, by the time of Malory, identified Britain with themselves.)

Malory was writing for the medieval mind, which was very different from ours. We need logic, and reason. Even if it is magic we need for it to make sense. The modern world is founded on reason. The medieval world was founded on superstition and faith. The world of medieval man was half magical, full of portents and supernatural phenomena. He would accept that a rock simply appeared, with an anvil on top of it and a sword stuck into it, with the helpful message that only the true king would be able to remove it. (Modern interpreters of the legend have offered more rational explanations for the origin of the sword.) When Arthur alone of all the knights who tried was able to remove the sword from the stone, it was accepted that he was ordained by God to be king, despite his youth and lack of battle experience.

There are two swords associated with Arthur: the sword in the stone that allows him to be recognized as king and that is broken in two during a fight with King Pellinore, and the magical sword Excalibur that is the gift of the Lady of the Lake. It is proof, should we need it, that the legend is a great deal more than an entertaining story. There is no fictional imperative to create a second sword: the first was god's message that Arthur was his chosen one, it gave him the authority to rule, it convinced the petty kings to accept this young untried adolescent as their ruler. It is hardly credible that it could be broken, and yet it was, and a second sacred sword, imbued with a different symbolism, makes its debut on the pages of legend: Excalibur.

Excalibur

The lake at their feet was calm as a mirror. As the darkness slowly lifted they began to see indeterminate shapes—trees at the water's edge, the round thatched huts of the marsh dwellers, the island. The early morning mist hovered over the surface of the water, muffling sound and bathing everything in ethereal light. The silence was broken only gently: by the occasional splash of a wading bird that momentarily disturbed the smooth surface and sent ripples scurrying to the farther shore; by a soft breeze that rustled the tree tops. Once in a while one of the horses would snort and shake its head, its bridle would jingle and its breath would condense and form a cloud of mist around its nose.

Most of the warriors were standing alongside their mounts but Arthur was seated on his white stallion. Like the morning he had an air of being newly minted, his young face with as yet no beard growth smooth as a woman's, his gray eyes serious and focused on the island as it emerged from the mist. He controlled the powerful horse with effortless grace, the two of them standing still as the trees yet radiating power and energy contained by a potent will.

He was still dazed by the events of recent days, the sword in the stone, his meteoric rise in status. He looked down at his new clothes. They had wanted to dress him in bright colors and jewels but he had chosen white—like his horse, a gift from Lancelot; like his white hound, Cavall; like a fresh sheet of parchment on which he would write his life story.

He gazed into the mist. His eyes, he decided, must be playing tricks in the shifting light because he seemed to see a hand rising from the water. The mist stirred and he could see that the hand was holding aloft a sword. He turned to call Merlin's attention to it but when he looked back it was gone.

The contours of the island were clear now. Apple orchards draped the shores and the lower reaches of a hill that rose steeply on one side, gently on the other, to a summit crowned with a circle of standing stones. And across the water, still trailing tendrils of mist, a black barge was approaching. The oars made no sound and seemed, magically, not even to disturb the water, but Arthur knew from Merlin that it was no magic but years of training. The barge made only a soft crunching sound as it came ashore. Arthur dismounted and handed the reins to a page, then boarded the barge, followed by Merlin and Lancelot and several of his companions.

The mist had completely dissipated by the time they reached the island. The sun had cleared the horizon and was illuminating the brilliant emerald of the trees and the myriad colors of the flowers. It glowed on the surface of the stones. Waiting for them on the shore was a delegation of priestesses in blue robes, led by the High Priestess, the Lady of the Lake. She was smaller than Arthur had expected, and was dressed in a flowing white robe. He had heard such tales of her power and wisdom that he had expected her to be physically tall as well, but as he was presented to her and felt the full force of her gaze he was in no doubt that her physical size in no way mirrored the force of her spirit.

"Welcome, Arthur of Britain."

Her voice was as mesmerizing as her presence. He nodded his thanks, not trusting his own to speak. She turned and led him towards the shrine at the foot of the Tor. Merlin had told him that it was a natural spring of fresh sweet water that had never failed, not even in times of drought when rivers shrank to a trickle and fields were barren and full of dust. From deep within the earth the sacred water flowed clean and cold, and since the earliest days the spring had been a shrine to the goddess. With the passage of time, the ground around it had grown higher, so that now the shrine was underground, a large, cool, man-made cavern. The priestesses gathered here within the womb of the sacred mother for their rituals to honor the cycles of Nature.

As he entered the shrine Arthur caught his breath, for lying on the altar in front of the sacred pool was the sword he had seen through the mist, clasped in the hand emerging from the water. The Lady of the Lake caught his eye, and from her shadow of a smile he realized that she knew about his vision. She lifted the sword and turned towards him.

"This is Excalibur, the sword of Britain. It is yours to use for as long as you defend her. This is not a gift, mark you, but a loan on sacred trust. You must promise to return it to me when you can no longer wield it."

It was a sword such as Arthur had never seen, indeed a sword of kings and emperors. The blade was smooth and so finely wrought that it sang. He reached out his hand and closed his fingers around the hilt. It was as if the sword belonged there, as if it had been made expressly to fit his hand and become a natural extension of his arm. He raised it, and felt the power flow through his arm and through his whole being, he tingled and glowed and vibrated, and saw in his mind's eye rapid images of the triumphs that lay ahead for him and Excalibur.

The Lady of the Lake signaled to one of the priestesses who came forward with a scabbard. This too the Lady of the Lake offered to Arthur. It was of fine soft leather, exquisitely worked with magical symbols embroidered in gold and silver thread.

"This scabbard was made for you, Arthur of Britain. It is woven with all the magic and spiritual protection of Avalon. As long as you wear it, though you may be wounded, you will never bleed to excess."

Arthur sank to one knee. "Thank you, my Lady. I give you my word that I will use your gifts well, and I will return the sword to you when the time comes." He rose, belted the scabbard to his waist and slid the wondrous sword into it. Then his solemnity vanished and he turned to Merlin with a radiant smile and followed the Lady of the Lake out in to the brilliant sunshine.

The symbolic meaning of the sword in many ancient myths is that it cuts away illusion; it eliminates the unnecessary; it is the sword of truth. A vital part of the spiritual journey is learning to differentiate between truth and illusion. Much that we have been taught as Truth may indeed have been true for our teachers but not necessarily for us. As we confront the challenges of the lower chakras, challenges to our survival, to our emotional bodies, and to the developing sense of ourselves, who we are, and who we choose to be as distinct from what others want us to be, it is necessary to find within us a capacity for discrimination, a truth meter that will help us to sift through the avalanche of information with which modern life bombards us for the nuggets that are true for us.

So take a break from reading now, repair to your sacred place, and follow the guided meditation to your sword of truth.

Sword in the stone meditation

In a safe place, free of interruptions, take a few moments to settle yourself comfortably, perhaps moving your body until you find the position that feels best for you, keeping your head, neck and trunk in a straight line to allow the energy to flow freely. Breathing deeply now, feel the gentle rise and fall of your abdomen as you breathe in … and out. Again, deep deep breath in … and out. And one more deep breath in … and out. And now relax your breathing, and allow your body to breathe itself.

Raise the shield of light from below, filling and surrounding your body with light, creating a protected space. Bring down the shield of light from above, balancing and blessing each of your chakras, Sahasrara at the crown, the Ajna chakra at the third eye, the Vissudha chakra at the throat, Anahata chakra at the heart, Manipura chakra at the solar plexus, Svadhisthana chakra just below the navel, and the Muladhara chakra at the base of the spine. And now breathing into your inner light at the heart center, expanding your inner light, so that you are now filled and surrounded by the triple shield of light, from below, from above and from within, grounded in physical reality, with an open and clear connection to the Source, honoring the light within.

Imagine that you are standing in a meadow at the very edge of an ancient forest. Behind you massive, wise old trees form a protective screen at your back as you contemplate, in front of you, a path across the meadow leading towards the east. It is a few moments before dawn, on the morning of the Spring Equinox, the day half way between the winter and summer solstices when the day and night are of equal duration. The quality of light is soft, and the eastern sky is awash in a delicate pink.

The trees behind you are emerging from their winter slumber, and are wearing delicate haloes of fresh yellow/green, not yet the full lush growth of summer. In the meadow before you, young shoots of grass and wildflowers are pushing their way up out of the ground, and here and there are splashes of color, the first blossoms. The air is crisp, cool, clean and fresh, and pregnant with possibility. As you begin to walk along the path, towards the east, imagine that you can feel the wind on your face, and breathe deep into your lungs the breath of life.

The path leads towards a small hill; as you get closer and the sky continues to lighten you see that on top of the hill is a circle of standing stones. It is a sacred place, a place of power where the energy of earth is especially strong.

As you enter the circle of standing stones you see that in the center of the circle is a large rock. At this very moment, the sun appears over the eastern horizon and a shaft of light illuminates a sword that penetrates the rock, so that the long shadow of the sword falls at your feet. As your eyes adjust to the brightness you can perceive a figure behind the sword in the stone. The figure is the guardian of the sacred sword Excalibur, the Sword of Spirit that penetrates the Stone of Earth, symbolizing perfect balance and harmony between heaven and earth, spirit and matter.

The guardian steps forward and asks you if you are ready to draw the sword from the stone. … Listen to your heart. If it is time, grasp the handle of the sword with both hands and draw it from the stone. Hold the sword upright, your hands clasping the hilt at the level of your heart and the blade pointing upward in front of your face … and step forward, into the stone.

You are the stone, and you are the sword, you are the meeting place, the bridge between earth and spirit.

The guardian of the sword is standing before you. Take some time to communicate with him or her, ask any questions you may have, or listen to anything the guardian has to say to you. Or perhaps you choose to commune in silence. If you have not yet drawn the sword, perhaps you yet have questions for the guardian.

...

If you have drawn the sword and stepped into the stone, take both sword and stone into your own being, and prepare to leave. If you felt the time was not yet right for you, know that you can return to this place at some point in the future. Thank the guardian of the stone and walk out of the sacred circle of stones, back down the path towards the forest. ...

Arthur's mystical, magical sword is an undisputed element of all versions of the legends. Excalibur, Caliburn, Caledvwlch: though its name and its genesis differ it is always a sword of great power, of venerated and sacred origin. With it, and with the scabbard imbued with the magical protection of the Lady of the Lake, Arthur is invincible.

Armed with the sword, Arthur is ready to fight his battles with the Saxons.

The Twelve Battles

They were long hard years. Every summer seemingly inexhaustible waves of invaders descended upon the shores of Britain. Arthur saw things he could not even have imagined in his worst nightmares in the haven of his years with Merlin, and at times the peaceful days of his boyhood seemed like a distant chimera. Reality was the clash of swords and shouts and screams and the smell of blood and guts spilling on the ground. The days and weeks flowed together. He slept in his clothes with armor and weapons at the ready, rose to meet the challenge of the day and fell on to his bed exhausted at night, to dream of the day's battle. And it went on year after year. He and his Companions were transformed from eager young boys into seasoned warriors, grim and determined. Arthur no longer thought of the idyllic times of the past nor looked forward to a time of peace in the future. The boundaries of his world were limited to the battle of the moment and where the next would be.

In the winters, when the islands were protected by rough seas, they retired to strongholds in the forest, licked their wounds, forged new weapons and trained new recruits. In the spring they waited, at first with excitement tinged with dread, later with weary resignation, for the hilltop beacons to signal the alarm. Arthur and the sword Excalibur were always in the lead, his sword doing the work of ten as he fought with inspired brilliance, courage and determination. He discovered a genius for strategy, and used to devastating effect the intuition honed in years of mystical study with his Druid teacher. When he fought he seemed to enter another dimension, following an inner voice that never failed him, inspiring devotion and unquestioned faith in those who followed him.

There was a moment, once, of respite. Melwas, the king of the summer country, invited Arthur and the Companions to the festival of the Winter Solstice. They observed the rituals in the circle of standing stones on top of the Tor, and later repaired to Melwas' stronghold for the celebratory feast. Melwas' household was not large but he offered a respectable spread, and had invited the priestesses from the shrine and the Lady of the Lake to participate. The Lady herself had declined but had given her permission to those of the senior priestesses who so desired to partake in the celebration.

Arthur found himself seated next to one of the priestesses, and he discovered that she was like no woman he had ever known. He was, in fact, relatively innocent of women. His life so far had been his early years of training, at Ector's court and with Merlin, and then the years of fighting. The priestess was intelligent, and learned, and genuinely interested in everything he had to say, listening gravely and offering insights that showed her understanding. He told her the tales of Mona that he had heard from Merlin, and how he had visited the island once. And she told him of Avalon and the Tor with its ancient circle of stones, where they still kept the old ways, the fires of Beltane and the seasonal celebrations offered to the Goddess. Of the mysteries she could tell him nothing, but she could tell him of blessing the fields and giving thanks for the harvest, and the myriad ways in which the spiritual community led by the Lady of the Lake served the people of the countryside.

And Arthur felt as comfortable with her as he did with Lancelot or Merlin, speaking eagerly and passionately of anything that came to mind. And she, like they, kept pace with him as they ranged over astronomy and philosophy and the mystery and science of nature. Only it was not at all like a conversation with Lancelot or Merlin, because he was deeply aware of the scent of her that was like spring flowers and autumn fruit, and of her eyes that were the fathomless blue of the deep ocean, of the warmth of her smile and her sometimes barbed wit. When she touched his arm while confiding a mildly wicked observation about old King Pellinore he felt his flesh tingle.

She was a priestess of Avalon and her body was her own. She was free to give herself as she chose. Mating, Arthur knew, was for her a sacred act, and had nothing in common with the frantic couplings of warriors after battle with the women who followed the army. Arthur had never been tempted, though he could have had his choice of any woman. But now: he felt stirred in a way he had never felt before, and felt the beginnings of a flush of embarrassment, but she looked at him directly. "Yes," she said, to his unspoken and unspeakable question, "Yes."

Even as he approached her chamber Arthur was torn between the sure conviction of their mutual understanding and the fear that he had totally misunderstood and that he was about to commit a grave offense. But she opened her door before he had a chance to knock and welcomed him in.

He awoke the next morning to find her sleeping beside him. He looked down at her face in wonder, and gently stroked her cheek. She stirred, smiling with her eyes closed.

"I was having a most wonderful dream. I dreamed I sat beside the High King at table and we shared the same dish. And we talked and talked, of so many things, and I learned that he is indeed a king of legend." She opened her eyes and touched his face. She smiled, teasing. "And he is also a man." She laughed. "And what a man!" She caressed

the back of his neck and as he kissed her Arthur felt as if he were on fire and dissolving at the same time.

Later, resting on his elbow, he looked down at her and caressed the outline of her face and jaw.

"What a queen you will be, Morgan." He kissed her gently. "I want to know everything about you. Where is your family?"

She shrugged. "I have a little brother somewhere. I have never seen him. And my sister is married to King Lot. But my family is the Lady and my sisters of the shrine. I came to Avalon when I was very young. This is where I belong. I think I have always known it. The Lady Viviane came to visit my mother when I was five, they are related somehow, and though I had never seen her before I … I knew her. And she recognized something in me. She told my mother that I must be dedicated to the goddess and be trained in Avalon. My mother did not want to let me go, she had already lost my brother, and my sister was not easy to love, but she could not deny the power of … my destiny."

Arthur lay back down on the pillow and she snuggled in the crook of his arm and caressed his chest.

"Lost your brother? He died then?"

"No. He was fostered somewhere. They would never tell me where, or why."

"So you came to Avalon?"

"Yes. It was so different from my home. Full of sunlight and apple trees. And the Lady. She opened my mind and nourished my spirit. I knew even at five that my spirit would have shriveled at Tintagel."

Arthur was suddenly tense. His arm tightened around her shoulders. "Tintagel? Your home is Tintagel? And your mother. Who is your mother, Morgan?"

"Her name is Igraine."

Arthur leaped out of bed and backed up to the window, horror on his face. He turned and rested his palms on the sill, looking out as he tried to control his breath and his voice. Morgan sat up in bed.

"What is it, Arthur?"

Arthur was breathing rapidly. He made several attempts to speak before he was able to say in a strangled voice:

"You are my sister, Morgan. My sister. By all that's sacred, what have we done?"

"You? You are the little brother they took away soon after he was born? I never realized ... I never ... But we sinned in innocence, Arthur. The goddess will understand, she will forgive us, she ..."

Arthur finally turned to face her. "It is not the sin, Morgan. It is ... Last night ... it was as if I have waited for you all my life. You have touched my soul. You are my beloved. But ... we cannot ... we can never ..."

The shock on Morgan's face dissolved into grief as she absorbed his meaning. She shook her head, tears streaming down her face.

Arthur had no choice but to put the memory aside and focus on war and the next battle: the planning, the execution, the aftermath. He and his cadre of Companions had been trained from childhood in the arts of war but their foot soldiers were not men born to fight; they had been born to till fields and raise crops and children but the eddies of fate had decreed otherwise. Trustingly, they followed their inspired young king into scenes of nightmare; some lost their limbs, others their lives, and some their reason, but few deserted or questioned the necessity of doing what they were doing.

After each battle the bile would rise in Arthur's throat as he gazed over the carnage-strewn field, but his voice was ever gentle, grateful and encouraging as he toured the field hospitals. Merlin, skilled in healing and herbal lore, was tireless too as he tended the wounded, and when his work was done he and Arthur would have some precious moments together.

Throughout those years Arthur crisscrossed the country, intuitively knowing where the next threat was coming from even before the beacons were lit, so that more and more often now when the Picts from the north swarmed over the Emperor Hadrian's wall, or the Saxons crossed the seas from the east or the Irish from the west, they found Arthur ready and waiting. The magical scabbard woven by the priestesses of Avalon became faded and worn over the years but never failed in its protection. Arthur was often wounded, but even deep cuts that would have spelled the end for other men did not bleed to excess and his recovery was rapid and complete.

Finally, a day dawned that began like many another. The sun rose over Badon Hill and glinted off the swords and pikes of hordes of men and women who were defending their homelands, their families and their king against an invader who had mustered all remaining allies and resources for a final desperate assault on the fertile island of Britain. And by the time the sun set, the invaders had been vanquished. Those remnants left alive fled to the shores and disappeared over the horizon, and the exhausted defenders cheered themselves and their king, put away their implements of war, and returned home.

We are told that there were twelve battles, though for most of them specific places have not been identified. Twelve is simply a mystical number that recurs again and again in mythology and in the natural world. There were twelve disciples of Jesus, twelve signs of the Zodiac, twelve battles of Hercules, and twelve tribes of Israel; there are twelve months of the year, twelve hours in the day, twelve days of Christmas. Arthur fought twelve battles, and then had twelve years of peace during which he created a society based on Right, rather than Might. Before he could turn his attention to implementing the ideas of his spiritual mentor Merlin for a society based on justice he had first to make the land safe, he had to satisfy the needs of the lower chakras, he had to find his own power and exercise it in the defense of Britain.

In the same way we, before we can focus on the spiritual development of the upper chakras, have to satisfy the needs of the lower chakras for security, and physical survival, and a secure sense of who we are in the physical world. Our battles are the challenges to our physical and emotional survival and growth that we encounter during the course of our development. Each chakra has its own physical, mental and emotional developmental tasks. At the first we have to learn how to walk and talk, to begin the development of our motor skills, how to bond with another, how to create a sense of safety and belonging and to trust in our own ability to provide for our needs. We learn that people and things exist even when we can't see them. At the second we learn about relationships outside the family sphere, and are challenged to allow our emotions their full range of expression and to decode the spiritual guidance encoded in our emotional reactions. Here, on the threshold of the third chakra challenges to our development of an individual identity, we gird ourselves with the sword of truth that will be our guide through the conflicting demands on our hearts and minds that is adolescence.

It is again time to close the book, to repair to your sacred place and prepare in the ways you have learned to enter your inner world as you follow the twelve battles meditation. Having reconnected with your own inner Excalibur you are ready to recognize some of your own battles, aware now of the inner strengths and resources that will allow you to resolve your challenges and nurture the development of your spirit.

Twelve battles meditation

In a safe place, free of interruptions, take a few moments to settle yourself comfortably, perhaps moving your body until you find the position that feels best for you, keeping your head, neck and trunk in a straight line to allow the energy to flow freely. Breathing deeply now, feel the gentle rise and fall of your abdomen as you breathe in ... and out. Again, deep deep breath in ... and out. And one more deep breath in ... and out. And now relax your breathing, and allow your body to breathe itself. Raise the shield of light from below, filling and surrounding your body with light, creating a protected space. Bring down the shield of light from above, balancing and blessing each of your chakras, Sahasrara at the crown, the Ajna chakra at the third eye, the Vissudha chakra at the throat, Anahata chakra at the heart, Manipura chakra at the solar plexus, Svadhisthana chakra just below the navel, and the Muladhara chakra at the base of the spine. And now breathing into your inner light at the heart center, expanding your inner light, so that you are now filled and surrounded by the triple shield of light, from below, from above and from within, grounded in physical reality, with an open and clear connection to the Source, honoring the light within.

King Arthur, Defender of Britain, was conceived at Spring Equinox. His birth at Midwinter Solstice symbolizes the rebirth of light in the depths of winter, when the sun begins its slow expansion of daylight that reaches its apex at midsummer. Arthur was to create a generation of peace during a time of chaos, and he was to create the idea of a national identity, a wholeness within British borders. He was to rule according to spiritual laws of justice, respect and honor, but first he had to make the land safe from the so-called barbarians who were invading from all sides. Arthur and his Companions of the Round Table fought twelve major battles before the Saxons were defeated and the land was safe.

Twelve is a magical number, a symbolic number that recurs over and over again in nature and in our mythology. Arthur's twelve battles symbolize the challenges that each of us faces as we develop the lower chakras and create our own sense of safety, security and belonging in the physical world; as we learn how to understand and use the language of emotion to further our development, and to recognize where our emotional energy is blocked or is leaking away; as we develop our intellect and strengthen our individual will. The tripod base of physical, emotional and mental development creates the stable and safe foundation that allows us to turn our attention inward at the heart chakra, opening ourselves to unconditional love, forgiveness and compassion. When the time is right, we then surrender the individual will, or ego, that we have so lovingly nurtured and strengthened, to the service of divine will.

As you imagine yourself filled and surrounded by the triple shield of light, from below, from above, and from within, and with the sacred sword of truth firmly in your hands, call forth an image of your own inner Arthur, the inner light that began a new phase of its journey within this physical body. The image may appear to you in human form, or in symbolic form, or perhaps in animal form. An image is not necessarily a picture in the mind, but more often it is an awareness, an inner knowing, a thought form. In order to continue its spiritual growth, and create wholeness within you—a balance of the masculine and feminine, and integration of the physical, mental, emotional and spiritual bodies—the inner light must first create a safe and secure environment within physical form, firmly grounded to the earth plane, knowing itself safe, stable and secure.

There were many challenges to meet and resolve during that phase of the journey, your symbolic twelve battles. Challenges to physical survival as you learned to provide food and shelter for yourself, and to nurture your physical health. Emotional challenges as you learned to create and nurture relationships. And challenges to your personal power as you developed your personal integrity and code of honor.

As you follow the development of your inner Arthur, your inner light, consider some of those challenges now, focusing first on one that you have resolved. ... You may want to consider the lessons and the gifts in a particular relationship; or in learning a skill, such as learning how to walk, or ride a bicycle, or read or drive a car, or perform a job; or the satisfaction you found in discovering and honoring your personal boundaries. ... When you bring that resolved challenge to mind, think about the inner resources that you discovered as you faced that challenge. ... What was your inner sword of truth? ... What strengths and capacities have you developed as a result of meeting that challenge? ...

Turn your attention now to a person, an issue, or a situation that continues to challenge you. It may have to do for example with your health, or with a relationship, or perhaps with an inability to protect your personal space and to say no. As you consider the strengths and capacities you gained from meeting that other challenge, how can those abilities serve you now? ... What new abilities need to be developed in order for you to integrate the sacred teaching that this challenge is offering you? ...

Remember that King Arthur did not fight his battles alone. He was with his Companions of the Round Table. Each of them brought to Arthur a particular gift. Who are the Companions of your inner Round Table? Who best can serve you now? Is it Lancelot, the Queen's champion, defender of the sacred feminine, the most gifted warrior? Or is it Gawain, with his open and generous heart? Or perhaps Galahad or Percival with their clear spiritual vision? Or perhaps it is something in your outer environment that can best serve you now: a friend, or a group, or an activity, an exercise perhaps, or changing your diet. Consider your inner resources, and also the resources in your environment. ... Which of those resources can be developed further? What new resources do you need to find? ...

And remember that, like Arthur, you have always available to you the guidance of your inner Merlin. Perhaps you would like to call forth an image of the inner Merlin, to help you to find the inner and outer resources that will support and guide you through this particular challenge.

In your own time, and only when you are ready, begin to bring your focus back to the outer world, bringing with you the insights and understanding you have gained. Take a few moments to write or draw about this experience in your Quest Journal.

Third chakra: Manipura

Symbolically, then, Arthur "remembered" who he was at puberty, the time of opening the third chakra when we claim our own identity and accept responsibility for who we are. The third chakra is where we come into our sense of self. At the end of the Wordsworth's quotation that introduced the second chakra the poet takes us to the frontier of the third chakra:

> *At length the Man perceives it [the vision splendid]*
> *die away,*

And fade into the light of common day.

The "vision splendid" that we brought with us and that continued to cocoon us in the early years of life fades away as we turn our attention inward, to focus on the development of our individual will, and on the "common day" of our physical experience on the earth plane. The dominance of the third chakra is the developmental stage that is the point of our furthest separation from an awareness of the spiritual dimension, and of our maximum focus on the self as a separate being. We begin life in total and unconscious immersion in what John Nelson calls the Spiritual Ground, and gradually move away from that as we fortify our ego boundaries and begin the development of a sense of self, of individual will. At the third chakra the full force of our energy is devoted towards the development of our individual identity. It is not until we energize the upper chakras that the "vision splendid" comes back into focus and we reopen to awareness of Wordsworth's "clouds of glory" that we brought trailing with us into our experience of physical life.

At the first chakra we did not know we were separate, either from Spirit or from our environment. If we were born into a loving and safe environment we internalized that love and sense of safety, and we formed the belief that the world was a safe place and that our needs would be met. We feel at home, and comfortable, in physical form. But if we were born into an environment that was hostile, violent, or abusive, even if the hostility and violence were not directed towards us personally, we internalized that too. We felt no separation between ourselves and our environment, so whatever happened in the environment happened to us. We programmed into the first chakra the belief that the world is not a safe place, and we continue to feel insecure and fear that our needs will not be met.

The good news is that we can reprogram the first chakra, or any chakra, at any time. Just as new generations of hardware and software enrich the capacity of the computer, so our knowledge and wisdom about the world and about ourselves enrich our lives, as we allow new understanding and insight to reprogram those unreasoned and uncritical beliefs that reflected our experience of the world before we had the cognitive and emotional capacity to evaluate our perceptions.

Changing a computer program—at least for the technologically-challenged among us—can be complicated and time-consuming but is eminently possible. Changing a chakra program requires consistent effort and can benefit from help—from books, friends, counselors—and is also eminently possible. It is not hard-wired into the first chakra that those abused or neglected in childhood have to spend their lives in a state of fear, or never be able to trust or bond with another. The emotional residue of those experiences is software that is amenable to change.

At the second chakra we saw ourselves as reflections of what others saw in us. In a loving environment what we saw reflected back to us was love, acceptance, competence and capability. We were praised for learning how to walk, how to talk, how to use the bathroom, how to throw a baseball and win a spelling bee. Throughout life we can build on that foundation and apply our belief in our own competence to new situations and challenges. We are more likely to know that if one way does not succeed, we will find another, and go in search of it without wasting time and energy in feeling discouraged.

If what we saw mirrored was criticism, we internalized that, and we may have developed a sense of incompetence or unworthiness. If we do not succeed on the first try we may give up, give in to a sense of hopelessness, or feel that we cannot do anything right. The second chakra stage of development is about seeing the self in relationships. If you think I'm okay then I must be okay. If you don't think I'm okay, if you criticize me or belittle me, then I am likely to believe that there is something wrong with me.

At the third chakra we accept responsibility for who we are. If we are not happy about how we think and feel we recognize that it is nobody's job but ours to change it, and we look for the resources and information that will help us to become the person we want to be. It is at the third chakra that we move into our own power. We decide for ourselves who we are. If we do not do that, if we continue to blame or place the responsibility for who we are outside of ourselves, we do not fully access the inner power of the third chakra.

One of the first concepts children learn at around age two when they begin to activate the second chakra is the concept of possession. They say "mine" almost as often as they say "no," the other great signal of differentiation: I and other. Ownership, at the second chakra, is a fundamental right, indeed the original wording of the Declaration of Independence defined our inalienable rights as the "pursuit of life, liberty and property." The changed wording from "property" to "pursuit of happiness" signaled the founding fathers' shift from a second to a third chakra focus for the ideals of their new republic.

A second chakra focus identifies personal power with money and possessions. The archetypal image of the male as provider, when masculinity and manhood are identified with how much money a man makes, has contributed a lot to the imbalance of yin and yang in our culture and within individual males. A man cannot be balanced and whole if his sense of himself and his power in the world rests on his income. He might feel a sense of personal power as long as he has a lot of money, as long as he is "successful" according to our present definition of that term, but the downside to that is if he loses his job, or his nest egg in the stock market, it will also mean a loss in personal power and in self-esteem.

Loss of sexual prowess as a man ages, like financial loss, is also perceived in our culture as a loss of manhood and often leads to a loss of self-esteem. In ages past, as a man aged he became a venerated elder, valued for his experience and wisdom. He was freed to focus on inner development and the spiritual connection once he was liberated from the insistent sexual demands of the second chakra. Now we no longer value the wisdom of the aged and seek to prolong sexual potency with artificial means.

At the second chakra, the possession of property confers status; the lack of it can lead to a lack of self-esteem and/or resentment towards those who have it. At the third chakra, there is the realization that real power is within, not in possessions but in the sense of self, in personal integrity and sense of honor. The pursuit of happiness means inner happiness, fully realized when we recognize that all we will ever need is already there within us.

Teenagers in this stage of development search for their own identity as they explore and develop the power of the third chakra, and they indulge in what to the adult world—whose memory of their own adolescence tends to be truncated—are incomprehensible behaviors: piercing and tattooing various body parts, dyeing their hair bright orange, speaking a foreign language full of trendy jargon that is foreign to older generations. They are trying on different identities, looking for the one that will fit and feel like their own. They seek acceptance and approval not from their families but from their peer group, and they may change peer groups as they develop and explore different ways of being.

Up to this point they have pretty much accepted the rules, opinions and value system of their parents. They may not have liked all the ingredients of the parental package but they did not seriously believe they could be different. Now they typically rebel and may reject all of those teachings, from the trivial—how to dress, what to eat, how to behave in polite society—to the most important— values, and religious or spiritual beliefs. The resolution of this stage of development is when the young adult arrives at a place of balance where he or she can evaluate both parental teachings and peer examples and accept those that resonate as truth, letting go of the rest and creating his or her own unique individuality.

The myth of King Arthur shows us the ideal circumstances for a third chakra transition. Arthur was trained in the martial arts and in the rules for a leader of his time by his foster parents, and he learned veneration for nature and respect for the dignity of his fellow man from Merlin. When the time came for him to claim his birthright his mentors stepped aside, showing him their faith in his ability to meet his destiny with grace and competence. As soon as Arthur took the sword from the stone his foster father Ector acknowledged him his sovereign and bowed the knee to him. His teacher Merlin prepared him for his coronation. Though Arthur faced opposition from some of the other petty kings because of his youth and inexperience or because he was an obstacle to their own ambitions, neither of his mentors said: "Are you sure you can do this?" or, "You're too young for this responsibility, let me help you a while longer."

In our world, few of us are blessed with such an ideal adolescent environment, and the rites of passage that used to carry the symbolism of attaining adulthood—the Bar Mitzvah, for example, or the Vision Quest—no longer involve the kinds of challenge that used to test the adolescent's mettle and give him a sense of his own power. The inner being of the teenager is crying out for freedom and self-responsibility, while the dangers of the modern world make it impossible for parents to allow it. Modern teenagers are in the historically unique position of confronting at the same time both unprecedented freedom—of the Internet, and the car, and the smart phone, and artificial escape into drugs—and the tightening noose of parental control and legal limits on their freedom of movement, exploration and self-responsibility.

The challenges of the modern world make this a particularly trying time for both parents and children. Parents have to walk the tightrope between providing the necessary protection for their children on the cusp of adulthood while allowing them the freedom to find their own individuality. In that search adolescents typically reject their parents' teachings, which can feel to the parents like a personal rejection. The wise parent knows when to slacken the rope and when to impose limits, but often parents are somewhere along the continuum between two extremes, rarely at the place of balance at the middle.

At one extreme there are parents who want to hold on to the full authority they had when their children were younger and they were the venerated kings of the castle, all-knowing and all-powerful. In their need to protect their children from the dangers of life they create rigid boundaries and try to maintain control over all aspects of their children's lives. This can create either total alienation—when their children realize they can never become their own person within the parental orbit and strike out on their own, rejecting the family altogether—or perennial children who continue to be dependent on their parents and never find the confidence to make their own choices.

At the other extreme there are parents who try so hard to be their kids' best buddy that they do not enforce any boundaries at all, which does not work either. Rebellion is part of the third chakra package; if adolescents do not have anything to rebel against because their parents give them total freedom, they do not have any testing ground for reaching their own decisions or the opportunity to discover their own uniqueness.

Parents could do a lot worse than look to the example of Count Ector and Merlin in their approach to their adolescent children. There comes a point when it is appropriate to risk trusting both in themselves and in the way they have raised their children, as well as in their children's own competence.

When the power of the third chakra becomes dominant during puberty, issues related to the development of personal power and self-esteem will surface and take center stage. We are not born with self-esteem: we develop self-esteem and a clear sense of who we are as separate individuals through our experiences, and from the examples that we find to emulate within our family and social group, among our teachers and role models, and from the written wisdom of our collective past.

If the first chakra is the center of our relationship with the earth and the physical plane, and the second our relationship with other individuals and with our emotions, the third is our relationship with the self, with our sense of integrity and our personal honor code.

This is not an easy transition, perhaps especially so now because we do not exactly live in honorable times. We assume that business people will cheat us if they can, and our admiration of the genius to make money is often forgiving of less-than-honorable ways of doing it. The deceptive and manipulative practices of the advertising industry have been adopted by our political leaders, and we take it for granted that their campaign promises are only a matter of saying what they think we want to hear so that we will give them our precious vote. And too often those tactics prove themselves effective. The brave few who dare to tell us the truth often do not get elected.

Whenever we do find a positive role model the media delight in digging around in the mud to find any shadow or stain on their character and integrity. The result is that we have very few role models of an honorable way to live, and in trying to figure it out for ourselves we are looking to our myths and history books. We are searching for examples of honorable lives, such as Arthur's, to guide us through the labyrinth of modern life.

The third chakra challenges us to step in to our own power and take full responsibility for who we are. Some of us find this to be empowering, and others find self-responsibility threatening. As long as we are part of a group there is no individual responsibility and some of us prefer it that way, but the third chakra pays the price. When the group takes responsibility it can be very comforting, but the price exacted by the group is the individual's power. The group's reason for being is not to empower the individual, but to take the individual's power and invest it in the group, whether it is a gang, or the Mafia, or a corporation, or the army. Or an ethnic group. Or an economic group. Or an academic group. Or certain kinds of family.

That is not to say it is impossible both to be an individual and be part of a group. The issue is whether we surrender our personal will to the group will. We cannot help but belong to some kind of group at each stage of our development because we are social beings, but we find as we continue to develop our own consciousness that we may have to leave the group that supports one level of consciousness in order for us to be able to move on to the next, and that can be a painful loss. One of the hardest things for substance abusers is that in order to stay clean they have to get out of the substance abuse group. They not only lose the substance, they lose their friends and their social network. The successful ones create a new group, of AA members perhaps, a group that supports where they want to be.

Very often it takes some kind of disaster to nudge us forward. We can get very comfortable where we are, and even if it is not comfortable it is at least familiar. We often do not volunteer to rock the boat when our lives are on more or less an even keel, so destiny intervenes to provide a challenge that will get us back on the track of growth. Probably all of us have experienced some kind of betrayal when something—or sometimes it feels like everything— we believed in failed us. Years later we can look back and recognize those times as turning points and see that if that level of reality had not failed us we would not have moved on to the next. Had I not been fired, for example, I would never have taken the risk to move to this job that I love. Had that partner not left me I would not have found the love of my life. Had I not been turned down by that university that was close to home I would never have been exposed to the research that triggered my passion. Each of those experiences may have been devastating at the time, and yet in hindsight it is clear that they were well-disguised blessings.

Death and resurrection are our constant experience as we shift focus to each succeeding level of chakra development; they are our initiation into a new level of reality. Dreams of death often refer to this symbolic death of one way of being in order to be reborn to a higher vibrational level. At the third chakra we die to group consciousness and family consciousness in order to be reborn as individuals. It is here, therefore, that everything that threatens our sense of self rises up and kicks us in the teeth, not because Source Energy is sadistic but to make us look at where we have invested our self-esteem: in the opinions of others? in material things? in our looks? in social status?

When self-esteem is invested in people or things outside of the self, we are in a very vulnerable position. We have what psychologists call "an external locus of control." We surrender our power to things, people and situations outside ourselves and beyond our control, and feel powerless to manage our lives. We might feel powerful as long as we have money, approval, social status, beauty, but if we lose any of those things we lose our identity and sense of self along with it.

At the third chakra we learn to value the inner self, who we are face to face with our own souls. We emerge from under the protective umbrella of the group power of the first chakra, and recognize the illusory nature of the money-power and status-power of the second chakra, and claim our real power: our inner strength and integrity. Once we recognize that power, nobody and nothing can take it away.

It would be hard to imagine any experience more dehumanizing than the Soviet Gulag, yet Alexander Solzhenitsyn survived it with his soul intact, and defied the might of the Soviet state to live on as his country's conscience and to write some of the most powerful works of the twentieth century. Primo Levi, Viktor Frankl, Elie Wiesel and a host of others survived the Nazi death camps with their humanity intact, and their example and their wisdom continue to inspire and enrich us.

Living with integrity, we learn from these inspiring and courageous examples, gives us a power that cannot be taken away. On the other hand, when we fail to act with integrity we can lose energy at this center. When we say, for example, "It's not personal. It's just business," as if business were somehow exempt from moral and ethical considerations, the third chakra pays the price. And we also weaken the third chakra when we fail to honor ourselves. Some of us are so afraid of a runaway ego that we go to the other extreme and denigrate our talents and capabilities, or hold on to past experiences of humiliation. However, feeling unworthy is the flip side of egocentrism; it is the same issue. Marianne Williamson reminds us:

> Our worst fear is not that we are inadequate; our
> worst fear is that we are powerful beyond measure.
> It is our light, not our darkness, that most frightens
> us. We ask ourselves, "Who am I, to be brilliant,
> gorgeous, talented, fabulous"? Actually, who are you
> not to be? You are a child of God. You are. And your
> playing small does not serve the world.

"Your playing small does not serve the world." It bears repeating because it is a transcendent truth that contradicts all those messages such as: "Who died and made you queen? Just who do you think you are? You'll never amount to anything. You're a screw-up, a loser, a wimp." Some parents think these kinds of messages encourage greater effort, they may offer them with good intentions, but the effect is not positive at all. Many of us heard those messages and a hundred other variations on the same theme so many times that they wore channels in the fabric of the psyche, and they keep replaying and replaying, as if the needle were stuck in the groove of an old record that keeps turning round and around, repeating itself *ad nauseum*. Those messages stifle initiative and ambition, and shred self-esteem.

The truth is, "You are a child of God. You are"; you are by definition a being of light, full of unlimited potential. This is the empowering truth of the third chakra, and when we can own it we serve not only ourselves but also the world. We develop a strong personal will in order to use that will in the service of divine power.

A person with a deficient third chakra, therefore, will have low self-esteem, low personal power, a weak will, and be easily manipulated. He or she may have a victim mentality and tend to blame others. Physically there may be poor digestion, eating disorders or ulcers, chronic fatigue or disorders of the organs in the central part of the body: stomach, pancreas, gallbladder or liver.

Excess energy at the third chakra can manifest as a runaway ego. Here the hunger for power is so dominant that it eclipses integrity and can manifest in aggressiveness rather than assertiveness, and a need to dominate others, often accomplished through manipulation. Someone with blocked energy at the third chakra does not engage in mutually respectful debate, but needs to prove themselves right and always have the last word.

At the third chakra, our moral development becomes a matter of personal choice. When the focus is on the lower chakras, we follow right action out of fear of punishment or embarrassment or social censure. Someone at this level of development will not rob a store in broad daylight when social authority is in place and functioning efficiently: policemen are patrolling, citizens armed with cell phones are on all sides, traffic is flowing and they know that the full force of crime control can respond in moments. But when that authority breaks down, as it did in New Orleans after Hurricane Katrina, and there is no fear of retribution, robbery in broad daylight was broadcast to the entire country.

Not only was there no fear of consequences, but the lack of authority fed into the shadow third chakra's hunger for pseudo-power. A healthy third chakra knows that real power is inner power, a healthy sense of self that encompasses valuing personal integrity. A weak third chakra finds a pseudo-power in manipulation and control over. And so we saw in post-Katrina New Orleans not only looting for material gain, but also looting for the tools of armed might, that were then used to intimidate and threaten.

We are not talking here, of course, about those who helped themselves to the necessities of life from grocery stores.

It was one of the tragedies of that experience that many of those trapped in their homes when the levees gave way and the city was flooded had not heeded the call to evacuate precisely because of the fear of looting. The thought process may have gone something like this: "If I have to choose between my home and possessions or my life, naturally I will choose my life. But what if I think I am choosing life and I leave my home and the hurricane changes direction at the last minute, as they so often do, and I return home to find my home looted or vandalized? I will have made the wrong decision.

It was not a wise choice at all but a wimpy one, and look at what it cost me." The fear of making the "wrong decision" keeps many of us paralyzed. "I hate my job but what if I change jobs and a week after I leave the company the stock soars and I would have received a windfall in bonuses or stock options? Won't I feel a fool."

A healthy third chakra knows there are no wrong decisions. There are only choices made to the best of our ability with the information available. And whatever the outcome, whatever the new choices to be made along the way, each one will be evaluated and decided upon and lived with, with no regrets or second thoughts or what ifs. Incalculable amounts of energy are wasted in looking back and wishing we had chosen differently, but it is not the choice that conditions spiritual growth: it is the attitude we adopt to whatever happens as a result of those choices.

A healthy third chakra is responsible and balanced, with healthy self-esteem, confidence, and an ability to meet challenges. We empower the energy of the third chakra when we take pride in ourselves, in our work, in who we are, and when we keep our promises and commitments to ourselves as well as to other people. We build self-esteem and self-respect by honoring ourselves: that is the challenge of the third chakra. At the first chakra we were part of the group and did not yet perceive our individuality; at the second chakra we allowed others to define us; now at the third we cultivate the inner will to reject others' judgments if they do not fit with our inner sense of who we are.

This can be an uncomfortable transition not only for us but also for those around us who are used to having us behave in a certain way that may be comfortable for them. Family therapists are all-too-familiar with the concept of the IP, the "identified patient," the family member who acts out the frustrations of the family unit and becomes the focus of the family's dysfunction. The IP gets blamed for everything that goes wrong, which frees the other family members from responsibility. It may take decades for the IP to decide to honor his or her third chakra and begin to refuse to accept that role, but when s/he does, it throws the family system into disarray and the fight to maintain the status quo can get very dirty.

Consider the classic middle child, whose survival mechanism is often to be the "good" child, the one who always tries to please, the peacemaker who apologizes even when not at fault. She may recreate the conditions of her childhood by marrying a clone of her father and continue the pattern of her childhood with her husband and her children.

If the marriage falls apart in spite of her best efforts to please she may finally decide she wants to recover her life, but she may find little support for her efforts within her family. The quest for self-discovery and empowerment is often a lonely journey, and it can be a cruel disillusionment to discover that family members do not appreciate the hard-won changes nor take any joy in the seeker's newfound happiness. They often would prefer her to be the way she was, always available to fulfil their needs, be someone for them to push around and feel superior to, someone to accept the blame for their own shortcomings.

As we claim our sense of self at the third chakra, any issues that threaten that sense of self come into consciousness and demand our attention. It takes courage and integrity to hold on to our own truth in the face of familial and societal pressures to conform to old ways of being and doing. Arthur's leadership of the British tribes was not easily won, and there was vigorous opposition to his new vision.

The Battle of Badon

Arthur left the celebrating warriors and walked outside into the cool air. Behind him there was music and laughter and drunken voices; ahead the world was as tranquil as if war had never been heard of. The moon was high in the sky and a gentle breeze swayed the treetops. As he walked down to the lake he could hear night creatures rustling. An owl hooted. There was the smell of wood smoke in the air. He sat beside the lake and watched the gentle ripples at the water's edge, absorbing the sense of peace and looking back on twelve years of fighting.

It had not been easy to unite the tribes. He had drawn the sword from the stone and the tribal kings had sworn allegiance to him as High King but the habits of centuries had been slow to dissolve. Celts were impetuous, passionate, and loved a good fight above all else. They had fought for centuries with each other, tribe against tribe—for land, for each other's women, for livestock, and for the fun of it—according to rules of honor accepted by both sides. What they knew of their history they had learned from the songs and stories of bards, songs designed to celebrate great battles and great warriors, stories that inflamed the passions and cultivated pride in individual tribal power.

From Merlin Arthur had learned a different kind of history, one that had come often to mind as he battled his frustration and near despair over ever uniting the tribes. "The land of Gaul," Merlin had said, "was a land of fierce warriors who far outnumbered the Romans. But Caesar was able to defeat the tribes one by one because they gave more power to their intertribal jealousies than to the might of the outside invader. And then Claudius crossed the waters to Britain and did the same thing here. And we still have not learned our lesson. I warned King Vortigern of it in my prophesy to him. Have you heard that story?"

Arthur had heard, as had everyone in Britain, the stories of Merlin's power, but he knew Merlin as a wise old man of the woods whom he loved with all his heart. He had never seen the Merlin of legend, a man whose word could command kings and strike terror in the wicked. He knew that Merlin had prophesied the death of Vortigern, and that he had been the right hand of Ambrosius.

"But please," he had said, "tell it to me again."

Merlin had smiled, and reached for his harp and strummed it in accompaniment to his story.

"After the Romans left Britain, Vortigern took power by killing the rightful king Constantine. Constantine's brothers, Ambrosius and Uther, were still very young. They were taken to Brittany and lived under the protection of King Budicius until they were old enough and

strong enough to return and claim their rights. In the meantime, the various Celtic tribes were once again fighting each other, and Vortigern, who had a Saxon wife, promised land to the Saxons in return for their help in establishing himself as High King.

"As you know, the Saxons were not content to stay within the boundaries established by Vortigern, and instead of continuing to be his supporters they too became a threat to him. Vortigern fled to Wales and told his engineers to build a tower on top of Mount Snowdon where he could retreat to safety. The engineers tried. Time and again they would work all day building the walls only to discover the next morning that they had collapsed during the night. Finally Vortigern in desperation called on his magicians. They told him that he needed to find a boy who had no father and sacrifice him so that his blood could be mixed with the mortar of the foundations, and then the walls would stand. That's an old superstition, you know. The ancient Celts would bury a human sacrifice head down in the foundation of their hill forts."

Merlin hummed for a while to the melody of the harp, a haunting minor key, while Arthur hung on his words, as mesmerized as if he were hearing the story for the first time.

"I was raised in the court of my mother's father, the king of Demetia, but my mother would never tell, in spite of threats and beatings, who my father was. Vortigern's agents learned of this, and took me and my mother to Vortigern. Thinking to protect me, she told some outlandish tale of my being fathered by an incubus." Merlin fell silent, and Arthur waited as an owl hooted close by, and other night creatures rustled through the undergrowth.

"In the beginning, I was trying only to save my life. I knew enough of engineering to know that the walls were falling because of some fault in the rock, and so I told them to dig under the foundation, and when they did they found a pool. It was then ..." a dramatic chord "... that I felt for the first time the power of spirit take over and flow through me. I do not remember what I said but others recorded it. I said ..." but Arthur could contain himself no longer. "You said that when the pool was drained they would find two dragons, one white and one red, and *they would fight bitterly, breathing fire. You said that the red dragon represented the people of Britain who would be overrun by the white dragon of the Saxons; that Britain's mountains would be leveled and the streams in its valleys run with blood. But after an immense effort the red dragon would regain its strength and would pursue the white dragon and tear its holdings down and defeat it."*

And Merlin had smiled.

This had happened, Arthur knew, when Ambrosius returned to Britain. He had created a coalition of the tribes that succeeded in driving the Saxons back behind their borders. But then Ambrosius died. His passing had been signaled by an omen seen the length and breadth of the land, a scarlet cloud in the shape of a dragon illuminated by the setting sun. From this omen his brother Uther had taken the name Pendragon and assumed the leadership of the British tribes, but though he was a great fighter he lacked the charisma of his brother and the tribes once again began to splinter.

Arthur whispered to himself the next part of Merlin's prophesy: "Then the Red Dragon will revert to its true habits and struggle to tear itself to pieces." Like his father and his uncle before him, it had been Arthur's challenge to convince the tribes that their "true habits" would bring about their destruction and that only together could they keep Britain safe. He had held steadfastly to that vision, throughout the squabbles and the inter-tribal conflicts and the taunts thrown his way by seasoned warriors that he was too young to understand the ways of the real world.

As Arthur looked up into the night sky he heard again the voice of Merlin telling him:

"Imagine, Arthur, a great river of energy that flows through the cosmos. It is the energy of the Source, and it flows only in the direction of well-being. It never flows in the opposite direction, and there is no opposing current. We can only allow, or disallow, the force of Source Energy; align ourselves with it, or allow ourselves to be swept into an eddy or even try to swim against the current. All the rituals and ceremonies of the Druids are designed to empower our alignment with nature, with the flow of life, the flow of the Source. You will need to *learn to feel that flow, and to align yourself with it, and when you do, you will be invincible; you and the land of Britain will flow together in the direction of well-being, peace and joy."*

The solution had been not to fight the tribes and their individual leaders, but to flow with them, gently guiding them in the direction of Light. Arthur had learned not to bully the various leaders but to listen to them respectfully, so that they each believed they had been heard and their advice followed. And he had forged an alliance of Companions who were faithful unto death. He had learned much from them, and they had learned to share his vision. Even those jealous and resentful of his power, such as King Lot of the Orkneys, had learned to accept the majority decisions and to recognize the benefits of cooperation.

Only later had Merlin told him the final part of the prophesy: "And then out of Cornwall will come the Bear, Artos, who will sweep the field clear." And so it had been, and now, peace. It was strange to think he did not have to rush off on the morrow to fight another battle. Arthur smiled to himself, and walked back to join the celebration.

Close the book, now, and repair to your sacred place for meditation. Explore the inner landscape of your third chakra and claim the fire of transformation.

Third chakra: the fire of transformation meditation

Before beginning this meditation, light a candle and place it in front of you, on a table or on your altar if you have made one. Take a few moments to settle yourself comfortably, perhaps moving your body until you find the position that feels best for you, keeping your head, neck and trunk in a straight line to allow the energy to flow freely. Breathing deeply now, feel the gentle rise and fall of your abdomen as you breathe in … and out. Again, deep deep breath in … and out. And one more deep breath in … and out.

And now relax your breathing, and allow your body to breathe itself. Raise the shield of light from below, filling and surrounding your body with light, creating a protected space. Bring down the shield of light from above, balancing and blessing each of your chakras, the Sahasrara chakra at the crown, the Ajna chakra at the third eye, the Vissudha chakra at the throat, Anahata chakra at the heart, Manipura chakra at the solar plexus, Svadhisthana chakra just below the navel, and the Muladhara chakra at the base of the spine. And now breathing into your inner light at the heart center, expanding your inner light, so that you are now filled and surrounded by the triple shield of light, from below, from above and from within, grounded in physical reality, with an open and clear connection to the Source, honoring the light within.

Take your attention now to the third chakra, at the solar plexus. Manipura means "lustrous gem." It is the jewel of the inner self, the power within, the unique, divine individual that is the essence of who you are. The element of the third chakra is fire. Open your eyes for a moment and focus on the candle flame ... and then as you close your eyes take the flame within, to the solar plexus, the third chakra. Imagine that you can feel its warmth spreading from this center throughout your being, warming, purifying, and transforming darkness into light.

Fire in the physical world transforms matter into heat and light. The symbolic fire of the third chakra gives us the ability to act and to develop our own personal power, to give voice and power to the King Arthur within, the best that we can be, taking responsibility for ourselves and living with integrity and honor. It allows us to create a sense of self, of who we are as individuals, distinct from the group and from those who guided and molded us in our early years. The fire of Manipura chakra allows us to develop autonomy, and to take responsibility for who we are; without it we can be stuck in blaming, which means giving away our power to others.

Adolescence is the time when we actively embark on the process of individuation. We begin to take from all the influences in our lives—our caretakers, teachers, authority figures, favorite rock stars, historical figures, political leaders, writers, movie-makers—those nuggets of their *truth that resonate as truth within us, and we let go of the aspects of their teachings and examples that do not. This is how we create our unique personality. When we are supported in this process we emerge from adolescence with all the tools necessary to build a successful, joy-filled life. We are self-confident, we live with integrity, we trust ourselves and our judgment.*

The young Arthur of legend was guided by enlightened beings who supported him and trusted him as he stepped forward to claim his destiny. Many of us are not so fortunate. Some of us were criticized for questioning and exploring, and we may as a result question ourselves and distrust our abilities. The third chakra is about self-definition, about honoring our own authenticity, our personal honor code and integrity. If we deny our authenticity through fear of criticism or shaming we waste our energy in trying to live up to the expectations of others and their definitions of what it means to be good.

So as you prepare to step forward to empower your inner Arthur you can invoke an image of your Inner Merlin to support you; the image may look like a person, perhaps even a Merlin you have seen in a movie and with whom you felt a connection, or it may be an image of your high self, the part of you that has one foot in the spiritual and the other in the physical. Or it may be a symbolic representation of wisdom and enlightenment. Or it may perhaps appear as an animal.

The color of the third chakra is yellow, and its symbol is a sphere. Breathe into the yellow sphere of light at the solar plexus and expand it, and now imagine stepping into it. Imagine yourself within the sphere of light. Allow the yellow light to permeate your being: yellow like the mid-day sun, like a field full of marigolds, or a ripe juicy lemon, yellow light permeating every single cell, every molecule and atom of your being.

With the intention of exploring the health and balance of your third chakra, begin to explore the sphere of yellow light. Notice any changes in the quality of color, or texture, or light. If you find places of shadow, you can—if it feels right to you—explore more deeply, and hold the intention of opening your consciousness to the awareness of what is contained within the shadow. Remember that shadow means only absence of light. Shadow places are places that are not yet developed. You can ask what needs to happen for you to bring light into the area of shadow. You may experience flashes of memory. If these become uncomfortable, you can move your consciousness outside the sphere and examine it from a distance that is comfortable for you.

King Arthur, though he had the support of his foster parents and of Merlin, was not universally accepted by the tribal kings who perceived in him a threat to their own ambitions. They said he was too young, that he lacked experience. Perhaps you were criticized or shamed as you began to spread your wings in adolescence. If in your exploration of the yellow sphere you should discover shame, examine the roots of this uncomfortable feeling. Is it shame about your body? Your emotions? Your sexuality? Your neediness? A feeling of not being good enough? As you listen to the voice of criticism in your head, whose voice is it really? Over time, you may have accepted that voice as your own, but whose voice was it in the beginning? ...

And now look for the rebellious voice, the authentic voice of your own inner wisdom that can question others' judgments and criticisms. Look within the yellow sphere for evidence of the inner voice of your own integrity; allow yourself to remember times when you have marched—in your actions, or perhaps in your thoughts—to the beat of your own inner drummer instead of automatically following the drummer of family, society, conditioning, expectations. Your reading this book is evidence that you have done that. Notice how it feels to honor that inner essence. What does that voice want to say? What does it need from you?

If the inner voice was silenced and not allowed to speak, or if it was threatened with harm if it did speak, it may take some time for you to find it and for it to feel safe enough to express its truth. Be patient. You are here, in a safe place within your own mind, and if you are consistent and loving with yourself you will find the inner voice. When you do, allow it to speak freely. It may be angry at first, and that anger deserves expression. It is helpful to support the free expression of anger energy with physical activity: running, or beating a pillow, or screaming in your car while stopped under an underpass, or writing, without regard to spelling or syntax, and then burning what you have written in a symbolic act of purification and release.

. . .

You may have found insights now, in which case you can store them on a mental shelf for retrieval and consideration later, or write about them in your Quest Journal. Or you may find them arising in the days and weeks ahead as you keep your heart and mind open and pay attention both to what is going on around you, and to the inner voice of your intuition. Often it is through discomfort or confusion that we are pushed in the direction of taking charge of our lives and claiming the power of the third chakra.

PART III

Summer
Camelot

Arthur once wandered into an enchanted land. He felt his strength and his energy slipping away from him and he had not the will to move. The leader of the enchanted land was something of a sadist who thought to amuse himself at the king's expense, and he told King Arthur that he would lift the enchantment and let him go free if he could discover the answer to a riddle: What do women really want? He allowed Arthur a year and a day to find the answer.

As Arthur rode away he met a repulsively ugly old hag. Her skin was like bark, her teeth were black and misshapen, her nose and mouth had slipped sideways across her face, and her hair was like dried up old moss. Though her appearance was vile, she was well spoken, and she told the king that she could give him the answer to the riddle. But in return he would have to give her what she wanted.

"And what do you want?" asked King Arthur.

"I want Gawain," she replied.

Gawain was the king's much-loved nephew, and Arthur would not ask such a sacrifice of him. But Gawain heard of the offer and made his own choice to sacrifice himself for his beloved uncle and king. He went to find the ugly hag, whose name was Ragnall. He took her back to court with him and married her with all pomp and ceremony. After the wedding when they retired to their room, Ragnall disappeared to slip into something more comfortable and Gawain tried to prepare himself to do his duty by her. But when she reappeared the ugliness had vanished and she was a beautiful young woman. She explained to Gawain that a wicked enchanter had put a spell on her, and that Gawain had partially broken the spell by agreeing to marry her.

"And now, my husband, you have to make a choice. I can be beautiful by night, and give you pleasure, and ugly by day, and others will pity and perhaps mock you. Or I can be beautiful by day, and others will envy you, and ugly by night, which will give you no pleasure."

Gawain thought and thought. And finally he said:

"No, my wife. The choice must be yours."

And with that, the riddle was answered and the spell broken. She was beautiful all the time. This simple truth—that what women want is the power of choice—like so many eternal truths in the Arthurian myth, was buried for a millennium and a half.

The Siege Perilous

She was slight, undernourished in fact. The fine bones of her cheeks were in sharp relief and her eyes, large and dark, dominated her face. Her dress was clean but it bore evidence of numerous repair stitchings and the color had faded to a nondescript beige. She stood in the entrance to the great hall of Camelot, unnoticed by the Companions seated at the round table who were busy talking to each other. She recognized none of them, though their names would have been familiar. Tales of their adventures were repeated the length of the land: Bedivere, Bors, Gawain, Lancelot, and all the rest. Their stories were as familiar as the stories of her own family. As she looked around the table she wondered which one of these Companions was Gawain, hero of her favorite story, the story she had first heard from her mother at the time of her first moon bleeding when her mother was teaching her what it meant to be a woman. As her gaze swept the company of Companions she wondered which of them had had the generosity and courage to free Ragnall to be her true self.

Her gaze came full circle to the empty chair. This was where petitioners sat when bringing their grievances to the king. King Arthur would give his ear to any who journeyed here on this particular day; he would always listen, and give fair judgment, but woe betide any who sought to take advantage of the king and try to use him unjustly. He could see into the hearts of his petitioners, it was said, and his punishment was swift and sure to those who deserved it. Many who had experienced the King's penetrating stare and suffered his just anger called that chair the Siege Perilous, the Dangerous Chair.

The king's seneschal rapped his staff on the floor and the hall became quiet. All eyes turned in her direction and she realized that the man directly across from her, facing the Siege Perilous, was King Arthur. He wore a simple white tunic, unlike many of the Companions who were richly clad, but his air of authority needed no gilding. From the far side of the hall she could feel the power of his eyes regarding her seriously yet, she felt, kindly. He nodded to her, and she tried to move forward, but her feet were as if nailed to the floor. She almost panicked, and turned appealing eyes to the seneschal. He gave her an encouraging smile and gently guided her forward to take her seat in the empty chair.

Her voice quavered as she told her story. Her parents had been murdered by a local petty chieftain who was now living in her family home and terrorizing the peasants. She had fled with her younger siblings and taken refuge with her uncle, who offered them sanctuary but grudgingly.

"And so I come to seek justice, my lord."

There were a few quiet moments, and then the king asked her some questions about certain details of her story. He looked around the room and the Companions, grave now, nodded their agreement. One of them rose, a young man, not one of the seasoned warriors, and asked permission to accompany her home and bring the king's justice to her tormentor.

"By all means, Gareth. Take ten men with you."

She slumped in the chair and could not find the strength to move. Tears were streaming and she could barely see. A strong and gentle hand helped her up and when she lifted her head to stammer her thanks she saw it was the king himself. His gray eyes were full of compassion. "I am deeply sorry for the loss of your parents," he said. "We can do nothing for them but offer prayers for their souls, but we can bring their murderer to his just desserts, and make it known that such injustice will always bring deserved consequences."

South Cadbury

Castle Cadbury

As you drive along a winding country road in the county of Wiltshire in southern England it is easy to miss the village of South Cadbury. A small church, a few cottages, the road takes a sharp turn left and you are once again surrounded by the lush green of the English countryside, the village already behind you. You must drive slowly, and pay close attention, to notice that just where the road makes that sharp turn left there is a rocky path to the right that leads steeply upwards. Follow it, and you will come to a gnarled old tree.

The tree guards the entrance to Cadbury Castle, considered by many to be the most likely site of Camelot. If so, it was not the Camelot of legend. There was never a castle here in the medieval sense, with ramparts and towers and crenellated walls. According to Geoffrey Ashe, the word "castle" is used in quite a number of places in south and southwest England to mean a hill defended by earthwork ramparts and ditches. The castle is the hill itself.

All that is visible now of the fortifications of Castle Cadbury are the earthworks that form a crown around the top of the hill, from which looking northwest you can see Glastonbury Tor. On clear days you can see past the Tor to Brent Knoll. These three hills are in more or less a straight line, and then across the Bristol Channel, on roughly the same line, is the Welsh hill fort of Dinas Powys. All four hills may have formed a chain of communication by beacon, to alert king and country to the arrival of Saxon raiders on the south or west coasts.

When the site at Castle Cadbury was excavated in the nineteen sixties, Ashe tells us, fragments of pottery were found there that match those found in Tintagel: non-British ware of high quality, used for expensive goods such as wine and oil imported from the east Mediterranean, and dated to the late fifth or sixth century, the time of King Arthur. The excavation also revealed that the hill fort had been first settled and fortified by British Celts during the last centuries BCE. Near the southeast bend of the top rampart was found the skeleton of a young male who had been buried head down in a pit, evidently as a ritual sacrifice. The purpose of such a human sacrifice would have been supernatural support for the wall, a practice that heralded Merlin's entry into legend and set the stage for his prophesy to King Vortigern.

Cadbury Castle apparently was the site of a last gesture of Celtic resistance to the Romans, and after the Romans finally stormed the hill fort they deported the remaining inhabitants. The site remained vacant for about four hundred years. It was refortified and reoccupied during the fifth century, the time of Arthur. A timber hall was built, and a gatehouse, and a wall sixteen feet thick around the entire perimeter, a distance of almost three-quarters of a mile. The archeologist in charge of the excavation, Leslie Alcock, concluded that Cadbury-Camelot was the headquarters of a king with resources of manpower unequalled, so far as present knowledge goes, in the Britain of his time.

Other historians locate Camelot in the city of Carlisle in northern England.

Wherever it was, and even if it was nowhere at all in the physical world, Arthur's Camelot was the high summer of his reign. He was born in the depths of winter, and spent the springtime of his early manhood fighting his battles and finding his own power. After the last of the twelve battles—the Battle of Badon Hill—the Saxon threat was for the time being eliminated, and Arthur was able to turn his attention to administering the peace.

Not only did Arthur take care of the threat from outside invaders, he also made the country safe from within. During the time of the *Pax Romana* the famous Roman roads had been safe for travel because they were patrolled by the legions, but for a hundred years or so those roads in Britain had not been either patrolled or maintained, and marauding bandits and pirates had made travel by road, or by ship around the coastline, a perilous undertaking. During the time of Arthur's peace, travel once again was safe. The Companions roamed the land and acted as Arthur's deputies in maintaining the values and standards of his reign.

It was a time to enjoy the fruits of the peace, to plant in the secure knowledge that the harvest would be gathered in, a time for entertainment—for country fairs and festivals—a time to settle down and raise families. Arthur built the fabled Camelot and established his court. Anyone in the kingdom could come to Arthur's court to voice grievances and be respectfully heard, with no distinction as to status or gender.

Within the great hall that was the central gathering place of any leader of the time, King Arthur is said to have had a round table. The symbolic significance of a round table is that everyone is equal: the table has no head. Arthur's round table has a long and sacred association. The circle has been revered as a perfect and therefore sacred shape since the beginning of human awareness, from Aristotle's celestial spheres to the Native American Medicine Wheel, from the Buddhist Wheel of life to the Wiccan circle of magic. The round table at the heart of Camelot is a powerful symbol for the ideals of Arthur's reign: balance, harmony, equality and respect regardless of gender or station. It also represents a balance of yin and yang energy. The round table was Guinevere's marriage gift to Arthur. The symbol of balance and equality that became the core symbol of Camelot was a gift of the feminine.

Fourth Chakra: Anahata

As we proceed through the chakras it is self-evident that we mature and develop physically, emotionally and mentally. We do not expect a two-year-old to have the physical strength and dexterity of a twelve-year-old, or a ten-year-old to have the cognitive capacity of a twenty-five-year-old.

We also mature in our spiritual understanding. At the first and second chakras spirituality means religion and the divine is God, out there and separate from us. The idea of God that we can understand as children is a God concretized and anthropomorphized. We are not yet ready for abstract concepts of divinity because we do not yet have the mental apparatus, and so we think of God as a father-figure, in some religious traditions kindly and loving, in others angry or jealous or punishing. Most of us probably had an idea of God that was something like the God Michelangelo painted on the ceiling of the Sistine Chapel: an old man with a white beard living among the clouds.

Michelangelo's Creation of Adam, Cappella Sistina, Rome

In the same way, in the dualistic world of the second chakra, ideas of evil are concretized into Satan, a cunning archfiend hell-bent on creating chaos.

As we moved away from our unconscious immersion in the spiritual realm that was our reality at the first chakra, we began at the second the process of development as individual beings. In our teen years, as we empower the third chakra in our search for our own identity, we typically rebel against everything we have been taught, and part of that rebellion may be questioning the God and the religious traditions of our childhood. We may experiment with different spiritual traditions, seeking the one that will satisfy our inner yearning.

The lower chakras have to do with physical reality and God is out there, different from us, and transcendent. The upper three centers have to do with our inner reality, our relationship to the power of will, the power of the mind, and the power of the spiritual connection, and we recognize that God is within us as well as in all things. The heart chakra is the central point of the human energy system, the point of balance and integration, the meeting place of heaven and earth, spirit and matter. It is the doorway into our internal world. The fourth chakra is the point at which we have completed our differentiation—our nurturing of the ego, the will, the self, what Michael Washburn calls "our separation in the service of transcendence"—and we begin the journey back to conscious reunion with the Source.

When we move into the fourth chakra, the lower chakra ideas of God begin to feel limiting. Perhaps the very term "God" begins to sound not quite right anymore because of its traditional limitation in the three major western religions to the divine masculine. We may begin to wonder what happened to the divine feminine. And we start searching for other words that are more inclusive: Mother/Father God, the Divine, the Universe, The Great Is, Universal Consciousness, The Great Holy Mystery.

The heart is the center of love. The term "love," too, undergoes an expansion of meaning as we transition through the chakras. The love that we experience during our journey through the lower chakras is love of a different quality than that of the heart chakra. The Greeks had different words for different kinds of love, but we have only the one word that we have to qualify if we are to be clear about our meaning. We could consider the love of the first chakra to be filial love, or love of family, love that is based on biological connections, a love that most of us can assume and presume upon, a love that has elements of duty and need. The love of the second chakra is erotic or romantic love, love that is founded on a sensual response. We call it "falling in love," that heart-stopping, stomach-fluttering, all-consuming passion when thoughts of the beloved fill just about every waking and dreaming moment. The love of the third chakra is the love and appreciation of self that manifests as self-confidence.

The love of the heart is unconditional, what the Greeks called Agape. It is love that is offered freely, not because it is loved in return, or because it is supposed to love, or because the recipient is deemed worthy of being loved. It loves because that is its nature, that is what it is. It is at the heart, therefore, that we learn the true meaning of forgiveness, and of unconditional acceptance of others wherever they are in their own developmental journey.

Billy Holladay sang of different kinds of love in her most famous blues:

> My man don't love me, he treats me so mean ...
> He's the meanest man I have ever seen
> But when he gets down to love me ...

The love that she yearns for in the first line is heart love. It is the kind of love that would be incapable of mean treatment, the love that wants the highest good of the loved one, the love that is nourishing, kind, considerate and tender. The love of the third line is the sexual passion of second chakra love, the love between partners that is exciting, wonderful, all-consuming—and can be fraught with ego traps. Love that is focused on the second chakra, primarily on sexual gratification, often seeks to have power over; it can be jealous, possessive, demanding, insecure. Heart chakra love is giving, understanding, accepting, and unconditional.

Unconditional. That is fourth chakra love, the love of the heart center. We love someone simply because they are: not because they love us back, or because they do things for us, or because we are supposed to because they are related to us. We love them just because they are. And this kind of love does not require that we know them personally. The love of the heart encompasses love of humanity, of the planet, of life, of all that is.

As human beings we require love to survive and thrive. Love is essential to our minds, our spirits and our physical bodies. There are studies of children raised in orphanages whose physical needs were provided for—they were fed, clothed, and sheltered—but nobody loved them, nobody picked them up and cuddled them. Most of them failed to thrive, and some of them died.

In another famous study rabbits were housed in floor to ceiling cages, all were fed exactly the same thing, at the same time, in the same amounts, but the ones in the lower cages thrived better than the ones in the upper cages. The researchers could not understand why. They had provided for all the variables they could think of so why were these rabbits not all responding in the same way? Because the research assistant was an animal lover, and when she fed the rabbits in the lower cages she would pet them and talk to them. She could not reach the ones in the upper cages so she just put their food and water in the cage. The rabbits that were touched and petted responded to the love energy of the research assistant's heart chakra, and that response was reflected in their physical growth.

Within a framework of chakra development, Arthur's time in Camelot would correspond to the development of the fourth chakra. First we have to provide for the needs of the lower chakras: the needs of physical survival, of a sense of safety and belonging in the physical world, and a sense of our own identity, who we are as individuals separate from the traditions of our group and family. Then we can turn our attention to our inner development, and it is at the heart that this process begins.

Romantic love in the outer world is expressed, traditionally, between man and woman. When we raise the energy from the second to the fourth chakra, that love is expressed on the inner planes by creating balance between the masculine and feminine aspects of our own being, by learning to love and nurture all parts of ourselves, and by bringing light into our places of shadow. It is not possible to love anyone else unconditionally until we can offer that quality of love to ourselves. It is at the heart center that the balance of yin (feminine) and yang (masculine) energy becomes the focus of development. We may be born with our yin and yang energies in balance but the process of acculturation teaches us to develop and emphasize one aspect or the other according to the sex of our bodies. One of the challenges of the heart chakra is to develop and express the shadow, the neglected masculine or feminine aspect of being.

We all, men and women, are made up of both masculine and feminine energy. Yang, or masculine energy, is about focus, direction and goal orientation. It is assertive and rational, and its verb is doing. Yin, or feminine energy, is receptive and emotional, and is about flow, intuition, and creativity. It is compassionate and nurturing, and its verb is being. Historically, societies have assigned masculine and feminine roles according to gender, without regard to the fact that our physical and emotional health, as well as our spiritual development, depend upon creating a balance of the masculine and feminine energies within us, whether we are male or female. Purely yin energy might be highly intuitive and creative, but without yang the ideas never make it into physical form. Purely yang energy is full of zip and enthusiasm, but without yin it lacks the creativity to give it structure. Both are necessary to the full expression of who we are.

For much of my adult life I accepted the standard feminist perception of the 1970s that the world was ruled by and for men. My developmental work was focused on healing the feminine energy within myself, in finding my own power as a woman and in countering the myriad messages that anything feminine is less important and less worthy. It was years before I entertained the notion that men could feel as stifled and entrapped as women.

At a point where I felt blocked in my spiritual development I was guided through a yin yang meditation in order to meet an image of my animus, the inner masculine or yang energy. He was a naked adolescent, and he was seriously ticked off. When I asked him what he was so angry about he said: "Isn't it obvious?" I looked more closely, and saw he had no genitals.

Masculine energy, in the world of my childhood, was angry, controlling, violent, unpredictable and dictatorial, and I wanted no part of it. I did not know that in cutting myself off from the masculine energy out there, I was denying an important part of myself. My animus, the masculine energy within me, had not grown beyond adolescence, and he was castrated. He was manifest in my life in unfinished projects, in great ideas that never went beyond hurried notes or sketches because they lacked the masculine energy to bring them into physical form.

I was not alone. In a spiritual workshop led by Gloria Karpinski that happened to be all women we were exploring archetypes of the masculine and feminine by listing words that described our inner images of yin and yang. All our adjectives for the masculine were negative. Someone said in a tone dripping with irony: "Well, why do you suppose that is?" and we all exchanged knowing looks and snickers. We were shocked by Gloria's comment that at least part of the answer was the wounded yang within us.

It is easy as we look around the world to see evidence of misguided yang energy and it is easy to assign the blame for it to men. We see it in patriarchal structures that limit the expression of yin: in the political and international arena, in business, in many religions, and within many families. Many women have tended to blame men for what is wrong with the world in general, and specifically for their own oppression, but it is not that simple. There are plenty of women who have supported the patriarchal structure over the centuries, and even now there are many who are threatened by the prospect of taking full responsibility for their own lives and who seek a mate who will take care of them and make decisions for them. It is not a matter of victim and oppressor. The lack of balance damages all of us, and damages our world.

Our sex largely conditions our gender identification and therefore the dominance of yin or yang. The people around us are likely to encourage certain behaviors based on whether we are little boys or little girls. A girl, for example, born to parents with traditional ideas of gender roles, may be called a "little princess" from the first moment when she emerges into the harsh lights of a delivery room. She may be coddled and protected and given constant overt and covert signals that she deserves *and requires* protection. She may internalize those messages and grow up believing that she can't survive alone, and that it is not okay to develop and express her masculine energy.

A small boy early on gets the message that it is not manly to cry, often internalized as a belief that it is not acceptable to express, or even allow himself to feel, the tender emotions. He learns to channel that energy into physical activity, or in less healthy ways such as violent anger. We may not, as a culture, like or want to encourage anger in males but we do not say it is unmanly to be angry, as we say it is unmanly to cry, or to be afraid.

Until relatively recently society provided both men and women with models of behavior that strictly delineated their respective roles. The archetype of the male was the provider, the decision-maker, a strong, largely silent, dependable presence. Fatherhood was mostly a matter of setting an example of what the male was expected to do and to be, a somewhat distant role rather than an intimate daily involvement with his children. The archetype of the female was the self-sacrificing wife and mother, a nurturing dependable presence in the home, financially dependent on her husband, and deferring to his wisdom and guidance.

Those are the cultural archetypes that we saw in television shows of the nineteen fifties and sixties. Women of that era were expected to be largely decorative; labor saving devices had greatly reduced the time spent on domestic chores while the post war economic boom provided the means to acquire luxury items such as fur coats and jewelry. The *Dick Van Dyke Show, Father Knows Best, I Love Lucy, Bewitched, I love Jeannie,* even *The Flintstones*— portray women as childlike, dependent and manipulative. The way a woman was groomed, the amount of time spent at beauty parlors and shopping, the clothes she wore and so on were an indicator of the financial success of her husband, when financial success was the primary criterion of manhood. The wife was a symbol of her husband's success in the material world, and marriage was a second chakra contract. He provided security and status; she provided a comfortable and welcoming home environment and dependable sex. Sex on demand was still considered a male marriage right; marital rape was still an oxymoron.

The women's movement of the early nineteen seventies challenged those roles. It was a drive towards creating a more healthy balance within women. The feminist pioneers were not satisfied with the limited and limiting traditional feminine roles of wife and mother and dependent, because their inner truth was crying out that they were capable and worthy of functioning in many different roles. Assertiveness training, one of the tools of the movement, is about developing healthy yang energy to complement—not replace—the highly developed yin. Women joined consciousness-raising groups, and read and wrote about their right and their ability to be strong and independent decision-makers. Many women in that first generation either lived without men or performed their traditional duties in addition to seeking fulfillment outside the home. A lucky few found men strong enough—in our terminology men with a healthy third chakra and a sense of self not dependent upon social approbation— with whom to share a life of equal partnership.

As women began to explore their power of choice and to demand equal status, men were faced with a situation for which they had no models and no experience. Keeping his woman "in her place" had been one of the criteria of the strength of the male, of his masculinity, of his membership in the men's club. Men married to feminist pioneers often had to face the derision of their peers and had to choose between them and the woman they loved and the mother of their children. Some found the strength to do it; others tried to maintain the status quo through asserting their will, sometimes through violence; some divorced and found a more traditional woman.

A generation later there was the beginning of a movement towards the development of healthy yin energy within men. In the nineties we saw more and more fathers who wanted to be a nourishing presence in their children's lives; more and more husbands who wanted a balanced partnership and shared responsibilities; more and more men who wanted the freedom to express a full range of emotion. At the same time, many men in our culture were feeling lost. They complained that they did not know any more what their role was, or what was expected of them. And because it was not manly to feel lost there was a backlash of anger, sometimes directed inward in helplessness and depression, and sometimes directed outwards in escalating crimes of violence against women.

Among women, too, there continues to be a lack of consensus. While many young women take for granted the rights and opportunities for which their mothers and grandmothers had to fight, and eagerly embrace the challenges that those opportunities bring, there are still many who want a man to take care of them. There are still women who expect to be paid for on dates, and expect the husband to shoulder the lion's share of household expenses regardless of the relative size of their incomes. At the other end of the continuum is the superwomen, women who have successful careers, who may have spent years as single mothers surviving on welfare while putting themselves through school. In a second marriage they may still feel they have to do it all, managing the home, the children, transportation to soccer and gymnastics, supervision of homework and so on, as well as the new roles of lover and partner.

When we look at the archetypal middle-class family of the mid twentieth century we see the working father, the stay at home mother, the 2.2 children, the house in the suburbs. The archetype clearly reflects the white middle class, not the vast variety of ethnic cultures which by now constitute almost half the population, but even there if we scratch beneath the picture perfect surface we may find women, like those portrayed in Marilyn French's *The Women's Room*, going quietly insane with the boredom and emptiness of their lives, eating themselves alive with resentment at being treated— whether with paternalistic indulgence or paternalistic abuse—as second class beings who are unable to think or act for themselves.

121

The movement that began with consciousness-raising groups and a few brave women claiming their right to be whole, self-actualizing beings, has matured a couple of generations later. It is no longer unusual to find women in all the professions, to find young girls and teenagers aspiring to careers in professions or occupations that were closed to their mothers and grandmothers. But we also often find that the pendulum has swung to the opposite extreme to create the phenomenon of the superwoman. Women by and large still bear the major part of the responsibility for running the home and raising the children, even when they have full time jobs outside the home. They feel they have to do it all. They have yet to find the place of balance.

In Arthur's Britain, infant Christianity existed within a context of enduring respect for a pantheon of feminine deities and by extension for women and for feminine qualities and values. Among the Celts women were the equals of men, in power and status. Geoffrey Ashe tells of this special feature of Celtic society, the unusually high status of women. Not only were women Druids, they also held royal power. Celtic queens ruled over tribal coalitions, and in matters of the bedroom a queen as well as a king could take a lover without social disapproval. In Arthur's time, such Christianity as existed in Britain was Celtic Christianity, a religious tradition that built upon the foundations of Celtic culture. It was only later that Roman Christianity—that had adopted the patriarchal structure of the Roman Empire—imposed its authority over the Christian world.

In the Middle Ages, the Age of Chivalry, when the most familiar of the Arthurian legends were collected and written down, the status of women was dichotomous. On the one hand they were helpless damsels in distress, fragile and chaste and dependent, with no power or learning or qualifications at all really except to be beautiful; and on the other they were temptresses who robbed men of their power. The medieval versions of the legends manipulated the stories to reflect these character types, most obviously in the characters of Guinevere and Morgan le Fay. Guinevere is the beautiful but powerless queen who spends her life embroidering; and Morgan le Fay is her shadow, the witch who is powerful but whose power is exercised in dark and evil ways. These archetypes are still alive and well in the depths of our collective psyche.

The fear of the latter cultural archetype has contributed greatly to the disempowerment of women. In the West our culture continues to embody a male fear of the mysterious feminine, as well as a female fear of the aggressive masculine. These fears have been manifested both in the inequities and imbalances in our society, and within our own beings, as both men and women have been afraid to honor and develop the complementary energy within themselves. The cultural archetype of the male as protector and provider, rational and unemotional, is an archetype that discourages the males in our culture from respecting and nurturing their feminine energy. And the archetype of the female as dependent, over-emotional, the self-sacrificing nurturer who always puts the needs of others before herself, is an archetype that discourages women from developing their own masculine energy.

As a result of the challenge to those archetypes during the last quarter of the twentieth century we are now in a period of flux. Out in the vanguard are those who have transcended the traditional archetypes and have created a new ideal of equality and balance: in the workplace, in the home, in politics, in the church, in sports. But that new archetype has by no means acquired universal acceptance and there are many among us who still experience resistance, fear, or resentment at the changing social environment.

One of the ways in which the dichotomy of roles has played out in relationships is that often women carry the burden of expressing emotion for both genders. And the more emotional she gets, the more he retreats and shuts down. Both are out of balance. The woman's heart chakra is overloaded, feeling the pain of the relationship, feeling the pain of the planet in many cases, which is at least part of the reason for the epidemic of depression among women. Men meanwhile shut down the heart because expressing emotion is not okay; it is a sign of weakness, and a source of embarrassment. They are more prone to heart disease from the constriction of the heart chakra.

I had a conversation once with an attorney at a neighborhood party. He told me that his specialty was criminal law. I had recently had my first exposure to the legal system with a client who was a battered wife and wondered how in the world attorneys and others who work at the courthouse deal with the toxic energy there. "By shutting down," he said. He mentioned several times that his shutting down had created difficulties in his marriage.

Marital discord as a result of shutting down the emotions is not a monopoly of the legal profession. Imagine the state of mind of a male emergency department physician or a forensic pathologist or a police officer, exposed day after day to the violence and cruelty in their community. If they have never learned how to be compassionate and detached at the same time it may be that the only way they know how to protect themselves from the cruelty and pain they witness is, like the above-mentioned attorney, to cut themselves off. They may begin to sound not only detached but cruel, because detachment without compassion can come across as cold and uncaring, hence the "black humor" of emergency departments and operating rooms.

Being afraid is not considered manly in our culture. When feeling threatened yang turns to firearms, alarm systems, big dogs, the martial arts, but a fear that is not acknowledged is the fear of his own feelings. Yang may sublimate fear in anger and fighting and shut down the tender feelings, which inevitably in time includes tender feelings towards a spouse and children.

Many men in our culture are more terrified of their own feelings (yin energy) than of any external threat. They are as terrified of their feelings as many women are of claiming their power (yang energy). Men often say they dare not get angry because the violence of their anger is such that they may not be able to control it, and I suspect that the intensity of the anger is such because many other "unmanly" feelings—fear, pain, hurt, grief, sympathy, helplessness—are channeled into an acceptable male emotion: anger. Opening the heart, for them, can be a terrifying prospect because it means exploring realms of emotion that are virgin territory.

In my practice I have encountered extreme examples of yin/yang imbalance: women who have been abused by practically all the men in their lives; men who have locked up their yin energy in order to play by the rules of what it means to be a man in our culture and who suffer emotionally and physically. Consider the man who has done his best to be what his culture and time have taught him a man should be: Strong. In charge. Taking responsibility. Making decisions. Being a dependable provider. In later life when all those duties have been discharged he might decide he at last deserves the freedom to pursue the dreams he had set aside: to play professional golf or tennis, to sell the house and buy a boat and travel the world, to move to Alaska and hunt. When he finds that the support and understanding he expects from his mate is not forthcoming he might feel abandoned and unjustly used. She might resent his new expectations of her because this new life that is his life-long dream is not what she signed up for, not part of their unwritten and unspoken contract with each other.

Both women and men contribute to imbalance in relationships and in society. It is not a matter of victim and oppressor, or generous provider and ungrateful recipient. Each of us makes our own contribution to the status quo, and the lack of balance damages all of us, individually and collectively. The controlling and oppressive husband that a woman attracts into her life reflects the restriction she has placed on the expression of her own yang energy; the needy, dependent and manipulative wife that a man attracts into his life is a reflection of his own powerless inner yin. Individually we are retarding our own development and the full and wonderful expression of the totality of our beings; collectively we are perpetuating patterns of imbalance and injustice that continue to create suffering.

When feminine energy is not balanced by the masculine compassion becomes pity, and nurturing becomes rescuing.

Compassion and nurturing are empowering to both parties; pity and rescue not only burden the rescuer but also devalue the targets of those sentiments, because the underlying message is that they are incapable of learning to take care of themselves. And if masculine energy is not tempered by the feminine, assertiveness becomes aggression, setting boundaries becomes extending boundaries and taking over the territory of others.

Taking over each other's territory has been the pattern of our recorded history ever since we changed the gender of God and the masculine became dominant. How far a ruler was able to extend the territory of his country was the criterion by which history judged him. There have been rulers who spent their lives in battle in order to build great empires, who were followed by lesser men, or at least lesser warriors, who allowed the empire to be taken away. Henry II built the greatest empire since Charlemagne, and his three sons lost it to the new European predator, Louis of France, whose father had lost much of the same territory to Henry.

One of Henry's sons was Richard the Lionheart, who was venerated for centuries for his gallant defense of Christendom during the crusades, but many now see those crusades not as an honorable defense of our spiritual heritage but as marauding escapades that violated the tenets of Christ's teachings. On their way to the Holy Land the crusaders raped and pillaged their way across Europe, leaving ravaged Jewish communities in their wake. The fourth crusade never even made it to the Holy Land but attacked Constantinople instead, a Christian city at the time. (In 2001 Pope Paul II apologized to the patriarch of the Eastern Orthodox Church, Bartholomew I, for the sacking of Constantinople by Crusader armies in the early 13th century.)

The denigration of feminine energy, both the feminine energy within men and women, and in the status of women in society, culture and religion, is not the way it has always been. The ancient cultures of Britain worshipped the Goddess, the feminine principle of divine creation, as did many of the world's traditional cultures.

Some three thousand years ago something happened that changed the gender of God. The three major western religions of Judaism, Christianity, and Islam all worship God the Father.

How that shift came about has had various explanations. Merlin Stone has uncovered evidence of widespread worship of the Great Goddess in ancient times in Europe and the Middle East, in Neolithic and Chalcolithic societies that were probably matrilineal. They were overrun by invading northern peoples who worshipped a supreme male deity and had patrilineal and patriarchal customs. Riane Eisler creates a compelling argument that the shift from a feminine to a masculine deity was a result of the invasion of male-dominated nomadic tribes into the partnership culture of central Europe. Leonard Shlain believes that the instrument of the change from a female to a male god was the creation of writing. This development changed the structure of the brain and shifted from right-brain dominance to left-brain dominance, from intuition to intellect, from image to word, from feminine to masculine.

For whatever reason, the Goddess, or the feminine aspect of divinity, has been neglected for a long time. The denigration of the feminine, and the idea of the feminine as the source of evil, goes all the way back to the beginnings of the dominant Western sacred text. Eve disobeyed God and ate the forbidden fruit in the Garden of Eden and tempted Adam to do likewise. The first woman, therefore, is held responsible for the fall from grace, and thereafter the book of Genesis is the genealogy of generations of males: Adam begot Sheth, and Sheth begot Enosh, and Enosh begot Kenan, and so on, as if none of them had mothers, or their mothers were irrelevant.

The theme persists throughout the Old Testament and the New and permeates Christian dogma. Delilah is a temptress who destroys the power of Samson. After all Job's trials, God rewards him for his faith with a new house and a new family, and "After this lived Job an hundred and forty years, and saw his sons, and his sons' sons, even four generations" (Job 40. 16-17). And his daughters? Immaterial. Mary Magdalene, of whom no negative word is to be found in the New Testament and who new scholarship indicates was a priestess and leader in the early church, mysteriously acquired the reputation of reformed prostitute. And even though the scriptures themselves—both the gospels of Mark and John—state that Mary Magdalene was the first to see the resurrected Christ, the tradition developed that Peter was the first witness to the resurrected Christ: Peter—enemy of Mary and of women, according to Elaine Pagels— took over leadership of the movement and changed the direction of the orthodox church away from balance of masculine and feminine and towards a strictly patriarchal structure that allowed no place for women or a feminine aspect of divinity.

The discovery of the Nag Hammadi documents in 1945 shed light on an early Christian church that is very different from the popular conception of a unified movement. These documents are third or fourth century Coptic translations of earlier Greek texts that were buried in the Egyptian desert. The early church was not, Elaine Pagels tell us, a golden age of unity and harmony that was later split, first into the church of Rome and the Eastern Orthodox church, and later by the Reformation into the many different Christian traditions that exist today. On the contrary, the first few centuries of the Christian movement were a time of intense and acrimonious debate: over the nature of Jesus; the place of women; the literal truth or symbolism of the resurrection; the nature of reality. The orthodox tradition prevailed because it inherited the power of the Roman Empire and it proceeded to eliminate the opposition. All that was known of that opposition, before the gnostic gospels were found, was what could be inferred from the writings of early church philosophers who were denouncing the ideas of the opposing sects.

The gnostic gospels reveal that among gnostic groups women were the equals of men in the early decades of Christianity; there were women who were prophets, teachers, traveling evangelists, healers, priests and possibly bishops. But within the orthodox church, that derived its authority from Peter and the fiction that he was the first to witness the risen Christ, are such Pauline dictates as:

"… the women should keep silence in the churches. For they are not permitted to speak, but they should be subordinate … it is shameful for a woman to speak in church," (I Corinthians 14, 34, quoted in *The Gnostic Gospels.*)

In the centuries that followed, as God became exclusively male and the feminine aspect of divinity was denied, the place of women within religion and within society became more and more restricted. There are indications, however, that reverence for the feminine face of God did not die but went underground. It has been suggested that the medieval troubadours who sang of their devotion to a usually unattainable woman were really singing their devotion to the forgotten divine feminine.

In a time when heresy—which meant anything not in conformity with official doctrine—was punishable by torture and burning, anyone who wanted to keep alive the idea of the feminine aspect of divinity had to be not only brave but highly inventive to disseminate forbidden truths under the nose of the ubiquitous and notorious Inquisition. So perhaps the troubadours, in their songs of devotion to unattainable women, and even Dante in his devotion to the unattainable Beatrice, were using the tools at their command to keep alive the idea of feminine divinity in a time when official doctrine blamed the feminine for the fall from grace, for tempting men away from God, and probably for crop failures and earthquakes.

Artists, too, incorporated clues clearly visible "for those who have eyes to see" in their paintings and frescoes. Whether or not the Priory of Sion ever existed—the secret society of *Holy Blood, Holy Grail* and the *Da Vinci Code* to name only two works that cite the apparently forged documents of the Priory—the fact remains that the symbolism discovered in the paintings of Da Vinci, Botticelli, Fra Angelico and others suggests that those artists were incorporating reminders of the denied divine feminine in their apparently orthodox works. Who can now look at the *Last Supper* and not see a woman beside Jesus? Perhaps Da Vinci was never the Grand Master of a secret society devoted to the divine feminine, but he did leave clues as to his thoughts about the masculine/feminine imbalance in the dominant religious hierarchy. And if Mary Magdalene was the wife of Jesus and sat beside him at the Last Supper, perhaps she is also the Mary in Michelangelo's *Pieta'*. The face and figure of the woman holding Jesus' crucified body are those of a young woman, not a woman in her late forties.

Michelangelo, Pietà

Elizabeth Cady Stanton, founder with Susan Anthony of the American Suffrage Movement and author of *The Woman's Bible* (1895), summarizes the biblical position of woman thus:

> The Bible teaches that woman brought sin and death into the world that precipitated the fall of the race, that she was arraigned before the judgment seat of Heaven, condemned and sentenced. Marriage for her was to be a condition of bondage, maternity a suffering and anguish.

Recent biblical scholarship shows the ways in which traditional patriarchal culture has distorted the role of women in the Bible. The discovery of the Dead Sea Scrolls and the Nag Hammadi Library has thrown new light on the place of the feminine in the early church that became the dominant western religious tradition. The reputation of Mary Magdalene, in biblical scholarship and in popular fiction such as *The Da Vinci Code,* is being rehabilitated, and the Goddess is once more finding reverence.

The earth, in ancient pagan traditions, is a feminine energy, and we still refer to our planet as Mother Earth. In the Kabbalah of the Jewish mystical tradition the first Sephirah on the Tree of Life, Malchut, is feminine. The Chinese Qi Gong and the ancient and modern Druids all tell us that the element earth and our planet are feminine. The snake that symbolizes Kundalini energy coiled at the first chakra at the base of the spine is feminine.

The element earth corresponds to the first chakra, to the physical aspect of our being. It is our strength and our stability, it is what grounds us in the physical experience, and it is the foundation upon which we build this specific life experience. The Earth, the mother, is the planetary vehicle for our journey in physical form, and our physical bodies are our connection to the earth, to the physical dimension.

The element that corresponds to the second chakra is also feminine: water. Where the earth is solid, strong and stable, water is fluid, and adaptable. While the element earth and the first chakra represent the stability and solidity of the physical body, the second chakra and water correspond to the volatility of the emotional body. The third and fourth chakras correspond respectively to fire and air, and are both masculine.

If any one of these elements were missing, or out of balance, the earth would not survive. So too within our beings both the masculine and feminine energies require nurture and expression and balance or we do not thrive as healthy beings.

The physical aspect of being in the West, like feminine energy, is often neglected in spiritual work, part of the legacy of a religious tradition that teaches dominion over nature, rather than harmony within nature, as well as the exclusion of the divine feminine, the earthy, regenerative, creative and intuitive aspect of being. We are living, now, with the consequences of that imbalance, as our disrespect for our planet has created a crisis that could prove our downfall. In this the ancients were wiser than we are. They recognized that the earth itself is sacred; that the divine is within all things, not separate and transcendent; and that there is no separating the health of the individual soul from the health of the planet. They knew that spiritual work is not something to be practiced on a specific day of the week, or at a specific time of day, but is in the way in which we live our daily lives, honoring ourselves, honoring each other and our world and all its dimensions.

One of the most beautiful and powerful choruses in the whole operatic repertoire is the chorus of Hebrew slaves pining for their homeland in Verdi's *Nabucco*. It expresses the longing of the heart in a way only music or poetry can, an indefinable emotion that the intellect expressed through prose can never capture. Music and poetry communicate directly with the emotions and the spirit, by-passing the critical, analytical faculty of the mental body.

I once sat enraptured in front of a huge canvas in the Los Angeles Museum of Art. I do not remember its title nor, to my shame, the artist. It had no "picture" or identifiable theme. If I were to try and describe it in words I could only say it consisted of variations of yellow. And yet it made my soul rejoice. Something reached out and into the very core of my being and drew forth an emotion that had been dormant for a long time. At another low point in my life I was brought back from the brink of despair by the American Ballet Theater.

An unfortunate facet of our yang-dominated culture is the assignment of low priority to the arts. We have decided, as a culture, that we are not willing to pay higher taxes in order to give our schools arts programs. Most of our schools no longer have orchestras. Our priority is to prepare our children for "success" in a technology-dominated world at the expense of the harmony of their inner essence. Arts are Yin. Technology is Yang. As in all things, we need both.

The first men in space were fighter pilots, scientists, engineers. Pure Yang, it might be supposed. And yet as they gazed back from space on the ineffable beauty of our planet they became poets and mystics. There is no language in Yang for the response of the soul to such experiences, and Yin finds a way—at those moments of transcendence—to make her presence and power felt. Whether we heed the call, whether we pay attention and work to integrate the moment of balance into a lifetime of harmony once the moment passes, is our choice and our challenge. Most of us have known such moments, however fleeting, as we read a poem, heard a particular piece of music, or watched a sunset: moments when we knew, deep within, the harmony of creation.

The series *Star Trek*, in its various incarnations, examined the issues of our time in the context of a future earth culture that had survived the nuclear age and learned to transcend the eye for an eye ethos of the first and second chakras. Arms in the *Star Trek* future are used defensively and as a last resort. One of the ways in which the series confronted contemporary challenges was to take some of our cultural archetypes and express them in extreme form. Vulcans are pure Yang, and represent our cultural veneration for reason taken to an absurd extreme. Our culture simply disparages emotions, and considers them a sign of weakness; Vulcans banish them completely to a deep and heavily fortified region of the psyche and live by the dictates of logic and reason. They believe themselves superior to humans because their decisions are made on that basis, uncontaminated by the energy of Yin.

Subsequent variations on this theme as the series, and we, developed were Commander Data and the Doctor-with-no-name, a machine and a computer-generated hologram respectively. They, unlike Mr. Spock, recognized their lack of wholeness and tried—in ingenious, inventive and often entertaining ways—to become "more human" by exploring and practicing the "non-rational" aspects of humanity: Yin.

We can program a machine to do left-brain functions, but the right brain includes the feminine qualities of intuition, and inspiration, qualities that are indefinable and unprogrammable and a vital part of who we are.

The imbalance in the world, and the damage to our natural environment, reflects the imbalance within us. As within so without. As the ancients knew, there is no separating the health of the individual from the health of the planet. It is not possible to separate our own personal health and growth from the health and growth of the totality of which we are a part. Balancing yin and yang energy within our own beings helps to contribute to the balancing of yin and yang on our planet, which is suffering the effects of several thousand years of imbalance.

Throughout recorded history we have known only what Rianne Eisler calls the "dominator" model of social organization. Within cultures this has meant the domination of one gender, one racial group, one economic group, or one social class over the rest. In international affairs it has meant the domination of the wealthiest and most militarily powerful countries. In terms of the ecology of our planet it has meant the dominion of man over nature and the exploitation and pollution of our natural resources.

Eisler makes a convincing case for the existence of a partnership culture in central Europe that preceded the dominator culture of our recorded history. Whether or not there was such a golden age in our past, it is vital—now that we have developed the technological means to destroy ourselves—that we learn to create such an age in our near future, that we begin to honor the divine in all people and in all things, giving each other and our planet the respect and honor they deserve.

What rings most false in the medieval versions of the Arthurian stories is the treatment of women, which is self-contradictory and unrealistic. It reflects the mores of medieval times rather than those of the fifth/sixth century, the time of King Arthur, when women and men held equal status in both the spiritual and secular power structures. By the time of the Middle Ages it was believed that women, like dogs, had no souls. At the same time, the code of chivalry demanded that women be revered and worshipped from afar.

This unrealistic dichotomy in the attitude towards women is manifest in the medieval Guinevere, a classic example of the Madonna/whore image of woman. She is the beautiful queen of the handsome and brave king who inspires the devotion of the knights: the Madonna symbol of chaste purity. But because she is a woman she is a slave to her passions and when she is suspected of adultery with Lancelot she brings the whole kingdom down: the whore symbol. (Though there have been numerous examples throughout history of men who have sacrificed everything to sexual passion, God the Father seems to be more tolerant of man's weaknesses and society has tended to blame the woman for tempting him.) Morgan le Fey and Nimue, who were powerful women and probably priestesses, have come down to us from medieval sources as wicked witches, one of whom imprisons Merlin and takes away his power.

The medievalist Norma Goodrich tells us that prior to the year 542 in Celtic Britain priests *and priestesses* were educated in reading, writing, astronomy, oratory, and philosophy; that Arthur's half-sister Morgan was such a priestess and her keen intelligence was recognized in early childhood. It was not until the sixth century, says Goodrich, that women were excluded from the priesthood and from schools by order of the Emperor Justinian.

In the early Celtic church there were women abbots of monasteries, and we know from the Irish epics that Celtic queens were leaders and warriors and that the culture supported a lusty sexual freedom for both sexes. It was a Celtic queen, Boudicca, who led the most successful and famous British revolt against the Romans in the first century CE. Even the eleventh century Geoffrey of Monmouth relates that after Uther married Igraine "they lived together as equals."

Guinevere was a Celtic queen and was more likely to have ridden beside Arthur than to have stayed at home embroidering. A Guinevere who is pure and chaste and spends her time cocooned in a castle doing needlework is much more a projection of the medieval idea of ideal womanhood than a realistic characterization of a fifth century Celtic queen. An ancient collection of Welsh tales, the *Mabinogion*, tells how Queen Guinevere took part in a hunt for the White Stag. Contemporary fictional accounts based on earlier sources rather than the familiar medieval ones, such as Stephen Lawhead's *The Pendragon Cycle*, offer a more realistic interpretation of Guinevere's character. Lawhead's Guinevere is strong and independent, magnificent in her battle dress as she rides into battle at Arthur's side. The relationship between her and Arthur is one of devotion, two equals in strength and resources, two heart chakras open and clear. (Lawhead ignores the Lancelot Guinevere aspect of the story.)

Medieval writers had to make the story morally satisfying within the context of the good/evil dichotomy prevailing at the time within the dominant Roman Catholic Church. From the point of view of medieval writers, if Arthur were indeed a good and noble king, who ruled according to just and moral laws, why did the kingdom fail? It could not be that God was unfair, and that he had abandoned Arthur for no good reason. It was not morally satisfying to the medieval mind that the coalition of Celtic kings led by Arthur would in time be overcome by hordes of Saxons, Angles and Jutes, just as Rome itself had fallen to Goths and Gaul to Franks. It was not enough of a miracle that Arthur created the coalition in the first place; or that he held it together through twelve mighty battles and twelve years of peace; or that he governed according to laws that were far in advance of his time.

There had to be some moral failing within the fabled Camelot to account for its fall, and because of the attitude of the Judeo Christian tradition towards the power of the feminine the failing was going to be due to a woman. Camelot fell, we are told by the medieval writers, because of the adulterous affair between Lancelot and Guinevere that caused dissension among the knights, and because Arthur had been manipulated into committing unwitting incest with his half-sister. It was Mordred, the product of their union, who was killed by Arthur in his final battle, and who in his turn inflicted a mortal—perhaps—wound on Arthur.

It is very probable that the love triangle of Lancelot, Guinevere and Arthur was invented by French medieval storytellers to discredit the English. The English and the French fought each other for centuries and it was a French medieval writer, Chrétien de Troyes, who first mentioned the adultery between Guinevere and Lancelot. If de Troyes intended to discredit and ridicule King Arthur by making him into a cuckold he obviously failed. The power of the archetypal symbolism in the myth has crafted this addition to the story to conform to the image of Arthur as a wise, compassionate, just and generous king. Arthur has continued to be loved and revered down the centuries because it is the deeper truth of myth that endures.

Here is the dilemma facing the medieval author. If the medieval reader is going to venerate Arthur, Arthur must be blameless, and yet at the same time he must do something that sows the seeds of his downfall. He commits the ancient sin of incest, but his sin is unknowing; at the time he does not know that his lover is his half-sister Morgan. It is she, like Eve in the Garden of Eden, who manipulates Arthur into wrongdoing and who bears the blame and the responsibility for the sin. Nevertheless, according to the pitiless morality of the time, Arthur had to be punished, and not only him but the whole country.

Several hundred years earlier, in the sixth century, the Goddess was still alive and well and Celtic women were strong and commanded respect. Morgan, Guinevere, the Lady of the Lake, and the teachers of Perceval, Goodrich tells us, were all powerful and well-educated women, equal partners in spiritual and temporal leadership. Let us imagine what the characters of Guinevere and Morgan, and the relationship between them, might have been like.

Guinevere and Morgan

Around the shores of the island were the round thatched huts of the marsh dwellers, the old ones, whose history on these islands stretched so far back into the dawn of time that they were almost a part of the land itself. In front of Guinevere, at the foot of the Tor, was the shrine of the sacred well of the Goddess, heart of Avalon and the seat of priestess training and ritual. On the far side of the Tor, close to the stronghold of Melwas, king of the summer country, was the small wattle and daub chapel of the Christians. It was the oldest Christian church in Britain it was said, built by Joseph of Arimathea when he came to Britain after the crucifixion of the Christ.

Guinevere did not feel she could calm her spirit in either of these sacred places. She walked by them and continued on along the shore of the lake. The surface was calm. Guinevere gazed over the water and breathed in deeply of the still, clean air. Water birds waded in the shallows; she saw the blue flash of a diving kingfisher and the momentary silver brilliance of his catch. But the tranquility of her surroundings did nothing to calm her inner anguish.

Arthur and Lancelot. The two loves were tearing her heart to pieces. She loved Arthur with all her heart and at the same time yearned for Lancelot. Why had the Goddess visited this torment on her? Whenever she looked on Arthur she was shamed by her secret longing. He was a kind and good and wonderful man, and he deserved a wife who lived only for him. And Lancelot loved Arthur with his whole soul and was equally tormented by his desire for her. Guinevere sank to the ground beside the still water, hugging her knees and resting her forehead on them.

There was no sound but a stirring in the air perhaps that alerted her to another presence. She lifted her head, and listened, but heard nothing more than the murmur of the gentle breeze in marsh grasses and the occasional cry of a bird. She slowly turned her head and caught sight of a figure standing a few feet behind her. With the sure instinct of a warrior she was on her feet with her knife in her hand before her brain registered that the figure was someone known to her and no threat.

Morgan wore the simple linen tunic of a priestess and her feet were bare, muddy from her walk along the water's edge. The two women faced each other, Morgan calm and self-assured, Guinevere still in an attack stance, until she took a deep breath, sheathed the knife and straightened.

"Forgive me, Morgan. I did not hear you come."

Morgan smiled and shook her head. "Nothing to forgive." She took a few paces forward until she was standing directly in front of Guinevere. As Morgan looked at her, Guinevere felt as if the other woman were looking into her very soul. Morgan held out her arms, without words, and Guinevere, warrior queen, bane of the Saxons and inspiration of Britain's warriors, dissolved into wracking sobs. Morgan held her gently, stroking her hair and murmuring soothing sounds. And Guinevere allowed herself to be comforted even though she knew she could never confess the anguish in her heart.

But Morgan had the Sight. "Yes," she murmured, "I felt the energy between you and Lancelot at your wedding. I knew then that there would be painful times ahead."

"You knew? Even then? Before I even knew myself?" Guinevere looked into Morgan's eyes but saw only compassion there. "And you do not condemn me?"

"For what? For loving? Love goes its own way and finds its own reflection quite apart from the will of the mind. You would never have chosen to fall in love with Arthur's dearest friend and companion, or indeed any man other than Arthur. It happened. And who am I, or anyone, to judge the flowering of love?"

They sat side by side on the grassy bank. The ways of the Divine Mother are often unfathomable, Morgan was thinking. She was remembering her own despair when she had discovered herself ensnared in a web of tangled emotions and conflicting loyalties. She had since learned that the world is not black and white, truth and falsehood, love and hate, loyalty and betrayal. Between all of those extremes there are infinite shades of gray, and negotiating the path of Light between them seemed sometimes to be a near impossible task.

Morgan came back to herself to find Guinevere looking intently into her face. Guinevere reached out and with the back of her fingers gently wiped away the tear that was meandering down Morgan's cheek.

"What is it?" she said.

Morgan smiled and shook her head. "I was just thinking, remembering. Something I thought was tucked away in the past ... a time when I was caught, much as you are."

"You? But I thought ... this is such a peaceful place, you honor the Goddess, your days are ordered by the seasons and by sacred ritual. Surely here the passions of the world do not disturb your spirit?"

Morgan smiled. "We may be dedicated to the Goddess but we are still human. We feel the physical pain of injury and the emotional pain of unfulfilled or conflicting desires." Her voice was husky. The discipline of years of training was failing her. She had never shared with anyone the secret wound in her heart, but here with Guinevere she found that the need to be silent and the desire to speak were battling inside her. Her face crumbled and she buried her face in her hands, sobbing. Guinevere put an arm around her shoulders.

"Morgan ... sister ... can you not tell me what is causing you such grief?"

And the words, so long held captive in the depths of her heart, erupted of their own volition.

"I bore a child ..."

"You bore a child? But surely Morgan, that is reason for joy ..."

"I bore a child ... to Arthur!"

The words were torn out of her throat in a note of despairing anguish, to reverberate in waves of shock on Guinevere's ears. Morgan sobbed against Guinevere's shoulder while Guinevere comforted her, moved beyond her own bewilderment by Morgan's grief. In her years of marriage to Arthur Guinevere had conceived only twice and had carried the babies only a few months. Her moon bleeding was irregular because—the healers had told her—of the life she was leading, but even now that the fighting was over she had failed to conceive again. But to learn that Arthur already had a child, and by Morgan! How could that possibly have come about?

Morgan's sobs were spent and she rested on Guinevere's lap, shaken every so often by shuddering breaths. At length she raised herself and wiped her cheeks with the edge of her tunic.

"It was during the early years of the wars, at a midwinter celebration at the court of King Melwas. At the banquet we sat together, and found we could talk about anything and everything. It was a moment out of time, a moment of escape for him from the constant thought of battle. We had not the remotest idea that we were close kin. We had never seen each other before. After my mother married King Uther I came here to Avalon to become a priestess. Arthur was raised by foster parents and even he did not know he was the son of the king and queen until he claimed the sword. I knew only that he was the new High King chosen by Merlin. It was not until the following morning, as we talked together and shared some of the experiences of our lives, that we realized who we were to each other and that we shared the same mother. We were both horror struck. But we agreed that we had sinned in innocence and that we would try to forgive ourselves and not speak of it again. He left soon after and I have not seen him since, except from a distance."

Morgan fell silent and gazed out over the water, as if gazing back through time.

"I did not even realize that I had missed my moon bleeding. When I started to feel sickness in the morning I thought I was ill and consulted a healer, who only had to look at me to know that I was with child. I did not believe her. I could not believe the Divine Mother could be so cruel. I decided to cast out the child, but found I could not. I could not violate all I believed in, I could not destroy the fruit of the Divine Mother's creative force."

There was a long silence. "Where is the child now?" Guinevere asked.

"In the Orkneys, with my sister Morgause. She visited Avalon a few months later shortly after the child was born. The child was male and could not be raised in Avalon, and I needed to find a foster home for him. Morgause was recently married to King Lot and expecting her first child, and she offered to take my son home with her to the Orkneys and raise him with her own children. I do not trust Morgause, she has ever been too interested in power, but I felt I had little choice. And at least the Orkneys are as far from Arthur as I could find. I did not of course tell Morgause who the boy's father is, though she is not without Sight and may know, or think she knows."

"And what ..." Guinevere could barely force herself to speak. "What did Arthur ...?"

Morgan had been speaking softly with her head bowed, but at these words her head snapped upright and her voice became fierce and intent. "I never told Arthur! And you must promise me, promise me Guinevere on all that you hold sacred, that you will never tell him either!"

"But ... he has a right to know... he has a son ..."

"A son by his half-sister! Can you imagine what the scandalmongers would make of that! He cannot know! Nor can anyone else. Promise me, Guinevere!"

"Yes, you are right, of course. I promise." She felt the grief of Morgan's loss as if it were her own, an aching loneliness of separation compounded by the fear of discovery and the threat to Arthur.

Morgan relaxed. She wrapped her arms around her bent knees and rested her chin on them. "They would not let me see him, you know, my baby brother. The night he was born I was banished to another room in the care of a nurse. I heard him cry, and I ran to the door, but the nurse would not let me out. And the next day he was gone. I learned later that Merlin had come for him, and had taken him far away to a place where he would be safe—from others who had ambitions, perhaps even from Uther himself. I think Uther thought of Arthur as a stain on the legitimacy of his kingship. It was hard on my mother to give up her newborn son, and then a couple of years later she lost me too—to Avalon. Uther expected to have another son, one whose legitimacy was beyond question, but my mother never conceived again."

Each of them turned inward, following a similar train of thought; of Igraine who lost two of her children and could not conceive again; of Morgan who lost her little brother and then her own son; and Guinevere who had not been able to carry a child to term. It was a cruel cycle of loss that each woman fought to understand.

"Secret messengers came to Uther from time to time and I knew they were bringing news of my brother, but whenever I asked about him my mother would tell me to forget about him. At that time I had no other recourse. Now I have the training and resources of a priestess of Avalon and I am able to follow the fortunes of my son in the sacred pool. I know that he is well, full of life and energy, running a little wild with his cousins perhaps but that is part of being young I suppose. I did not have that kind of childhood. I was the only child at Tintagel, and I came to Avalon when I was five. I found great joy here, but of a different kind than battle training and running wild in the woods."

The sun was beginning to set and the clouds in the western sky were scarlet and edged with gold. The brilliant colors were reflected in the still waters of the lake, and the sun seemed to sink into its own reflection as the light took on the mystical quality of crepuscule.

"What are we going to do?" Guinevere's voice was bleak.

Morgan sighed. "I am going to live my life as a priestess of Avalon and hold the secret of my son in my heart. I have learned that sometimes truth is divisible and self-contradictory. When faced with compelling and conflicting truths, or loyalties, or beliefs, or duties, or desires, or feelings, all we can do is be true to ourselves. Only you can know what that means for you. It is important only that your intention is pure, and your intent I know is not to hurt Arthur."

Far, far to the north, on the outer fringes of the British Isles, Mordred stood at the edge of the training field watching his foster brothers learning to wield the great sword. He was struck anew by the *physical differences that set him apart from them. With their fair hair, stocky builds and ruddy complexions they were the obvious spawn of King Lot. They were loud and clumsy, charging around the field like young bulls. Mordred was slender and dark, and moved with grace and control, qualities—unbeknownst to him—that he had inherited from his father. From his father too he had taken his thick, black hair and the deep gray of his eyes, so different from the bleached blue eyes of Gawain and his brothers.*

The qualities he had inherited from his mother, Morgan of Avalon, were not visible to the naked eye: a certain knowing, an awareness of things that should have been beyond his ken and that he was careful to guard within his own mind. Not that his noisy, blustering, innocent foster brothers would have believed him anyway.

He was not only markedly different from his cousins in his looks and manners. He was unlike them too in his interests. They would have mocked him for his love of learning had not the directness and strength in his steady gaze checked their impulses; that, and his obvious superiority in swordsmanship and other, less honorable, forms of fighting. He was a year older than Gawain and far beyond him in skill and ruthlessness. Even all four brothers together could not have bested him, not yet, but they nursed the expectation that one day they would.

The voice of the sword master roused him. "Mordred. Over here." He walked, with his usual grace and air of self-containment, over to where his cousin Gawain was waiting. He picked up the practice sword. As he faced Gawain his stance was relaxed, his face betraying nothing of his recent thoughts. Gawain was as usual angry, his feelings clearly written in his face and posture. As they began to circle each other, Mordred awaited his moment and allowed Gawain to dissipate his energy in wild swings of his sword. Gawain's movements were clumsy and without plan. When Mordred did move in, there was controlled savagery in his fighting and in moments Gawain was lying in the dust. With a bow, Mordred returned the practice sword to the sword master and turned away. Gawain stood and dusted the dirt from his pants and retrieved his sword; humiliation fed his anger and he shouted to Mordred's retreating back:

"I will be king of Lothian and you are just a bastard, Mordred! Son of no father! Your mother's just some priestess who happens to be my mother's sister and you are nobody. Nobody!"

Mordred did not turn. He kept walking with his loose, graceful stride and no one could have known by looking at his face how deeply his heart was wounded by Gawain's taunts.

From the window of her room high in one of the towers of the castle Queen Morgause had watched the whole drama. Her face wore a small, secret and malicious smile. "Yes, my little bastard Mordred," she murmured, "for now you may continue to think you are nobody. But you are my passport to power; you are my death grip on the conscious of the king. One day we will leave this barren rock at the end of the world and take our rightful place. In Camelot."

In the Arthurian myth we have an example of what a healthy heart chakra looks like: a balance of masculine and feminine, yang and yin; a balance of assertiveness and nurture; acceptance without judgment; and unconditional love. If we discard the medieval frosting regarding the status of women we find women who are strong, in positions of both temporal and spiritual leadership, as well as creative, intelligent, and nurturing. And in Arthur we have an example of a male whose feminine energy is developed and in balance. Arthur is a warrior and a brilliant military strategist; and he is also just, kind, compassionate and respectful. He knows how to wield the sword to protect his kingdom from threat, and he also knows how to nurture the kingdom in time of peace. He does not abuse his power as High King, but has the strength and the honesty to follow right action.

The theme of yin and yang balance is woven into the structure of the myth, both in the characters and situations, and in the symbols of the sword, the round table, and the Holy Grail. It is Merlin, archetype of the divine masculine, who places the sword in the stone and engineers the test of Arthur's kingship; who gives him, in other words, the right to rule. And it is the Lady of the Lake, archetype of the divine feminine, who gives him Excalibur, the sword of power that gives him the means to rule. The round table, Arthur's symbol of justice and equality, is a gift from the feminine: Guinevere. The martial arts vanquish the invaders and bring peace to the land, and the feminine arts influence the quality of that peace. The Holy Grail, focus of the spiritual quest, is a cup or chalice, an ancient symbol of the divine feminine.

Arthur's example of a healthy and balanced heart chakra survives the medieval doctoring of the legends. In the context of the time, we would expect the response of a High King to the adultery of his queen with his closest friend and Companion to be one of anger and revenge, a shadow second chakra response. The erotic and romantic love of the second chakra, if it does not encompass also the love of the heart, needs to possess the beloved, to be the exclusive lover, and when betrayed responds with jealousy, rage, perhaps violence. We would expect that in a culture dominated by second chakra attitudes towards sex and romantic love—as the medieval culture was—a man who did not respond in that way would be lampooned as a cuckold and would lose the respect of his warriors and of his people. This was no doubt the intent of Chrétien de Troyes in inventing or repeating this part of the legend.

But this does not happen. Arthur loves both Lancelot and Guinevere, and he views their love for each other with the compassion and understanding of the heart. Operating from his fourth chakra, the love he bears for both of them is compassionate and forgiving, and for his generous heart Arthur is loved, both by his own people in the legends, and by the legions of readers of the legends down through the centuries.

Again, contrary to accepted practice, Arthur continues to honor Guinevere even though she does not bear him an heir. We can appreciate how radical an attitude Arthur's is by comparing him with, say, Henry VIII, some thousand years later, who divorced or executed four queens in his quest for a son and heir. (One of his six wives died giving birth to the son who would have saved her, and the sixth outlived him.) It is one of the most delicious of historical ironies that in spite of all his efforts Henry was succeeded by his daughter Elizabeth, who became a far more powerful monarch than he. She is remembered for laying the foundations of the British Empire, and he for being a fat tyrant.

Among the Celts women were of equal standing with men, and if Arthur as some scholars have suggested lived in the north of Britain, behind Hadrian's Wall, his attitude towards Guinevere and Lancelot would not be so surprising. But if Arthur lived in the south—in the land of Tintagel, Castle Cadbury and Avalon—then he was a Roman Briton, product of four hundred years of assimilation. For him to continue to honor Guinevere as his queen and not hide her away in a monastery—in spite of her inability to bear a child and not to mention her love for Lancelot—was not in keeping with the dominant attitude. But then we are not talking about an historical document; we are talking about a myth, and a myth communicates its spiritual truth directly to the deeper levels of knowing within us. We do not condemn Arthur for being a wimp; we love him for his tolerance and understanding and we perceive those qualities as evidence of his strength.

If we look at the love between Lancelet and Guinevere as Arthur did, through the doorway of the fourth chakra, the heart, rather than from the perspective of the second chakra, there is no betrayal, and no judgment. Love is love. At the same time, Arthur knew that he lived in a predominantly second chakra culture. Others would see betrayal, even treason; they would judge, and would demand retribution. As long as the relationship between Lancelot and Guinevere remained between the two of them there was no problem. When it was forced into the open by the younger coterie of knights who were still operating from the second chakra, a second chakra response was inevitable. Arthur, like Arjuna in the Bhagavad-Gita, had to do his duty within the context of his times, holding himself apart as judge and letting events take their course. Guinevere was found guilty of treason and condemned to death by burning. She was rescued by Lancelot and they fled, she to a convent and he to his own castle.

The contrast between cultural morality, embedded in the second chakra, and the nonjudgmental acceptance of the heart, appears again and again throughout the myth. Uther lusted after Igraine and used magic and manipulation to bed her. The result was the conception of Arthur, light of Britain. The conception of Galahad has all the same elements of illegitimacy, enchantment, trickery, and betrayal. Elaine disguised herself as Guinevere to lure Lancelot to her bed. He made love, so he thought, to the wife of his king. And yet Elaine knew, Malory tells us, "that same night should be gotten upon her Galahad, that should prove the best knight of the world," because he would find the Holy Grail. Spirit does not use pure unsullied vessels but seems rather to seek out examples that challenge our assumptions of right and wrong.

Those assumptions are challenged again as we contemplate the heart chakra in the story of Isolde and Tristan, one of King Arthur's Companions. Isolde the Fair is married to King Mark of Cornwall, but is in love with Mark's nephew Tristan. Mark requires that she undergo a test of fire to prove her innocence. She is not burned. Spirit, therefore, does not condemn her for loving Tristan, but Mark seeks to imprison both of them, despite the evidence of divine protection, when he discovers them in bed together. Only when they are dead, for love of each other, does Mark relent. He buries them side by side at Tintagel, and from their bodies grow a vine and a rose, which grow together so closely entwined that no one can separate them. The second chakra, in the person of King Mark, views Tristan and Isolde as treasonous and adulterous, but the higher view of the fourth chakra finds them together in eternity, not burning in hell but forever alive and closely entwined in a vine and a rose.

Lancelet was probably a late addition to the story, and yet for most of us the love triangle of Lancelet, Arthur and Guinevere is the heart of the legend. Even now we are still stuck in the second chakra when it comes to romantic love.

Relax now, in your sanctuary, and begin to explore the relative power of the yin and yang energy within you; to open your heart and mind to the needs of the under-developed aspect of your being and recruit the inner resources that will help you to create the balance that will allow you to actualize more and more of your unlimited potential. Begin with deep breathing, raising the light of earth, invoking the light of spirit and breathing it into each chakra, breathing into the inner light at your heart, creating the triple shield of light.

Balance of yin and yang meditation

Begin as always with deep breathing, and invoking the Triple Shield of Light.

For King Arthur, twelve years of peace followed the twelve battles. He built Camelot, and established there a place where all—regardless of gender or wealth or station—could come and be heard in an atmosphere of acceptance and respect. The country was safe, not only from outside invaders but also from bandits and thieves, and travelers were safe to go their ways along the country's roads, or by sea around the coasts, without fear of molestation.

This was the summer of Arthur's reign, a time to enjoy the fruits of the peace, to be free to plant and harvest, to settle down and raise children.

So imagine now that it is summer. It is noon, and the sun in its journey across the sky has reached its zenith. It is high in a clear sky, its light so bright that the sky overhead has almost lost its color and only nearer to the horizon is it a clear blue. You are in a meadow, and facing south. The grass is high, and filled with wildflowers of red, yellow, orange, pink, blue and purple. This is a magical meadow. The air is pure, and you can breathe easily and comfortably. There are no allergens in the air, nothing to impede your free and natural breath. As you walk through the meadow, imagine that you can feel the hot sun on your head and shoulders. You can perhaps hear the swishing sound of the grasses as you walk; maybe there is a gentle breeze that barely disturbs the air, and the hum of insects. Everything is hot, and bright, and as you look down at the ground you see that your shadow is small, confined to the space around your feet.

You turn towards the north and enter the forest now, and experience the cool shade. The trees are in the full radiance of their summer growth, forming a rich, almost impenetrable canopy of shade as you walk beneath them. At your feet are ferns and mosses, and plants that have adapted themselves to deep shade. There is a great variety of shades of green, and here and there perhaps the brilliant yellow of a hosta; if you look closely there are tiny wildflowers of yellow and blue. In the distance you can hear or imagine the sound of a stream, bubbling and gurgling as it flows over rocks.

Summer is a time of brilliant sunlight and obvious contrasts of light and shadow. As you stand now at the very edge of the forest you are aware of that contrast: the deep cool shade of the trees, and the brilliant hot sunlight and colors of the meadow.

In your journey of development through the chakras, you have experienced the challenges of making a home on the physical plane. Of creating a sense of belonging and safety within physical form, meeting the challenges of survival and providing for your physical needs, creating a solid and stable foundation on which to build the rest of your life. You have spent time withdrawn from the awareness of spirit, focusing inward and building a sense of self and strengthening your individual will. You have fought your twelve battles and established your relationship with power in the outer world.

And now, in the summer of development, it is time to focus on the heart and begin the journey on the inner planes. The heart is the center of love and compassion. It is a different quality of love from the filial love of the first chakra, or the romantic love of the second. The love of the heart is unconditional. It is like the love of a flower, that does not ask if you deserve to enjoy its beauty or its fragrance, but freely offers itself.

The romantic relationships of the second chakra are based perhaps on physical attraction, or on a need to find a completeness that we were lacking. A relationship of the heart is founded on unconditional acceptance: it is physical, and emotional, and mental, and spiritual, a bonding on all levels of being. It can be a commitment to a person, or to a social cause, or to a spiritual path. The challenge of the heart is to refine our capacity to love, to love others not because they love us, or because they do certain things or fulfil certain roles, but simply because they are. This kind of love begins with unconditional love and acceptance of the self, in all its dimensions. Bringing light into our places of shadow is a lifelong journey, and it is at the heart that we focus on bringing balance to the masculine and feminine aspects of our being.

Here, at the edge of the forest, you can step right, into the bright light of the sun, the masculine energy of the element of fire. And then you can take a step left into the cool enveloping shade of the forest, into the nourishing and receptive feminine energy of the element earth. Right, into fire, and left, into earth. Right into fire, and left into earth. Where do you feel the most comfortable? Stay in that comfortable place, close your inner eyes and experience it fully.

With your inner eyes still closed, turn to face the opposite. If you are in the forest, you will be facing the bright sunlit meadow. If you are in the meadow, you will be facing the cool shady forest. Within that other environment, invite an image of the shadow or under-developed aspect of your being. If your feminine energy is dominant and you are most comfortable in the forest, look within the shimmering sunlight for an image of your yang energy, an image that represents the animus, the masculine energy within you. If your masculine energy is dominant and you are in the bright, hot meadow, it will be an image that represents the anima, the feminine energy within you. The energy that is dominant does not necessarily conform to the sex of your physical body.

Examine the image closely. Notice every detail, walk around it and examine it from different angles and different directions. Ask the image if it is willing to talk to you, and tell the image that you are willing to listen. Ask the image what it needs in order to grow into its full power. Listen. ...

Gently now, and in your own time, begin to bring your focus back into this place and this time, bringing with you any insights you have gained, and take some time to write or draw your experience in your Quest Journal.

The challenge of the fourth chakra is to refine our capacity to love, ourselves as well as others, and to seek out and eliminate all the barriers and obstacles to an open heart. We violate the energy of the heart when we act in unloving ways and when we hold on to negative emotions towards others or towards ourselves.

As we look into the heart chakra we may find that we are limiting our choices by holding on to past negative experiences. What if you fell deeply in love at the tender age of sixteen with a man with black curly hair? He dumped you and you were devastated, the utter devastation that only a sixteen year old can feel. And as you look honestly into your own heart you find that you still do not trust men with dark curly hair. It may just be that your soul mate has dark curly hair but with this mindset you will never give him a chance.

Releasing that old painful memory may be relatively easy if you know you have moved on with your life and that old hurt is just like something forgotten in the basement. In that case simply bringing it out into the light may be enough to let it go. But you may find that letting go is more of a challenge. Perhaps you still cry when you think about it, or still have feelings of abandonment. Journaling around your feelings for that lost love can be helpful; talking with him or her in your imagination and giving yourself an opportunity to say all the things you never got to say can also be very therapeutic; writing a letter that expresses your feelings likewise.

And you can be as angry and profane in the letter as you want. You are not going to send it. You can write it over several days or weeks, as other thoughts come to mind, and when you feel it is finished put it away for a while. When you reread it a few weeks or even months later you will know if it is time to burn it and create a ritual of release. It is often more of an emotional release to have such a confrontation in your own mind through imagery or letter writing rather than face-to-face, because you maintain control and do not have to deal with any defensive backlash. If necessary you can talk to a therapist. You will know when you have reached a place of being ready to forgive and release.

Sometimes when we look into the heart we find that we are holding on to resentment. At the heart chakra everything and everyone we need to forgive comes into consciousness and it can be very uncomfortable. We might find ourselves remembering things that happened years ago that we thought were long forgotten. They erupt into our minds seemingly out of nowhere and they still have a negative charge. It is as if they have been hanging around in the subconscious waiting for just the right moment to say, Hello, I'm still here, remember me? Though we may still have conscious memories of the major traumatic events of our lives it can be the small, forgotten, seemingly insignificant things that accumulate into a toxic residue: guilt about cheating in the third grade; anger because your kid sister got more attention than you; hurt because somebody made fun of you the first day in kindergarten. When we open the heart chakra these painful memories emerge so that they can be forgiven and released. They are the practice runs for the greater challenges to forgiveness and compassion.

A lot of us have a distorted perception of what forgiveness is. Some of us refuse to forgive because the person who in our perception wronged us will not admit they did anything wrong. But we are the ones hurt by that. Forgiveness is not so much an act of altruistic generosity as it is an act of love for the self: forgiveness heals the forgiver. My mentor in counselor education used to say that lack of forgiveness is giving someone you don't like rent-free space in your mind. Thoughts of the wrong we perceive was done to us choke off the free flow of energy through the heart

Or we might say: I can't forgive because I'm still angry. But forgiveness is not an emotion; it is an act of will. It is something that we decide to do because we recognize that it is the best course of action for us, for our peace of mind and our growth. It is not a matter of doing what we are "supposed" to do. The concept of forgiveness has broken out of the religious mold in recent years and there is a sizable chunk of research that validates the healing power of forgiveness. Science is catching up with what religious traditions have taught for centuries and there have been numerous studies on the therapeutic power of forgiveness.

When we decide it is time to forgive we do it as often as we need to; we say the words and perhaps imagine the person or situation we are forgiving, and we know we have finally forgiven when we can think of that person or situation and it does not pinch any more, there is no emotional reaction to it.

Forgiveness does not come naturally to us. "Revenge is sweet," so they say. "Revenge is a dish best served cold," as if it were something to be relished, at leisure. "An eye for an eye, a tooth for a tooth," says the old Hammurabi Code, which has been widely misunderstood as license to give back whatever hurt or injury we have received. It was actually a giant leap forward at the time, around 1780 BCE, an admonishment to make the punishment fit the crime instead of imposing draconian punishments that were wildly out of proportion to the crime, something that had still not been learned almost three thousand years later when a peasant could be hanged for poaching.

The Hammurabi Code was superseded by the Christian teaching in Matthew to "turn the other cheek." Which means that the spiritually evolved response to evil, or injustice, is the polar opposite of revenge: it is forgiveness. Right? Yes, but at the right time. Forgiveness does not mean condoning the wrong. It means freeing up the energy consumed by holding on to anger and resentment, so that it can be put to better use in creating the life that we want. Feelings of hurt, betrayal and anger, and thoughts and plans of revenge, keep us locked in a victim consciousness that is painful and disempowering; they consume enormous amounts of energy and can create depression, listlessness, hopelessness and even despair. However, even if the key to honoring the heart chakra lies in forgiveness it does not always mean that the appropriate response to somebody taking advantage of you, or treating you badly, is immediate forgiveness. Sometimes in the quest for emotional and psychological healing there are intermediate steps to forgiveness. Similar situations can contain different emotional and psychological challenges and different spiritual lessons for different people.

Let's say you find yourself working for someone who seriously pushes your buttons. He is arrogant, unpredictable, egocentric, and he makes you so angry you just want to scream. Going to work is a chore, you lose all sense of accomplishment and fulfillment, and over time the stress of continuing to work in such an environment begins to give you headaches, insomnia, digestive problems, immune deficiency.

Possibly you can look back over your life and see similar situations in your past, and recognize a pattern. Not necessarily with a boss, but perhaps with a family member, or a romantic partner or partners. How have you responded in the past?

If a pattern keeps repeating itself, if you keep encountering a similar set of circumstances that evokes a similar emotional response in you, the chances are that the way you have responded in the past has not been the most beneficial for you. Perhaps you have told yourself to rise above it, to accept responsibility for where you are and make the best of it. Perhaps you have fought it. Perhaps you have walked away. And now perhaps you have decided that you are supposed to just forgive but it's *really hard.*

If telling yourself to "rise above" an abusive situation is your usual response, it may feel like what you "ought" to do according to the moral or religious teaching you have received, but if the pattern keeps recurring in your life that response may not be what this particular situation is giving you the opportunity to develop. Perhaps your soul wants you to learn how to be more assertive, so that you create balance in your life.

If, on the other hand, your usual response pattern is to fight, then perhaps your challenge in that same situation is to try and see the other person's point of view, to develop empathy so that you broaden your horizons by learning to look at the world through another lens and discovering inner dimensions that have been closed off from your perception. Perhaps when you look inside you discover that this obnoxious person is mirroring your own arrogance and egocentricity.

Or maybe learning to walk away would be a productive skill for you, so that you learn to pick your battles and become more discerning. When you fight *everything* people stop taking you seriously, you become labeled a chronic complainer and limit your options for gaining what you want.

If, on the other hand, it has been your pattern to walk away from uncomfortable situations, and yet the uncomfortable situations continue to be attracted into your life, perhaps developing assertiveness and self-confidence is the appropriate response.

You may ultimately decide to quit the job anyway, but when you quit after having mastered the skill of assertiveness, or discernment, there will be no need to recreate similar circumstances in the future and you will attract the job of your dreams: satisfying, challenging, fulfilling, financially rewarding. When you quit under these conditions you can forgive totally and even feel gratitude to the obnoxious one for having given you the incentive to develop the ability to stand your ground, or pick and choose where you will take a stand instead of being at the mercy of a knee-jerk aggressive response.

Ultimately the goal is forgiveness and release, but there may be intermediate steps that are important to your emotional and psychological well-being, as well as to your spiritual development.

When the forgiveness is not only an act of will but a true emotional release it does indeed bring all the promised rewards: self-empowerment, better health, greater energy, better relationships, and a happier and more fulfilling life.

We open and empower the fourth chakra, therefore, when we forgive unconditionally, ourselves as well as others. Spiritual teachings are in our daily experience, and opportunities to practice are never in short supply. Where better, for example, than in our primary relationships and in what we perceive in our parents' relationship are we to be challenged in our development of complementary energy? If we grow up with a father who is violent and unpredictable, and a mother who is long-suffering and chronically depressed, those primary perceptions of yang and yin will be programmed into the first chakra until we can forgive and bless them both for the opportunity to learn. We often do not learn as much from perfectly balanced models as we do from the imperfections of role models and teachers who express imbalance and prod us into a reaction, into suffering and pain that becomes the crucible in which we forge our sword of truth.

Life in the physical world is the laboratory in which we test the truths of our intuition, and in which we are tested. We can do all the positive affirmations in the world, meditate, practice yoga postures and deep breathing, follow a vegetarian diet, undertake a pilgrimage to a sacred place and have a sublime spiritual experience, but if we ignore the opportunities for growth in our daily experience we will not move forward. At the heart chakra that means forgiving those who have wronged us, even if they do not say they are sorry, even if they do not acknowledge they have wronged us, even if we will never understand why they wronged us.

Many of us who find it a challenge to forgive those we perceive as having wronged us find that the next step—self-forgiveness—is even harder. Guilt can be like a hard crust that encases the heart and in time can create physical symptoms. Often when I work with clients suffering chronic pain we find that guilt is the obstacle to healing. Guilt over one episode of infidelity, even though it may have been confessed to and forgiven by the spouse and by God, can create a lifetime of crippling back pain if it is not forgiven also by the self.

A major obstacle to self-forgiveness can be the belief that we deserve to feel guilty. What we did or said or felt was wrong, so we believe that the burden of guilt is no more than just. But a burden of guilt contributes nothing to spiritual development. What will contribute to development is sincere contrition, and making whatever amends we can make, either to the person we wronged or to some other if that person cannot be found or has passed over. And just as we can find emotional release by expressing anger or hurt to an image, in the same way we can talk to an image of a loved one who has passed over, offer our apologies and ask for forgiveness. In the many years that I have used this procedure with clients there has not been one occasion when the image was angry or unforgiving.

Very often there is a burden of guilt that is not a result of self-judgment but is a judgment imposed from outside: a distraught parent who blames a six-year-old for letting his two-year-old brother fall in the pool; a father who communicates conscious or unconscious messages that he really wanted a boy, or if he has a boy who is a computer whiz that he really wanted a football player; a mother on emotional overload who lets slip that her most recent pregnancy was a mistake. What can be a moment's distraction for a parent can become a lifetime sentence for the child, who absorbs that negative judgment deep into the psyche where it festers and colors his or her self-perception.

Discovering such an origin for the vague and undefined guilt we have lived with can lead to a justified anger. This too must be honored and expressed, either directly or through journaling or counseling, though ultimately the goal is to extend compassion and forgiveness to the one who imposed it.

Take a break now to practice the forgiveness meditation. When you feel it is time to forgive, when you feel you have understood the sacred teaching in a particular situation or relationship and are ready to let go of the anger or judgment or resentment or feeling victimized or whatever the negative emotion is, this meditation will give you a tool and an imaginary context in which to do it. It may take several repetitions until you feel that the forgiveness has "taken." When you can think of the person or situation and there is no knee-jerk painful emotional response, you will know that you have freed yourself and are no longer losing energy over it. Begin as always with deep breathing and invoking the Triple Shield of Light.

Forgiveness meditation

Knowing yourself safe within the Triple Shield of Light, imagine that you are walking through an ancient forest such as existed in the time of King Arthur; you are surrounded by massive trees—oak, ash, birch, and many other species. You are walking on a carpet of fallen leaves, and you can perhaps imagine hearing the swishing sound that your feet make, and the sound of the breeze in the treetops; there is the occasional cry of a bird, and you can perhaps imagine the breeze caressing your hair. You breathe deeply of the air that smells pure and fresh.

Imagine now, that up ahead you see an opening in the trees, and as you come close you find a clearing, a perfect circle bordered by twelve mature oak trees. Their branches intertwine over the clearing forming a natural cathedral, a sacred space, perhaps created by the Druids. Within the circle the air is still, and the silence is complete.

Waiting for you in the center of the circle of trees is someone whom you have decided to forgive. When you are ready, enter the circle and stand before them. And say to them:

I forgive you for all the times you have hurt me, consciously and unconsciously, real and imagined, intentional and unintentional, past, present and future. (Or you can be more specific about what they did.) I forgive you.
I forgive you.

And I ask for your forgiveness, for any time I have hurt you, consciously and unconsciously, real and imagined, intentional and unintentional, past, present and future.
Please forgive me.
Please forgive me.

Then turn; behind you is a mirror, and as you look at your reflection say: I forgive myself, for all transgressions, conscious and unconscious, real or imagined, intentional and unintentional, past, present and future.
I forgive myself.
I forgive myself.

Surround the other person in a bubble of light, cut all energetic connections between your bubble and theirs, then thank them for coming and tell them to leave.

We can close off the heart when we do not allow others to love us, when we are so afraid of being hurt that we never let anyone get close. The heart can atrophy from lack of loving nourishment, it can feel cramped and squeezed inside the chest wall, or feel as if there is a heavy weight pressing down on the chest so that taking a deep breath is difficult or even impossible.

Heart love is the essence of the message of Jesus. One side of the heart coin says "Love thy neighbor as thyself" (Mark 12:31 and Matthew 22:36-40) and the other says, "Judge not" (Matthew 7:1-3). For the self-absorbed, loving the neighbor as much as the self is the challenge. For the self-sacrificing, loving the self as much as the neighbor can be an even greater challenge. And what about judgment? Notwithstanding the biblical injunction our Anno Domini history is full of judgment: the Crusades and the Inquisition; the countless religious wars; the pogroms; the exclusion of African-Americans from white churches; the exclusion of women from the priesthood; the persecution of homosexuals; the judgment of the millions who follow a different spiritual path and are deemed unfit to enter the kingdom of heaven. Such judgment is inimical both to the teachings of Jesus and to an open and loving heart.

Dan Brown worries at the end of the *Da Vinci Code* about what the consequences would be of forcing the Catholic Church of today to admit to a two thousand year error in suppressing all knowledge of the divine feminine. The church provides a moral compass for millions of people; what would happen to them if it were discredited?

The question presupposes a black and white world, an either/ or choice. From the perspective of chakra development there does not have to be a choice. There are those comforted and guided by the church who accept its stories as literal truth, and those who feel free to make their own interpretations of biblical teachings and accept only those that resonate as truth for them. And now that the Inquisition no longer burns heretics at the stake those who seek a different face of the divine are free to follow their own hearts and search for an experience of divinity in their own way. The obstacle to all of us living harmoniously in this world together is judgment, trying to prove one way right and the others wrong.

Imagine two women, Carla and JoAnn. Both are gifted, both do well in school and have promising beginnings to their careers. Both marry in their early twenties and make the decision to quit the work force and devote themselves to their children during their first years of life. When their fairy tale marriages end in divorce and their husbands abdicate responsibility for the children, each of them has to find a way to survive. They discover that picking up their careers where they left off is not an option. They have to take jobs below their skill level that pay less than they are worth in order to work part time and structure their time around the responsibilities of home and children.

Carla grieves the loss, looks reality in the eye, and sets about building a new kind of life. She researches aid programs and is not too proud to take advantage of them; she is grateful for the job she has that allows her the freedom to pick her children up from day care and take them to the pediatrician when they are sick. Even though money is tight she recognizes that this difficult stage will pass. She creates a network of friends, other women in similar situations, who share babysitting and offer emotional support.

In later life she looks back on this time of her life as the time when she found herself and her strength, and when she is ready for another committed relationship she attracts a man who is himself well balanced and who complements her strength. Her relationship reflects the balance within her own healthy heart chakra: a heart that knows gratitude, forgiveness, compassion for self and others, and unconditional love. Through her response to this experience Carla not only opens her heart; she strengthens her first chakra by affirming that she can provide for her own survival needs, and the second by taking responsibility for her circumstances instead of blaming her ex-husband, and the third by boosting her personal will and self-esteem.

JoAnn on the other hand is angry and bitter. Her thoughts are dominated by what she has lost. She hates her job and feels demeaned by her changed social circumstances. She feels abandoned not only by her husband but by the social circle that she shared with him, and is not interested in finding new friends in the same situation as she. There is no joy or satisfaction for her in providing for the needs of her children and herself; she just wants to find another man who will support her and relieve her of her burdens. When she falls in love again, she will likely attract a man who will dominate her, whose price for financial support might be total submission.

It is hard to rejoice in the qualities of self-reliance when you are a single mother struggling to fulfill both parental roles, earn the family bread and raise the children. It can feel overwhelming to do it all alone. And many in that situation harbor a secret fantasy that someday Prince Charming will appear to relieve them of all those burdens, a man who will adore them and their children and provide for all their needs. And meantime the heart chakra suffers from the resentment, anger, and lack of forgiveness. And the domino effect weakens other energy centers: a continuing fear of being unable to provide for the self at the first chakra, a tendency to blame others for misfortune instead of accepting the opportunity for growth at the second, diminished self-esteem at the third.

A healthy, balanced and open heart chakra belongs to those who love all parts of themselves and others unconditionally. Heart love is not so much an emotion as an energy, the energy of the flower that freely offers its beauty and fragrance. It does not ask if you deserve it, or if you appreciate it, it simply offers its gifts freely and unconditionally. Lori Myles-Carullo in her memoir *Beauty's Way* describes a moment of heart awakening in the gift of a flower during a walk along a dusty road in Costa Rica:

> In the midst of the weeds [was] a beautiful little pink wildflower, brimming with the simple ecstasy of existence. She was so small that I had to kneel down in order to get a better look at her, and I was awed by how such a tiny part of existence could be so intricate in beauty. I observed the various shades and hues of pink at her bubble-like core, a hundred fragile tendrils making their way up to bright yellow nodules at the tip of each one. This little flower was clearly an exquisite gift of life, beautiful simply for beauty's sake ... What a perfect metaphor for awakening.

Unconditional love of others also means that we love them enough to let them experience the world in their own way. There are people on this planet who sincerely believe that loving you means they get to tell you what to do. Have you ever heard, or perhaps even said: "I'm only telling you this because I love you"? Unconditional love means unconditional acceptance of another, whether or not we agree with their choices.

Wounds to the heart chakra can manifest as either deficiencies or excess. A person with a deficient heart chakra might be antisocial and unable to make friends, be judgmental or critical. Loneliness can lead to depression. An excessive heart chakra might manifest in codependency, in being demanding clingy, or jealous. Either can lead to physical malfunctions of the heart, lungs, breasts and arms.

A healthy, balanced heart chakra is compassionate and loving—of the self as well as others—with a sense of inner peace and balance. We all, in the process of living, have accumulated hurts both big and small to the heart. In this meditation, inspired by Belleruth Naparstek, you can explore a pathway of healing for the heart. Begin as always with deep breathing and invoking the Triple Shield of Light.

Meditation for healing the wounded heart

Imagine now that you are standing in front of a Celtic spiral, and imagine that this spiral is the symbol of your heart. As you contemplate the spiral, you become aware of a presence beside you. A presence that is loving, compassionate, and wise. It is the Inner Healer, and you know, without knowing how you know, that this presence is deeply familiar. The Inner Healer has been with you since the beginning of time, knows you intimately and has only your best interests, your highest good, at heart. Perhaps the image of the Inner Healer appears as Merlin, or an animal, or a curandera, or a shaman, or an older version of yourself, or a sacred being.

With the Inner Healer at your side you magically enter into the spiral that is the symbol of your heart. And you find that the outer circle of the spiral is full of debris. Stop for a moment, and scuff the debris aside with your shoe. Beneath it, there is an ancient cobbled road. And you become aware that the road, even though it might have been neglected for a long time, is strong and stable, able to bear the weight of heavy traffic. The stones are worn smooth on the surface, yet still perfectly fitted together, resting on a deep and stable foundation.

Breathe deeply, aware of the loving presence of the Inner Healer at your side. You look around and you recognize the debris. It is the accumulated hurts, some major, many of them minor, of your life's journey. Perhaps there are garbage dumps of guilt, or self-blame, rejection and unworthiness, broken dreams.

You continue, your Inner Healer at your side, along the cobbled way, and ahead of you now the road seems to enter a tunnel, but as you get closer you realize it is not a tunnel at all, but an opening into an ancient forest. The cobbled road runs through it, spiraling down into the center of your heart, and the trees on either side have grown over it so that their branches interlace overhead. And as you get closer you become aware that the road through the forest is suffused with a gentle light that appears to be coming from the trees themselves, as if their inner life energy were visible to you, creating a soft glow that surrounds you as you enter the forest. The light reflects off what look like jewels in the forest, the eyes of the forest creatures who have come to accompany you on your journey: gentle deer, soft lovable rabbits, strong bears, protective tigers and lions, wise owls, sharp-eyed hawks. They accompany you as you continue along the cobbled road, sharing their gifts with you, creating a kind of honor guard, frank and sincere in their devotion. You turn to your Inner Healer and find yourself smiling, as you take a deep breath of the sweet, clean air of the forest, breathing in the oxygen that is the gift of life offered by the trees.

As you continue walking, you become aware of the sound of water. The ground continues to descend, spiraling down towards the inner core of your heart, and as you follow the sound of water you come upon a small stream flowing down the side of the mountain. The sunlight reflects off the droplets of water as it hurries over the rocks. Lush green ferns line the steam, and soft velvety mosses cling to the rocks and roots of trees. Perhaps you dip your hands into the cool water and take a drink. The water is fresh, pure and sweet.

You and your Inner Healer follow the cobbled road alongside the stream as it flows downhill; it is joined from time to time by other steams and becomes a river, and at the foot of the mountain where the river slows you decide to step into it, and surrender to the flow. You find you are able to float easily and safely, that the river cocoons and supports you as you flow downstream. And where the river flows into the sea, a gentle current gently deposits you and your Inner Healer on the bank. You walk across the sand to where the land meets the waters. All the elements meet here in perfect harmony: the fiery sun is sinking low into the sky, creating a beautiful palette of color in the western sky; the water is a deep blue, the sound of the waves soothing; the air is fresh, salty and clean; and the earth beneath your feet is stable, strong, supportive and nourishing.

This wondrous, safe and beautiful place is the inner landscape of your heart, the essential core of your being, beautiful, whole, balanced, harmonious, and full of light. Look around you. This is the essence of who you are: whole, pure, harmonious, balanced. This is the part of you that has never been, and will never be, touched by trauma, by disappointment, by betrayal, by feelings of inadequacy, all the tests that your personality encounters on the upper levels of your heart that interface with your environment. They do not penetrate here. This part of you is inviolate, and it is the deepest, truest, most real part of who you are.

Rest here a while, with your Inner Healer, and allow yourself to be reminded of your own inner harmony, of who you really are at the core of yourself.

And when it is time to leave, you return on the cobbled way alongside the river and the mountain stream and back through the forest, following the widening rings of the spiral. And along the way, nestled in hidden places, you may find broken pieces of your heart that were left behind during times of hurt and trauma. And you discover that each piece has been carefully polished and protected by a forest creature, who offers it back to you. And perhaps you accept one or two, and they slide easily back into their place. Perhaps you accept all of them, or perhaps some of them you leave for another time.

When you emerge from the forest and into the outer spiral perhaps the cobbled road seems clearer, and the crust of debris looks a little different. Or perhaps a lot different. And as you allow your heart to heal you find you are more open, and that the pure light of your inner being radiates ever more brightly and contributes to the greater illumination of the world.

And so, together, you and your Inner Healer come back out of the spiral of your heart, and with a smile your Healer withdraws for now, making it clear that he or she is available to you any time you wish. And you come gently back into present time and space, breathing easily, bringing with you a sense of wholeness, peace and harmony, and spend some time with your Quest Journal.

PART IV

Autumn
Avalon

Glastonbury Tor

[After the Crucifixion] St Joseph of Arimathea, one of the few followers of the new religion who seem to have been wealthy, set sail as a missionary, and after long voyages came to that cluster of little islands which

seemed to the men of the Mediterranean something like the last clouds of sunset. He came upon the western and wilder side of that wild and western land, and made his way to a valley which through all the oldest records is called Avalon… Here the pilgrim planted his staff in the soil; and it took root as a tree that blossoms on Christmas Day…

G. K. Chesterton, *Short History of England*, 1917.

Within sight of Castle Cadbury, just twelve miles away, is Glastonbury Tor, an oddly shaped hill with a tower at its summit. Around the base of the hill is the modern town of Glastonbury that boasts the ruins of a Gothic abbey and monastery, as well as a mystical heritage that has made it a kind of New Age Mecca. Glastonbury claims to be the Isle of Avalon.

It was here, according to legend, that Joseph of Arimathea—the Joseph who donated the Holy Sepulcher in which Jesus was buried—made landfall when he sailed westward after the crucifixion. The surrounding area was drained in the Middle Ages and is now fertile farmland, but in Joseph's time, and some four hundred years later in Arthur's time, it was largely under water, and the Tor—that rises some five hundred feet above sea level—was an island except perhaps for a month or so in the summer when the surrounding wetlands dried out.

Joseph stuck his staff in the ground on what is now called Wearyall Hill. His staff took root and grew into a thorn bush that blossoms at Christmas. The original Holy Thorn was cut down by a Puritan during the British civil war, but there are numerous offspring of the bush in and around Glastonbury and one of them was replanted on the original site in the 1960s. One of the interesting things about this thorn bush, according to Geoffrey Ashe, is that when it was examined by a botanist who was not told where it came from, it was pronounced Syrian. And it does bloom around Christmas, which is something of a miracle in an English winter.

The tower on top of the Tor is all that is left of a medieval church dedicated to St. Michael. Tor simply means "hill," and there is nothing mystical about that, but it is almost impossible to talk about the Tor without getting mystical. It is said to be at the intersection of two ley lines, the lines of power that are the earth's meridians or energy pathways. There are traces of paths, or terraces, that encircle the Tor, indicating that at some point in its history the hill was artificially shaped, but exactly who did it and when and why is the subject of great debate. There are many so-called "sensible" explanations, but they tend to contradict each other. One such explanation is that they are terraces formed for medieval agriculture. They were no doubt used that way in the Middle Ages, but the terraces—or whatever they are—are probably much older.

Marion Zimmer Bradley in *The Mists of Avalon* describes the terraces as a processional way, used by the priestesses of Avalon in their rituals to honor the Goddess. There are modern mystics in the town of Glastonbury who offer seekers the experience of climbing the Tor and tracing the terraces as a symbolic journey through the chakras. Ashe suggests that the terraces formed a complex labyrinthine pattern, a spiral design that turns up also in Crete, Italy, Ireland, Scandinavia and elsewhere. If so, it probably dates from the age of Stonehenge and Avebury and other vast ritual works of the second or third millennium BCE.

Mazes used to be linked with beliefs about the Underworld, and the Tor is spoken of in legend as being hollow, a point of entry into the Underworld. In contemporary times Ashe heard local tales of a chamber below the summit, or a well sinking far into its depths. Some intrepid explorers are said to have found a way in and to have come out insane. Dowsers have claimed to detect a network of subterranean waterways, even an underground lake.

The archeological excavation of the Tor in the nineteen sixties found traces of human activity in prehistoric times, and of fairly large buildings and continuous settlement during the time of Arthur. If a local chief had a fort on the Tor, says Ashe, that would create a link with the oldest known story bringing Arthur to Glastonbury, written down in 1130 by a Welsh monk. The story goes that Melwas, the ruler of Somerset, carried off Arthur's wife Guinevere and kept her in his castle until she was either rescued by Lancelot, in some versions, or released through negotiation mediated by Merlin in others.

At the foot of the Tor is Glastonbury Abbey. The ruins that remain are only a sad and haunting shadow of what must have been a magnificent structure. Somewhere within the ruins of the abbey is the site of the tiny wattle and daub chapel built by Joseph of Arimathea, reputedly the first Christian church in Britain. Glastonbury Abbey used to be the most powerful and wealthy abbey in Britain, and perhaps for that reason came in for particularly harsh treatment when Henry VIII had his squabble with the pope and decided to break with Rome and declare himself the head of the church in England.

England was Catholic at the time, and Henry was married to Catherine of Aragon, sister to the king of Spain. She was older than Henry and had been married to Henry's older brother Arthur; after Arthur's death Henry married her—having obtained a papal dispensation to do so—in order to hold on to the alliance with Spain. She bore Henry a daughter, but he wanted a male heir, and after twenty years of marriage and six children either stillborn or who died in infancy Catherine was not likely to have any more children. And, in any case, Henry had fallen deeply in lust with Ann Boleyn. He asked the pope for an annulment and the pope refused. Henry renounced the pope and declared himself head of the church in England, which not only gave him the freedom to divorce Catherine and marry Ann, but also gave him an excuse to take over all the monastic lands, to enrich his own coffers and reward his supporters and favorites.

The last abbot of Glastonbury, Michael Wilding, refused to take the oath to the king and was subjected to that particularly barbaric and grisly punishment for traitors: he was hung, drawn and quartered on Glastonbury Tor. The abbey buildings were looted for their treasures and then abandoned, and in succeeding centuries were used as a ready stone quarry providing material for building houses and even a road. When the land and rectory came up for sale early in the twentieth century the sales ad focused on the rectory, and of the abbey said only: "interesting ruins on the grounds." After an appeal to the public for funds the site was bought by the Anglican Church, which maintains it still.

The only one of the abbey buildings to have survived intact is the abbot's kitchen. In the days before hotels and motels pilgrims— and travelers generally—would spend the night at the nearest abbey. Depending on your social station you would be entertained royally at the Abbot's table and housed in comfortable quarters, or you would be given a space on the floor in the kitchen. In the abbot's kitchen at Glastonbury is a prayer—dating back to the sixth century—that is a charming common sense approach to spiritual and physical nourishment.

> Give me a good digestion, Lord,
> And also something to digest
> Give me a healthy body, Lord
> With sense to keep it at its best.
>
> Give me a healthy mind, O Lord
> To keep the good and pure in sight
> Which seeing wrong is not appalled
> But finds a way to put it right.
>
> Give me a mind that is not bored,
> That does not whimper, whine or sigh.
> Don't let me worry overmuch
> About that fussy thing called "I".
>
> Give me a sense of humour, Lord,
> Give me the grace to see a joke.
> To get some happiness from Life
> And pass it on to other folk.

Another offspring of the Holy Thorn is to be found in the Chalice Well Garden, site of a natural spring at the foot of the Tor. Legend also tells that Joseph of Arimathea brought with him to Britain the chalice from the Last Supper, filled with the blood that dripped from the crucified Christ. He hid the chalice in the well, which is why the water runs red. The water runs red also because of its iron content.

The well was probably a sacred site from ancient times. Natural springs were sacred places to the Celts and probably those before the Celts, and were dedicated to the Goddess, the feminine principle of the creative force. The Avalon of legend is the abode of the Lady of the Lake, the mysterious figure who gave Arthur his magical sword.

After the Battle of Camlann the dying Arthur was taken to Avalon for healing by four queens or priestesses, and the Avalon barge, sailing off into the mists, is the last we hear of Arthur. Because the legend does not tell of his death, even though Thomas Malory's account is titled *Le Morte d'Arthur*, in myth Arthur is "the once and future" king. There is no grave, therefore he is not dead but sleeping, and will return at some future time to lead his people again.

Glastonbury Abbey records would have us believe that Arthur was buried in the grounds of the abbey. Geoffrey Ashe tells us that a Welsh or Breton bard supposedly divulged the secret of Arthur's burial place to King Henry II. Henry passed this news to the Abbot, and a few years later in 1190 the monks excavated the spot. They dug down seven feet and unearthed a stone slab. Under it was a lead cross about a foot long, with a Latin inscription. *Hic iacet sepultur inclitus rex Arturius in insula Avalonia.* Here lies buried the renowned king Arthur on the isle of Avalon.

Nine feet farther down they found a rough coffin made from a hollowed-out log. Inside were the bones of a tall man whose skull was damaged, indicating that he had apparently been killed by a blow on the head. Some smaller bones, and a scrap of hair that crumbled away when touched, were explained as Guinevere's. The bones were placed in caskets, and in 1278 they were transferred, during a state visit by Edward I, to a black marble tomb before the high altar of the main Abbey church. (We can imagine what Johnny Cochran would have had to say about that chain of evidence. There were almost a hundred years between the time of the graves' discovery and the bones being reburied inside the abbey.) Not even the bones remain. The archeologist Leslie Alcock tells us that the tomb was broken up during the Reformation and the bones dispersed.

Most historians believe this story is a hoax. There had been a fire at the abbey and money was needed for rebuilding, and what better than the grave of King Arthur to attract pilgrims and donations? There could also have been a political motive. Some historians speculate that Glastonbury called itself Avalon and claimed the graves of Arthur and Guinevere to give legitimacy to King Henry II. By claiming the Celtic myth of old Britain as the myth of the Norman conquerors, Henry could simultaneously steal the thunder of Celtic Welsh patriots and encourage a kind of early nationalism centered on himself.

In the early nineteen-sixties the archeologist Ralegh Radford excavated the site of the original burial and found traces of the monks' digging. Deep down, at a spot suggesting a person of importance, he discovered stone slabs such as were used to line ancient burials, and these were disarranged, as if a large object, possibly a coffin, had been dragged out. His findings, however, support only the existence of the grave of an important person, possibly a king. Not necessarily Arthur. The inscribed cross has disappeared. There is a drawing of it; the lettering is untidy and rather crude, and might suggest a date long before 1190 when it was supposedly found. Norma Goodrich, who theorizes that Avalon was not Glastonbury but the Isle of Man, believes that the abbey grave was that of a Saxon king and queen some centuries after Arthur.

Fifth chakra: Visuddha

Avalon symbolizes the spiritual context of the reign of King Arthur. It was the Lady of the Lake, representing Avalon and the mystical heritage of ancient Britain, who gave Arthur not only the sword Excalibur, but also a scabbard with magical qualities. In Malory's telling of the legends, Merlin asks Arthur which he likes better, the sword or the scabbard. Arthur replies that he likes the sword better.

> "You are the more unwise," said Merlin, "for the scabbard is worth ten of the sword; for while you have the scabbard upon you, you shall never lose a drop of blood, however sorely wounded you may be, and therefore keep the scabbard always with you."

The sword that Arthur drew from the stone served to legitimize his right to be king. The sword Excalibur, with which he fought his twelve battles and which gave him the power to protect his kingdom and his people and create a society of justice and equality, belonged to the Lady of the Lake. The second sword is proof, should we need it, that the legend is not simply fiction with no spiritual foundation. There is no fictional necessity for a second sword. The first sword is magical, it is the gift of God, or Merlin; why could it not serve as the magical or sacred sword with which Arthur fights his battles? Yet it is broken in a fight with King Pellinore and a different sword, imbued with different symbolism, becomes the symbol of Arthur's power.

In terms of the mythical structure of the story, the sword from the stone takes its leave of the pages of legend because it has served its purpose: to prove to hardened and ambitious warriors that their sacred duty was to give their allegiance to an adolescent boy with no experience of war; to renounce their own ambitions to be High King and follow the High King chosen by God, who had made his wishes known through the test of the sword in the stone. The exigencies of the myth then require that a sword imbued with the power and purpose of the feminine be introduced into the story. Excalibur was the sword of destiny, the sword of ancient Britannia, that could be wielded only by the king. It was not given to Arthur but only loaned; it was his to use only as long as he was king. Even though it came to symbolize the qualities of the Round Table fellowship it was not Arthur's to bequeath to a chosen successor, but was to be returned to the Lady of the Lake when his life was over. It was she who chose who would wield the sword.

The magical scabbard served the prosaic first chakra purpose of protecting Arthur's life. In the days before antibiotics even a superficial wound could be fatal; it was in fact a relatively superficial wound that killed Uther, because he continued to fight and did not take care of it. The scabbard was not a powerful enough symbol on its own to carry the power of the feminine; that was to be the sword of destiny, the sword of ancient Britannia, the sword of truth.

The sword of truth is the gift of the fifth chakra. The fifth chakra is the center of speaking our own truth: our own truth, not necessarily the accepted truth of our group, family, society or culture. At the first chakra the group tells us what truth is, and we accept the ideas and values of our family, religious faith, or community. At the second chakra our ideas of truth are heavily conditioned by the opinions of others. At the third chakra, in adolescence when we forge our own identity, we begin to evaluate the various authorities in our lives and sift through the many "truths" that compete for our allegiance. As we take from those sources the ideas and beliefs that resonate as truth within us we begin to develop our own unique individual will, and to formulate the Truth that we express at the fifth chakra.

The fifth chakra is also the center of our surrender to divine will. In the three lower chakras we develop personal power; at the fifth chakra we surrender that personal power to divine power, and trust that whatever is right for us will manifest as we embark consciously on the quest for the Holy Grail, the quest for enlightenment. This is not always an easy transition. For a lot of us the concept of surrendering the will we have so long and often painfully developed and nurtured is a major challenge to our sense of self. Surrender can feel like submission, or sacrifice, and that is not a comfortable feeling, nor one that our now strong individual will can readily accept. When we say "Thy will, not my will," it sounds a lot like the duality that we are trying to get away from.

In truth there is no paradox. If we have done our preparatory work well, by the time we reach the fifth chakra "Thy will" *is* "my will," there is no difference once we have bathed in the universal love of the heart. We are in alignment with our divine purpose. "Thy will" is the will of the divine within, the spark of divinity individuated within our beings that is at the same time part of the great Oneness of Spirit, and is the chariot that carries us home.

As mentioned earlier, there are similarities between the levels of the chakras and various developmental theories. In the cognitive developmental model of Jean Piaget, for example, the first chakra is sensorimotor, the second concrete, the third formal-operational. There are clear parallels between the challenges of the chakras and the developmental tasks identified by Erik Erikson, and with Abraham Maslow's hierarchy of needs. However, most developmental theories stop at the fifth chakra, because—as John Nelson reminds us—historically the upper levels of consciousness have been considered pathological. In the Western psychological tradition we have not differentiated between mystical and psychotic experiences.

In *Healing the Split*, Nelson suggests that mystical experiences and madness are both openings to the Spiritual Ground, but at opposite ends of a continuum. Schizophrenia typically develops in the early twenties, and Nelson theorizes that in terms of chakra development schizophrenia manifests when an individual has developed as far as the third chakra and then regresses: to the second chakra in cases of paranoid schizophrenia, to the first in cases of catatonia. Such an individual is wide open to the lower energies of the Ground without any of the filtering mechanisms that provide protection, and is prey to terrifying hallucinations and voices that can command violence to self or others.

At the other end of the continuum, an individual who is operating at the fifth chakra or above will reopen to the Spiritual Ground in full consciousness, on a firm foundation of well-developed physical, emotional and mental bodies. They too may see visions, or hear voices, but the experience is one of transcendent joy, and the voices are loving and empowering.

It is vital in Nelson's opinion that mental health professionals distinguish the difference in order to decide upon the appropriate intervention. Helping them to do so was one of his motives for writing his book, and he articulates the dilemma with the following example.

What if a person on the threshold of a spontaneous spiritual awakening were to experience visions? And what if they did not understand what was happening and went to see a traditional psychiatrist? In all probability they would be given anti-psychotic medication that would shut the process down.

And what if, at the other end of the continuum, someone were experiencing hallucinations or delusions that signaled the first stages of schizophrenia and were to consult an alternative healer who recommended meditation? Meditation could fragment still further their fragile ego boundaries, hastening their regression and compounding their suffering.

At the mystical end of the spectrum is a spiritual opening that results from disciplined spiritual practice, and disciplined spiritual practice does not mean we have to stand on our heads or meditate for hours a day. It means working our way, consistently and with determination, through the issues presented in our daily lives at each of the chakras. When we are prepared and spiritually mature, an opening to spirit is a mystical experience; or those wonderful moments in deep meditation when we feel like we know everything; or artistic inspiration.

At the other extreme are uncontrolled openings to the spiritual dimension, because we never developed any ego boundaries, or our boundaries are incomplete. In the spiritual dimension are not only what Nelson calls higher order energies, but also lower order energies, undeveloped or misguided souls, as well as the energy of our collective fears. The psychic membrane, or ego boundary, that we develop during our journey through the lower chakras serves as a filtering mechanism to protect us from lower order energies. Without them, we can be prey to horrifying visual and auditory hallucinations.

In her moving and compelling account of her experience with bi-polar disorder, Jay Redfield Jamison describes a manic episode that is a wondrous adventure:

> ... I found myself, in that glorious illusion of high summer days, gliding, flying, now and again lurching through cloud banks and ethers, past stars, and across fields of ice crystals. Even now, I can see in my mind's rather peculiar eye an extraordinary shattering and shifting of light; inconstant but ravishing colors laid out across miles of circling rings; and the almost imperceptible, somehow surprisingly pallid, moons of this Catherine wheel of a planet. I remember singing "Fly Me to the Moons" as I swept past those of Saturn, and thinking myself terribly funny. I saw and experienced that which had been only dreams, or fitful fragments of inspiration.

After this episode, Jamison sank into a suicidal depression, but like many who suffer bi-polar disorder she resisted medication for many years because she did not want to lose the highs.

One way to conceptualize bi-polar disorder, what used to be called manic-depression, is incomplete psychic membranes that allow us—unpredictably and uncontrollably—sometimes to be open to higher order energies, that can be mystical experiences like Jamison's, and sometimes to lower order energies, the terrifying hallucinations and voices of despair that characterize psychosis.

When we look beyond the surface differences of the various theories of human development and seek the underlying spiritual truth, not only do we find many correlations between the chakra system and psychological theories of development, but also between the chakras and the four worlds of the Kabbalah; with Jungian psychology; and with the four elements of pagan tradition. And we find the same warnings about the dangers of unaccompanied or premature journeys into the spiritual realm.

The Kabbalistic World of Action corresponds to the first chakra and the element Earth; the World of Formation to the second chakra and the element Water; the World of Creation to the third chakra and the element Fire. The World of Emanation, the element Air and the Collective Unconscious contain the upper chakras, which are refinements of the stages of spiritual opening and of the qualities we need to develop in order safely to dissolve the protective boundaries that have shielded us—as long as we were unprepared—from the full force of spiritual power.

To the unprepared, that power can cause a literal burn out, as some intrepid or naïve experimenters with psychedelic drugs have discovered to their cost. Psychedelic drugs blast open psychic boundaries. Without a stable physical, emotional and mental foundation the user can lose his or her tether to consensual reality, sometimes permanently in terrifying and spontaneous flashbacks. John Nelson suggests that the reason why some people in the 1960s had good trips on LSD and others bad was a matter of their spiritual maturity. For someone operating more or less consistently at the fourth chakra or above, LSD can be the catalyst for a mystical experience. But those primarily focused on the second or third chakras have not yet adapted to the higher vibrational frequencies of the spiritual realm and for them opening the psychic membranes is premature and leads to painful and frightening, even dangerous, experiences.

Mitchell Chefitz in *The Seventh Telling* describes the Chariot, a meditational journey through the four Worlds of the Kabbalah to the presence of God, based on the visions of Ezekiel. To undertake that journey without guidance and without the appropriate foundation is a perilous enterprise. Warnings about the dangers of delving deep into the mystical worlds are to be found in the story of four rabbis who descended into paradise. One looked and died. Another looked and lost his mind. The third looked and became estranged from tradition. Only Rabbi Akiba returned safely. Only he descended and ascended in *shalom*, which in this context means safety.

The Catholic Church taught that the uninitiated should not even attempt the journey. Mystical experiences were not for the rank and file but only for saints and mystics whose writings, like the Bible, were to be interpreted for the faithful by the church hierarchy. The Church has been accused of guarding the mysteries in order to concentrate its own power, and while there may be some truth in that there is also concern for the safety of the flock, taking to an extreme the role of fatherly guide and protector.

Intense meditative practices if used inappropriately can provoke a premature opening. Spiritual energy in the yogic tradition is known as Kundalini and is symbolized by a snake coiled at the base of the spine. As we mature through the chakras the snake uncoils and reaches up the spine, energizing each chakra. There are practices in Kundalini yoga to stimulate this process, traditionally closely supervised by a guru. But if we do them before we are ready, hoping perhaps to shortcut the sometimes difficult and uncomfortable route to enlightenment, we can raise the energy prematurely and catastrophically. We can cause physical or psychological harm, because the body and mind must gradually adjust to higher vibrations of energy, a process that occurs naturally as we pursue chakra development systematically.

In the Arthurian legends, this leg of the spiritual journey is symbolized in the quest for the Holy Grail. Those Companions who lacked a solid foundation and a clear spiritual focus failed in their quest for the Holy Grail: some of them perished; Lancelot for a while lost his reason; some abandoned the quest. Their experiences mirror those of the second century rabbis who descended into paradise in the Kabbalistic story

Personal gurus and teachers of Kabbalah are not easily found in these times, and the chakra system—and the example of mythological figures such as King Arthur—can teach us how safely to undertake the journey. By systematically following the blueprint for healthy chakra development, using the tools available to us to resolve and release the baggage we have accumulated, healing our wounds and building our strength on all levels of being, we prepare the stable foundation that will support our safely opening the upper chakras. We honor and nurture ourselves on all levels of being, recognizing that the physical, emotional and mental bodies are the vehicle for spiritual development, and create the tripod base that supports a safe journey to enlightenment, however we choose to call it—the World of Emanation, the Collective Unconscious, the Spiritual Ground—to look upon the face of God/Goddess.

We can nurture our physical bodies by eating healthy and nourishing foods, in the proportions that are appropriate for our ideal weight and size; by drinking plenty of water; getting adequate rest and some form of regular and enjoyable exercise. Arthur and his Companions from their youth undertook rigorous physical training, necessary in times of war and maintained in times of peace through games and contests. In the yogic tradition, the postures and breathing disciplines of Hatha Yoga tone, stretch, strengthen and balance the physical body so that the demands of the body do not detract from the development of spirit. It is not easy to focus on meditating when your back is aching or your intestines are in spasm or your neck is stiff. This is not to say of course that those with physical disabilities or chronic illnesses are also handicapped in their spiritual development, only that within our physical parameters—whatever they are—we are conscious of our physical needs and nurture them. There are modified yoga postures for the wheelchair-bound, and studies have proven the benefit to both muscle and skeletal tissue of even mild exercise and strength training.

We nurture our emotional body by paying attention to our emotions, allowing them appropriate expression and seeking to understand what they are trying to tell us. Emotions are communications from the depths of our inner wisdom. They tell us when we are in harmony with source energy and when we are not. Uncomfortable emotions are a signal that we are out of alignment. We are in alignment with source energy when we are happy and express the inner joy that is the essential nature of our being. The emotions of sadness, irritation, frustration, depression, are messages, signals from our inner wisdom that something needs attention.

We can open ourselves to understanding those messages and encourage the emotional energy to flow by giving ourselves permission to feel, working through a negative emotion by talking to a friend or counselor, writing in a journal, screaming under a highway bridge or at the ocean, crying at sad movies, beating up a pillow, punching or kicking a bag. And at the same time we can nurture the emotional body by taking the time to relax deeply on a daily basis, and by doing those things that we feel are emotionally nourishing—a massage, perhaps, or a hot bath, relaxing with a favorite book or movie, time with loved ones, playing and giving free reign to our inner child, laughing at a favorite funny movie.

We nourish our intellect by taking the time for activities that are mentally stimulating: in conversation perhaps, or reading, or learning something new, or watching interesting television programs or movies.

It is only when we have cleaned the junk out of the basement of the personal unconscious, disciplined the mind and nurtured the physical and emotional bodies, that we are ready to undertake the quest for the Holy Grail.

The fifth chakra, then, is the center of speaking our truth and the power of choice, and we can lose energy at this center when we let others define our needs and wants and make choices for us. How do you feel, for example, when someone asks you to do something you really do not want to do? Many of us have a hard time saying no, but when we say yes in this situation we are saying no to the fifth chakra. We are violating our boundaries and giving away our power. When we give our power away to someone else by allowing them to control our actions, the energy of the throat center—instead of being the expression of truth and divine will that is the gift of a healthy fifth chakra—becomes toxic. We may do whatever we have agreed to do but we resent it. We may have thoughts of anger towards the other person or towards ourselves. If it gets bad enough we may have thoughts of violence or revenge. And those thoughts, over time, can poison the system, keep us stuck, and block the awareness of our connection with the Divine Source.

The same mechanism of surrendering our power is operating in the case of addiction. When we are addicted we have given away our will to the addictive substance: nicotine, alcohol, cocaine, food; or the addictive habit: gambling, sex, exercise. We are not the ones in control of our thoughts, feelings and actions; we are controlled by the addiction. The defining factor in addiction is whether we have the power to control it—in the case of food or exercise—or give it up altogether—in the case of harmful substances or habits.

Physical manifestations of a deficient fifth chakra can be a fear of speaking out, a weak voice, or problems with the throat, ears and neck. Constant throat clearing can be a sign that there is a block at the fifth chakra, a sign that we are holding back from speaking our truth, keeping quiet because we are afraid or we want to keep the peace, or we have been conditioned to believe that what we have to say is not important. If you should find that people you are talking to are constantly asking you to repeat yourself, or saying they can't hear you, it may be because of a fear of speaking your own truth.

One way to encourage the development of a clear voice is through chanting.

Chanting meditation

Take a break now and settle yourself comfortably in your sacred space. Take some deep breaths and invoke the Triple Shield of Light. Take a deep breath into the abdomen and on the exhalation chant the sacred word "OM." Perhaps this first time your voice will be soft, even tentative. Focus on increasing the power of the sound and notice the change in the feel of the vibration at your throat. Deepen the breath and notice how that allows you to prolong the length of the chant, as well its power. Chant the word for as long as feels comfortable to you, and then relax into the silence, feel the vibration created by the field of sound around you and the responding harmony within you.

Chants are available in many languages and in many musical styles. As you proceed you can sing along with recorded chants, or perhaps join a chanting group. I highly recommend the CDs of Snatam Kaur, which are in Sanskrit. Every sound has a vibration, and every letter in Sanskrit corresponds to a particular vibration. Each chakra is symbolized by a lotus flower with a specific number of petals; each petal corresponds to a sound vibration and when we chant that vibration it stimulates the corresponding petals of the thousand petalled lotus at Sahasrara, the crown. Sahasrara is correlated with the brain, and as the human brain controls the physical body, Sahasrara controls the chakras. The petals of the chakras stimulate the petals of Sahasrara, and vice versa.

Many Sanskrit chants invoke the qualities of various Hindu deities. The deities embody certain aspects of the Divine, and the

185

vibration of a particular chant echoes the vibration of that aspect. The purpose is not to worship the deity, but to evoke those qualities from within the self. When you chant about the compassion of the Creator, for example, the vibration of the sound awakens and evokes that compassion within your own heart.

So perhaps you will choose to experiment with different kinds of chant and find those which feel most harmonious to you. As you develop the strength of the fifth chakra through chanting you will notice a greater facility and flow in two major areas of growth at the fifth chakra: the communication of your truth and the expression of your creativity.

If one extreme of dysfunction at the fifth chakra is a weak voice or an inability to speak your mind, at the other excessive or blocked energy here can manifest as too much talking and an inability to listen, a loud and dominating voice and frequent interruptions. Balance at the fifth chakra requires the practice of listening skills and paying attention to what someone else is saying instead of jumping forward in time to whatever you are going to say back to them, or cutting them off in mid-sentence.

Someone with a fifth chakra that is in healthy balance has a resonant voice and is a good listener; has a clearly developed knowledge of his/her own truth and communicates that truth with clarity and power; and recognizes the necessity for expressing creativity.

We heal the fifth chakra by learning good communication skills, by honoring our boundaries and speaking our own truth. Some of us though do not even know what that truth is. Imagine a woman, let's call her Eleanor, who has never considered that her own desires are even worth voicing; she may in fact no longer know what they are. Perhaps in childhood she had accepted that her older brother's needs came first: he was the one with new furniture in his room while hers was second hand; he was the one who went to expensive schools and had his choice of colleges; he was the one who watched television or played basketball with his father while she did household chores. At the dinner table she sat silent while the rest of the family discussed sports or politics or TV shows. If she dared to express an opinion it was greeted with derision or ignored as irrelevant. (The Italian writer Natalia Ginzburg describes such scenes from her own childhood, though her response was to train herself to speak very fast in order to get a word in!)

In all likelihood in her marriage Eleanor will follow the same pattern, and follow her husband's lead in choice of friends, entertainment, vacations. He will set the rules in the household and she will comply, keeping the home, herself and her children immaculate to do him honor, entertaining his business associates, and staying home while he plays golf or drinks with his friends. Perhaps at some point she visits her family doctor when she is feeling down and receives—instead of understanding and counseling—a prescription, and embarks upon years of dependence on anti-depressants and anxiolytics in various combinations and in increasing doses.

Perhaps at some point she is divorced or widowed but continues to be treated by her children as if her reason for being were to serve them. She does not dare to say no because her greatest fear is that they will abandon her. Only by fulfilling everyone else's needs does Eleanor believe she is of any value, and it does not occur to her than she can be loved for herself. She is a constant loser in the game of trying to figure out what others might want so that she can provide it before they can criticize her, because living by others' rules is always a losing proposition.

Eleanor speaks in a barely audible whisper, as if afraid of being noticed. Clearly she has weaknesses at all developmental levels but here we are concerned with her voice, an indicator of a weak fifth chakra. A place to begin her recovery could be with the issue of boundaries and learning to speak her own truth. She first has to discover what that truth is because she has never thought in those terms before. One way to rediscover her own truth can be through Interactive Guided Imagerysm, creating an image of the "inner advisor"—that part of us that embodies our own deep inner wisdom—who can provide reassurance and direction. It may take months of contemplation and practice through imagery before Eleanor is able to say no for the first time to one of her son's constant demands for money, and she will probably do it in fear and trembling, but if she is consistent and patient he may come to accept the changes in her, and even over time learn to respect her new-found strength and growing self-confidence.

"Over time" is a key phrase, because as we learned at the third chakra those around us who are used to our behaving in a certain way are likely to pull out all the stops in their efforts to turn back the clock. It is very convenient for a family such as Eleanor's to have someone available to fulfil their needs, including their need to have someone to blame for everything that is not working. They may be highly resistant to that someone's efforts to change, and go for the jugular in their criticisms of new behavior. When support for growth and healing is not forthcoming from within the family it may be necessary to distance oneself from them for a while so as not to allow them the opportunity to sabotage the healing process. The initial stages of a journey such as Eleanor's can be lonely, until new friendships that support the new level of functioning can be created.

As with change at any chakra, change at the fifth demands consistency and courage, and can benefit from a supportive friend, minister or counselor who can remind us in the dark and lonely times of the rewards of self-nurture: confidence, stability, an ability to laugh and enjoy life, the ability to attract friends and partners who value us for who we are and not simply for what we do for them.

Learning to speak our own truth often feels threatening, and can create a lot of painful backlash before it begins to feel liberating and empowering. We can begin by imagining speaking our truth, by writing in a journal or by transferring our experience on to a third person through story writing.

Meditation for speaking your truth

In a safe place, free of interruptions, begin by taking some deep, complete breaths, bringing the breath consciously down into the lower part of the lungs so that the abdomen expands on the inbreath, and deflates on the outbreath. Perhaps you would like to spend five or ten minutes chanting.

Bring up the shield of light of earth; bring down the shield of light of spirit; breathe into the heart and expand your inner light. Filled and surrounded by the Triple Shield of light you can allow yourself to sink safely down to deeper and deeper levels of mind, deeper levels of awareness, deeper and deeper levels of knowing. Imagine that the Triple Shield carries you to a place that is beautiful and welcoming, a garden perhaps, or the beach, or a forest clearing. Or perhaps you would prefer a structure of some kind. If so, create the structure that is perfect for you ... furnish it with your favorite colors ... so that it is comfortable and welcoming.

Spend a few moments becoming familiar with this place, with the feeling of being safe and relaxed.

When you're ready, think about a person in your life to whom you find it a challenge to speak your mind, to speak your truth. Perhaps they are dominating and intimidating; perhaps they seem fragile and you are afraid of hurting their feelings; perhaps you fear they will be offended; perhaps they are demanding and you have developed a habit of going along with whatever they want from you.

Before you create an image of this person, invoke the presence of a spiritual being to support you. Perhaps Merlin, or the Lady of the Lake, or an animal helper. Or perhaps there is a guardian angel that you have called upon before. Perhaps you invoke an older version of yourself, an aspect of you that is wise and strong. This inner helper is compassionate, wise, and loving.

And when you feel ready, create an image of the person to whom you have decided, perhaps for the first time, to speak your truth. When the image is clear, surround them in their own Triple Shield of Light, and move them far enough away from you so that your shield of light and theirs do not touch each other. Thank them for coming, and tell them that there is something you want to say to them, and that you don't want them to speak, just listen.

And then say to them whatever it is that you want to say, that you have been holding inside and have felt inhibited about saying. Perhaps you need to express anger, or disappointment, or to say no.

Take your time. Perhaps the first time it is enough to create the space and summon the image. And when you are ready, thank them for coming and tell them to leave. Watch as they turn and walk away, out of your consciousness for now.

The twin challenges of the fifth chakra at first sight can seem contradictory: on the one hand to speak our own truth, that requires a strong personal will, and on the other the surrender of our individual will to divine will. In truth, there is no conflict. Our truth, at the fifth chakra, *is* the truth of divine will. We have found the place of alignment with the flow of Source Energy, and we willingly surrender to that pure positive flow.

The awakening of the fifth chakra comes to the companions of King Arthur as the vision of the Holy Grail.

The Vision

This was to be Galahad's first festival as a Companion and he felt as if he were a different person from the untested youth who had celebrated the summer solstice in the great Stone Henge on the plain. Then they had gathered an hour or so before dawn and had waited in the still chill air of a midsummer night for the rising sun to strike the heel stone and cast its shadow into the welcoming embrace of the circle of stones.

Now it was night and they were gathered within the sacred circle on top of the Tor. As they waited in darkness the moon rose above the horizon and cast them in a silver glow. The moon's light reflected off the surface of the lake at the foot of the Tor, creating a bridge of light to the land. The king stood by the altar stone, Merlin at his side. As always King Arthur wore white, and his tunic and cloak seemed to glow with an ethereal inner light. The Companions and Druids formed an inner circle within the circle of standing stones.

Galahad became aware of women's voices chanting. A line of lights traced the processional way around the Tor as the priestesses of Avalon climbed the Tor and chanted the words of power. The deeper voices of the Druids already within the sacred circle answered them now, and as the priestesses came closer the air began to pulsate as the power built.

Galahad had heard the teachings about Samhuinn every year of his life: that Spirit is infinite and unknowable, that it is both masculine and feminine, loving and firm, compassionate and wise. It both creates and destroys, destroying illusion and the unnecessary. It was this latter aspect of the infinite divine mystery that presided over the lunar fire festival of Samhuinn, a feminine aspect of spirit called Cailleach. She sent the winter snows to cleanse the country of autumn's debris, to harden the ground and quicken the roots and seeds that lay dormant. She sent the winds that stripped the branches bare of the last remnants of dead leaves.

The circle hummed with power. The column of priestesses entered the sacred space and disposed themselves around the circle, alternating priestess and Druid to maintain a balance of yin and yang. The Lady of the Lake took her place beside Merlin. Galahad's scalp prickled and he felt as if he might even levitate as the Lady raised her arms and ceremonially blessed the four directions and the four seasons. Each participant turned with her to face south, west, north and east. She laid a branch of yew on the altar to symbolize the eternity of spiritual life and turned back to face the circle. Her voice was low and musical, and carried without effort to everyone present, so that each of them felt as if she were speaking intimately to them personally.

"We have reached the time of Samhuinn, which is no time. The old year has ended and the new year is not yet begun. We stand outside of time and the veil between the worlds is thin. We honor the memory of *our loved ones who have passed. We honor ourselves and our predecessors with blessings from the earth."*

Priestesses bearing bread, salt, wine and honey made their way around the circle of participants. Galahad took a piece of bread, dipped it in salt and honey, and took a goblet of wine. When everyone had been served they stepped forward to the fire in the center of the circle and ate and drank together, then the Lady cast the remaining gifts of the earth into the fire so that the essence of the earth's bounty could be released to nourish the spirits of those who had passed over. The chanting began again, and the high melodious voices of the priestesses and the deeper harmony of the Druids led them into meditation.

Afterwards they could never agree on what happened next or on what each of them had seen. There was a sudden whooshing sound and the circle was flooded with light. Each one of them had a vision, but not the same vision. They agreed that there was a woman, and that she carried a vessel of some kind that she offered to each in turn. Some, whose ancestors had come from the far-flung reaches of the eastern empire, saw a woman in swirling robes and with slanted eyes, the Goddess they called Kwan Yin. For others she was Isis, or Tara, or Ceridwen, or Mary the Magdalene.

Balin, whose foster parents had raised him in the Christian faith, saw Mary the mother of Jesus. "She wore a blue robe," he told them, "and her face was ever young. She offered me wine in a cup such as Jesus himself must have used. It was wooden and worn smooth and yet it glowed with an inner light. It must be true what they say, that Joseph of Arimathea brought the cup of the Last Supper to these isles."

Others saw the Great Goddess in her various manifestations: as the Maiden, or the Mother, or the Wise Crone, and the cauldron she carried was large, or small, or silver, or beaten gold, or ceramic, or wood. It contained sweet mead, or beer, or wine, or fresh spring water. What they did agree on was that they had shared something wondrous and had been fundamentally changed by it. Each knew that they must seek this Holy Grail and bring it out into the world, to share the joy of looking upon the face of the Divine.

The Quest for the Holy Grail

The Holy Grail is a relatively late addition to the Arthurian legend. Chrétien de Troyes wrote about it in his *Perceval, Le Conte du Graal,* sometime after 1181. The Grail legends were grafted on to the Arthurian story and grew into it, feeding on the roots of the legendary king.

It was not Arthur himself who undertook the quest for the Holy Grail; it was the best of his Companions. ("Knight" is a feudal word, part of the trimmings added to the legend by the medieval writers who collected the stories, as are shining armor, jousts, and the denigration of women.) Arthur did not have to search for enlightenment; he was already there. He knew that the Holy Grail is within, that enlightenment is not a final destination but a way of being, and that he could not lead anyone there but only show the way by living a life that was honorable and true. He could not teach his Companions what he knew but only encourage them to follow their own hearts and to seek the Holy Grail in their own way.

Troyes, the home of Chrétien, is the city in the Champagne region of France where the Knights Templar originated, and it is perhaps no coincidence that the Holy Grail makes its debut in the Arthurian legend a few decades after the Templars' return from the Holy Land. The nine founding Knights Templar went to Jerusalem to protect the holy places, and were headquartered in the Temple of Solomon doing nobody-is-quite-sure-what for nine years before returning home and overnight becoming rich and powerful. The belief is that they found something under Solomon's Temple, something of immense significance. Possibly the cup of the Last Supper; or documents; or treasure.

After they returned home in 1129 the Templars began an immensely successful fund-raising and recruiting campaign and for the next couple of hundred years were perhaps the most powerful force in Europe, taking a leading role in the Crusades, developing a banking system, ferrying pilgrims to the holy places and protecting them *en route*. Then, in a sting that would be the envy of the CIA, the combined armies of the Pope and the king of France rounded up the Templars on a Friday the thirteenth, a date still considered unlucky today. The Templars were tortured and executed in inventive and horrific ways, accused of heresy, homosexuality and devil worship, but the general consensus is that they had become a threat to the secular and spiritual power hierarchies. Their purported treasure was no doubt also an incentive, but the treasure was never found and the Templars' fleet of ships disappeared. Perhaps, as some believe, some of the Templars escaped and sailed to Scotland with the Holy Grail.

Another story of the origin of the Holy Grail is that the cup of the last supper, in which was collected the blood of Jesus as he hung on the cross, was taken by Joseph of Arimathea to the Isle of Avalon in Britain and was hidden in the sacred well at the foot of Glastonbury Tor.

Whatever its origins, the search for the Holy Grail has become the heart of the Arthurian legends. It has been suggested that Arthur thought up the quest for the Holy Grail to keep his Companions busy. Once there were no more Saxons to fight, what was a warrior to do? But that is not the reason. The Companions went in search of the Holy Grail not because they were bored, but because the time was right. They had reached the stage of development where they were ready for the inner search for truth, the opening and development of the fifth, sixth and seventh chakras.

In the Hindu tradition, the culture traditionally has supported physical, emotional and cognitive development within the chakra framework. It is accepted that in childhood we prepare to take our place in the physical world; that in early adulthood we focus on establishing our families and careers; and that we spend our middle years nurturing family and career. And when those tasks are completed, when our children are grown and we retire from our employment or pass on the family business to our children, then we can retire from the world and pursue the development of spirit. We can focus our attention on the upper chakras.

The Companions of the Round Table followed this pattern. Under the guidance and leadership of Arthur they fulfilled their roles in the physical world. They made the land safe, and helped Arthur to establish a society founded on kindness, justice and mutual respect (first, second and third chakras). Then Arthur opened the door to spiritual reawakening by showing them how to open the heart and balance yin and yang energy (fourth chakra). In their quest for the Holy Grail, the Companions of the Round Table withdrew from the mundane world and surrendered their individual will to divine will. They gave up everything they knew to follow the quest, trusting in the unfolding of divine will (fifth chakra). They wandered the land and confronted many challenges, seeking the truth within themselves and bringing light into their shadow spaces (sixth chakra). Only three of them, Perceval, Bors and Galahad, found the Holy Grail (seventh chakra). Gawain and Lancelot did not, though Gawain was permitted a brief sight of it.

Perceval, the hero of the first Grail story, grows up in the depths of the forest with his mother. His father and two older brothers have been killed and Perceval's mother is determined to shield her youngest from the life of violence that she perceives knighthood to be. In spite of all her efforts, Perceval one day sees five knights riding through the forest. He has never seen armor before and takes them for angels. (They are clearly wearing medieval armor of metal; sixth century warriors would have worn polished leather.) When they explain who they are Perceval determines to become a knight himself, and sets out for King Arthur's court.

In the course of his knightly wandering Perceval comes across the Grail Castle and is welcomed by the wounded Fisher King. He witnesses the ritual of the Grail procession, but because he does not ask the right questions he is not blessed with the sight of the Grail. He has to undergo many more adventures and learn a whole lot more before he will be ready.

Some of the other adventures of the knights have been collected by Andrea Hopkins. Lancelot finds an ancient chapel in the forest, abandoned and half ruined. An iron grille blocks the way in. Inside he can see an altar richly draped with cloths of silk, on which stands a tall silver candelabrum with six white candles. He lies down to sleep on his shield, and dreams that a sick knight arrives. The six candles begin to burn and the Holy Grail appears on a table of silver. The sick knight sits up, approaches the holy vessel on his hands and knees, kisses it, and is healed. When Lancelot awakens he rushes away, blinded by tears because he knows that the mysteries of the Holy Grail will remain hidden from him.

As Bors is riding through the forest he encounters two knights who have stripped and bound his brother Lionel and are beating him with a thorny branch. As he is about to ride to his brother's rescue, Bors sees an armed knight carrying off a beautiful young woman. Bors has to choose between leaving his brother in the hands of his tormentors, or abandoning the young woman to be violated and dishonored. After praying for divine protection for his brother he gallops off in pursuit of the ravisher, rescues the damsel and restores her to her father, and takes off again after his brother. On the way he meets a cleric who tells him his brother is dead, and shows him the body. Bors lays the body in a chapel; the cleric promises to conduct a service on the morrow and invites Bors to spend the night in the nearby tower.

In the tower Bors is wined and dined and offered all manner of enticements by a group of young women. After a while in comes a beautiful lady, who makes it clear that she wants Bors. When he politely declines, she threatens to throw herself from the tower and take twelve of her maidens with her. Though he pities them Bors does not consent to mortal sin, even to save their lives. When they do throw themselves off the tower they turn into fiends. They fly off and the tower disappears, along with Lionel's body.

The next day Bors finds his brother, and hears a voice telling him to head for the sea where Perceval awaits him. They are joined by Galahad, who has had adventures aplenty of his own. They set sail together and have several more adventures before arriving at the castle of Corbenic, where they witness the ritual of the Grail. Galahad dies in a state of ecstasy, Perceval lives out his life as a hermit, and Bors rides home to Camelot to tell the story.

And where is Merlin? Merlin in his dotage became besotted with a young and beautiful enchantress who robbed him of his power. Or he was tricked, perhaps poisoned, by Morgause or Morgan or Nimue. He was imprisoned in the cave under Tintagel where his wails and howls still echo through the darkness, (especially when there is a strong wind.) Or he was caged in a crystal cave on the shores of Scotland.

These fantasies of Merlin's end reflect the beliefs and prejudices of the medieval era, like the fiends in the story of Bors. The major female characters in the Arthurian myth, Goodrich tells us—Nimue, Cundrie, Morgan, and the Lady of the Lake—were priestesses, healers and spiritual teachers, educated and wise. Cundrie is said to have lectured on astronomy in Arabic. But in later centuries, when women were considered chattel, were not allowed access to education, were believed to have no souls and not much of a mind, the idea of a female apprentice to Merlin would have been unthinkable. That he would willingly and freely offer to a woman the secrets of his power—the secrets of chakra development— would have been a concept outside the parameters of the medieval mind. Women who did have power were by definition witches and sorceresses whose souls were in pawn to the devil. So while the idea of a female successor to Merlin was absurd, the idea that a woman should succeed in tricking, poisoning or bewitching him was not at all outside the realm of belief.

What is more likely is that Merlin faded from the story when his work was done. His purpose was to create Arthur, to keep him safe, to nurture his mind and spirit and ready him for his great work. Merlin continued to be Arthur's mentor, friend and counselor as he established his kingdom, but by the time of the quest Merlin has disappeared from the pages of myth because it was the Inner Merlin that the questers followed: sixth chakra wisdom and seventh chakra reunion with the universal soul. This part of the spiritual journey is one that has to be taken in solitude. Teachers and mentors can teach by example, but the doorway to mystical experience is not wide enough for two.

Arthur continued to function as king, interacting with armies and administrative leaders as well as with the questers. He continued to occupy the central point of balance of the heart chakra, functioning both in the physical world and in the spiritual by illuminating the way for the questers. Arthur's quest was to create the conditions under which a quest for the Holy Grail could take place: the conditions of physical security, and a context of values embracing principles of justice that would support the inner search for transcendent truth.

The quest for the Holy Grail is the search for enlightenment, and it is an intensely personal journey that each of us undertakes in our own way and in our own time. It is the soul's longing for the spiritual connection that is the ultimate goal of yoga. To look upon the Holy Grail was to look upon the face of God, and it was fatal to look upon the Holy Grail unprepared, just as it is dangerous to raise Kundalini energy prematurely, or to force an opening of the sixth and seventh chakras through the use of drugs before the body and psyche are prepared through consistent and systematic preparation of the lower rungs of the ladder.

This is not to say that the challenges of the lower chakras do not constitute spiritual work. They are lower in the sense that they necessarily come first and are located in the lower half of the body. They are not lower in any other sense, not less important, not less spiritual. In a spiritual tradition that teaches transcendence of the body, rather than integration of body and spirit, there is often the perception that taking care of our physical bodies is somehow antithetical to spiritual growth, and that we should learn to ignore the body and focus our attention on the higher spiritual realms. Many spiritual self-help books and workshops focus exclusively on the upper chakras, and we are perhaps familiar with the phenomenon of spiritual seekers who are "flaky," who cannot get anywhere on time, who are disorganized, disconnected from physical reality and out of touch with their emotional energy. They may say they come from some other place, and that this is not home for them, or that they do not know how to behave, react, or be here.

That this is not home may well be, but it begs the question of why we are here. This is not home for any of us in the ultimate sense. It is our home for the experience of the learning that we have chosen to undertake. Learning how to be comfortable and safe in the physical is part of that learning, as is learning how to integrate emotional energy, how to refine the intellect, and how to develop a strong personal will in order to offer that will to the service of the divine.

Healthy and balanced lower chakras are the necessary foundation for reopening to spirit. The body and mind accommodate to higher vibrational energy as we prepare to reopen to full spiritual awareness by meeting and resolving the challenges presented to us in our daily lives at the various levels of the chakras. It is not safe to spend an hour or so in Kundalini practice or meditation and then go through the day ignoring the signs in the everyday world of the challenges—tests in Holy Grail terminology—to be faced and resolved.

At the other extreme are those of us who are so comfortable in the world that we focus exclusively on sensual pleasure and have no impetus to develop further. The physical world feels so complete and satisfying that the very idea of an unseen, empirically unverifiable spiritual dimension is unnecessary, or even absurd.

It is in the sense of being ready that Galahad was pure and deserving of finding the Holy Grail and Lancelot was not. Lancelot was not "worthy" not because he was stained with the sin of adultery, but because he was not ready. Purity has come to be associated with virginity, or chastity, as we see in the story of Bors. This comes from a lack of appreciation of the spiritual aspect of sexuality and an identification of sex with manipulation and unhealthy sensuality, or the shadow side of the second chakra. Purity in the context of the quest means purity of intention, purity of the heart and the spirit, the purity of focus that can only come when the challenges of the lower chakras have been resolved. Gawain's tests of fire and water are assumed in the legends to be tests of his virginity, just as Bors' vows of chastity were put to the test, but we can interpret that symbolically to mean that if we are focused on the second chakra we are not ready for the sight of the Holy Grail. It is not our literal virginity or chastity that is important, but whether or not we have transcended a second chakra focus.

In the legends, the Holy Grail was many different things besides the well-known cup or chalice. It was a book associated with blinding light, a book perhaps written by Christ. It was a stone fallen from heaven, or a stone that had the power to grant eternal youth. It was a shallow dish. It was a spear, or a sword, or a vase. The specific physical object could take many forms because it was not the object itself that was important. What was and is important is what it symbolized.

The most common depiction of the physical form of the Holy Grail is the cup that has been Christianized as the chalice from the Last Supper, but for many ancient cultures, including the Celtic, a bowl or a chalice was a symbol of the Goddess, of the feminine face of Spirit. A chalice or magical cauldron symbolized the sacred womb of the Goddess. In the Middle Ages, a time of masculine energy triumphant and dominant, it makes sense that the focus of the spiritual quest would be the symbol of the divine feminine, in order to bring the energies into balance. Without acknowledging and honoring the feminine and creating balance within their energy field those well-intentioned Christian knights of the Middle Ages had no hope of attaining enlightenment.

There are ancient Middle Eastern legends suggesting that Jesus was married to Mary Magdalene, and that at the time of the crucifixion she was pregnant. After the crucifixion she escaped with Joseph of Arimathea to Egypt, and then to southern France where a cult of Mary Magdalene still flourishes. Her daughter, the daughter of Jesus, was named Sarah. The term *Holy Grail* was originally written as one word: *Sangraal*. Divided after the "n," it becomes *San Graal*, a holy vessel. Divided after the "g," it becomes *Sang Raal*, or *Sang Real*, which means "royal blood." The vessel therefore could have been Mary herself, and the blood the royal blood of Jesus that she carried in her womb. In that case, the tales of Joseph of Arimathea's having accompanied the vessel containing the blood of Christ would refer to his having accompanied the "vessel" Mary Magdalene, who carried the living blood of Jesus in her womb.

The origins of these legends are explored in Margaret Starbird's *The Woman with the Alabaster Jar: Mary Magdalen and the Holy Grail*. Her work, together with the thesis developed by Michael Bargent, Richard Leigh and Henry Lincoln in *Holy Blood, Holy Grail*, are woven into Dan Brown's *The Da Vinci Code*. Bargent and his colleagues write that early Christian communities were led by both priests and priestesses, and practiced equality and harmony between the sexes. According to *Holy Blood, Holy Grail*, the later church, with a strictly patriarchal structure, deleted all references to the divine feminine from the bible, introduced the slander that Mary Magdalene was a reformed prostitute, and eradicated the descendants of Jesus.

Whether the Holy Grail was a physical object, or the living blood of Jesus, it symbolized the same thing: the yearning for the spiritual connection, for reunion with the divine source, for en-*light*-enment, which is no more than the recognition that the light within and the light without are the same.

Probably the oldest surviving account of Perceval's quest for the Holy Grail, according to Norma Goodrich, comes from a Welsh collection of ancient druidical tales called the *Mabinogion*. Perceval was the seventh son of seven sons. Seven, like twelve, is a mystical number. There are seven days in the week, seven chakras, seven candles on the menorah, seven Roman Catholic sacraments, seven levels on the Kabbalistic tree of life.

The number seven recurs in *The Interior Castle* by St. Teresa of Avila (1515-82), who wrote that there are seven mansions within the soul, and that meditation will lead us safely to the highest mansion in the center of the castle. We could say that the mansions correspond to the seven chakras. We gain access to the mansions through meditation and self-knowledge as we progress through the chakras towards reunion with the divine source at the seventh, or central, mansion.

St Teresa's concept of seven mansions is reminiscent of Mitchell Chefitz' description of the Work of the Chariot in *The Seventh Telling.* The Chariot is based on the vision of Ezekiel in the mystical *merkavah* process of the Kabbalistic tradition. As the seeker descends in meditation through the worlds of Action, Formation, Creation and Emanation, he or she encounters angels guarding the entry to seven succeeding temples, each one presenting a challenge, some memory or experience that has been walled off from consciousness because it was too threatening or too painful to face. As each temple is opened through the process of descent, encounter, reconciliation and transformation, that part of the self that has been locked away is reintegrated into the whole, expanding horizons and creating a transformation within the soul. With each encounter the seeker becomes stronger, more powerful, able to receive and perceive more expansively. The seventh temple leads to an experience similar to Ezekiel's that is given as an act of grace: "It's as if God himself sends out a coach and four to bring you home."

Jungian analysis, or self-exploration with a counselor, psychiatrist, or psychologist at ease with the concept of spiritual awakening can follow a similar pathway.

Whether we follow the model of St Teresa, or the *merkavah,* or the chakra system, or transpersonal psychology, or Psychosynthesis, the process is the same: to clear out the debris in the personal unconscious that stands between the self and the Self, between the individual soul and the universal soul, between separation and oneness. In the Arthurian myth, that process is presented as a series of tests, or initiations, that the questers have to confront.

Like the other components of myth, initiations in various cultures around the world involve similar features: sacrifice, monsters, and physical danger of various kinds. Lancelot crosses a bridge of swords; Gawain walks through fire and water; Perceval duels the Red Knight. When Perceval first arrives at the Grail Castle he does not find the Grail because he does not ask any questions. In other words, he is not ready. He still needs to grow and gain in wisdom before he will be prepared for the sight of the Holy Grail. Perceval becomes wise partly through experience and partly through the guidance of women, or in other words through the balancing of yin and yang energy. When he returns to the Grail Castle a second time he is prepared, and is rewarded.

The quest for the Holy Grail, or the search for the spiritual connection of the seventh chakra, is not a final goal but a process, a way of being in the world. The tests confronted by Perceval and the other Companions symbolize the challenges we all face as we continue our spiritual development. The challenges of the lower chakras, as Caroline Myss explains, have to do with our relationship to power in the outer world: challenges to our sense of safety and our belief that we can provide for our own needs at the first; challenges in relationships both with other people and with money, sex and authority at the second; challenges to the development of healthy self-esteem at the third. The challenges of the upper chakras have to do with our relationship to power on the inner planes: the power of the will, the power of the mind, and the power of the spiritual connection. The lessons are more subtle, and more refined. When are we being compassionate, loving and giving, and when are we being over-compliant and giving away our power? How well do we differentiate between thoughts that come from divinely inspired intuition, and thoughts motivated by fear?

The debate over whether or not the Holy Grail is a chalice or Mary Magdalene's womb focuses attention on the physical substance—a chalice or the DNA of Jesus—rather than on the symbolic meaning of the Holy Grail. In so far as it draws attention to the divine feminine and the need for balance on all levels of being it is a step in the right direction, but it loses sight of the fact that the quest for the Holy Grail symbolizes the search for enlightenment, the process of tempering and purifying each individual soul. That is a journey undertaken soul by soul, in response to specific life circumstances, and has nothing to do with having possession of a physical object or carrying the DNA of Jesus. Jesus did not become a light of the world because he was born of a royal line; the power of his teaching and of his example was not on account of the genetic makeup of his blood but the purity of his soul. If someone were to find the chalice of the Last Supper or the bones of Mary Magdalene they might experience fame or wealth, but not automatic enlightenment.

Alchemy, an ancient science and speculative philosophy known in ancient China, India, Greece and Egypt as "the Art," sought to understand man's relationship to the cosmos and exploit it for his benefit. The goals of alchemy were largely understood in material terms: to transmute base metals into gold, to discover a universal cure for disease, and to unlock the secret of immortality. In China, the quest was primarily for immortality, as if man could conquer his fear of death by conquering death itself. In medieval Europe, the quest was primarily for gold.

We can imagine those scientist/philosophers over the centuries, huddled over their instruments of varying degrees of technological sophistication, heating various concoctions of chemicals and trying in vain to discover the secrets of eternal life and material wealth. In truth, in the symbolic language of the chakras, eternal life is our birthright and the gold is the gold of enlightenment. Through the purifying fire of our life lessons we transform the "base metals" of our physical existence into a vehicle for the gold of our eternal spirit. As we develop the chakras, following the example of King Arthur, our physical, mental and emotional bodies become an instrument for the expression of light and truth. Then we will have found the Holy Grail.

Sixth chakra: Ajna

All that we are arises with our thoughts.
Speak or act with an impure mind
And trouble will follow you
As the wheel follows the ox that draws
the cart.
Speak or act with a pure mind
And happiness will follow you
As your shadow, unshakeable.

Dhammapada

The directive of the sixth chakra is to seek Truth, but there are as many different kinds of truth as there are different kinds of love. There is that which is true for a particular place and time and cultural reality, and there is transcendent truth, that which is true for all time and all places. The moral code of a particular culture—that culture's definition of right and wrong that is a product of its religious traditions, its economic system and its philosophical heritage—is not always the same as transcendent truth.

In fact, they are often very different. Sexual mores, for example, change from culture to culture, yet within a given culture are often perceived as spiritual imperatives. In the western culture any kind of male/female bonding outside marriage is acceptable except the sexual. Some cultures do not permit of any male/female interaction outside marriage while others are accepting of sexual freedom for one or both sexes. Or we can consider alcohol, which is prohibited by Islam but accepted by Christianity. Jesus drank wine. His first miracle, in fact, was changing water into wine at a wedding. Or we can consider telling the truth. "Thou shalt not bear false witness" is taught to us as an absolute, but what if there is a conflict between the literal truth and a higher truth, for example to do no harm?

In his autobiography *Emergency Exit* the Italian writer Ignazio Silone tells how he and his classmates were taken to a puppet show by their priest. When the puppet villain asked the children to tell him which way Punch had gone, with one voice they told him the wrong direction. Later the priest charged them with having told a lie and said they must beg for forgiveness. Silone refused, and had to spend the day on his knees. At the end of the day the priest asked him if he had learned his lesson. "Certainly," the young Silone replied. "If the devil ever asks me for your address I will give it to him."

The priest had not moved beyond the literal truth of the second chakra, the stage of cognitive development that Swiss developmental psychologist Jean Piaget called "concrete operations." The truth of the sixth chakra is more subtle. We recognize here that truth is not black and white, and we develop the skill of discernment. The truth of the sixth chakra can be tricky because it is very easy for us to rationalize what we want to be true. There are those on the spiritual path who constantly use the phrase: "I was led to …" Often no doubt they are being divinely led in a particular direction, and sometimes "being led" towards doing something is really being afraid to do something else.

How do we know when a gut feeling is divine intuition and when it comes from fear? They can feel very similar. It is one of the challenges of the sixth chakra to develop the power of discernment, and to differentiate between fear, superstition and intuition. Many of us receive emails, some even supposedly blessed by the Dalai Lama, that offer spiritual insights and then a warning that if we do not pass them on we will break the energetic link and suffer some dire consequence. But Spirit does not threaten.

To believe in a non-rational reality is not necessarily to be gullible. Spirituality is not anti-intellectual; we honor and respect our intelligence and learning as well as all other aspects of being. We seek to balance within us the archetypes of intellectual and mystic; they are not mutually exclusive. It is as important to develop and discipline the mind, and to use critical thinking skills in evaluating information and experience, as it is to nurture the physical body and to learn to understand the messages encoded in emotional responses. These three—the body, the emotions and the mind—form the stable, safe launching pad for a full reopening to Spirit.

We find the same tripod foundation in the Kabbalistic tradition. The intellect is one of the four worlds of the Kabbalah, the World of Creation; the body corresponds to the World of Action; and the emotions to the World of Formation. These three form the necessary foundation to safely open to Spirit, the World of Emanation. The study of Torah disciplines the mind, just as Hatha Yoga disciplines the body and psychology helps to understand and refine the language of emotion. All these disciplines are the means to the end of reunion with the Source. To pursue Hatha Yoga simply as exercise, or to study Torah as an end in itself, makes of those disciplines the goal itself, rather than the means to the goal of mystical experience.

Within eastern spiritual traditions the sixth chakra is the "third eye," the center of wisdom and intuitive insight. Some of us have tended to confuse or even equate psychic sensitivity with spiritual refinement, but it is wisdom, not psychic power, that is the goal of the sixth chakra, though psychic sensitivity may develop as a side effect. Psychic power is not the same as spiritual development. There are countless books and spiritual workshops that promise to develop psychic power, as if psychic sensitivity were a barometer of enlightenment, but psychic power without the wisdom that comes from spiritual development is dangerous. Intuitive insight is very seductive; it confers great power that if not managed with compassion and respect can feed a runaway ego.

This is part of the reason why in times past this knowledge was shared only with those who had undergone long and rigorous training. Psychic ability can be a by-product of opening the sixth chakra, but it is not the purpose of opening the sixth chakra. It is possible to be psychically sensitive without being spiritually evolved. Some people are born with psychic ability, but they still have to work their way through the developmental challenges of the lower chakras if they are to be balanced and whole and able to use their gifts safely and for the greater good.

We saw in the twentieth century a prime collection of tyrants who tried to harness psychic power: Hitler used the sacred symbol of the swastika which has been forever polluted for many of us; both the KGB and the CIA conducted experiments with psychic energy and none of us believes that their purpose was spiritual development. The energy is neutral; it can be directed for good or ill. And the safe way, for the individual and for society and for the planet, is to pursue spiritual development methodically, following the blueprint of the chakras, or the example of mythical figures such as King Arthur.

The body, the emotions and the mind constantly exchange energy. Each aspect of being influences the others, even though we may not be consciously aware of it. Negative thought patterns create uncomfortable emotions and in time have a detrimental effect on the body. Physical pain can contribute to feelings of depression and to thoughts of resentment. Feelings of depression are often accompanied by physical exhaustion and thoughts of hopelessness. On the other hand when our thoughts are focused on people or situations that bring us happiness, our mood lifts and we feel better physically.

Thought is pure energy. Feelings are denser. The body denser still. When we consciously decide to change some aspect of being, because we know that such a change will bring us closer to the happiness and fulfillment we want, we can choose to focus on any one of them and the change will impact, sooner or later, all other levels. Behavioral therapy intervenes at the densest, physical level. By making a conscious choice to change a certain behavior, with consistency and effort the change will eventually become rooted and will affect not only the behavior but the thoughts and feelings that underlie the behavior. This is approaching change from the first chakra, the physical, and the tools of behavioral therapy are physical: keeping lists, setting goals and identifying the necessary steps to get there, having a schedule. It takes time, and effort, and discipline.

Or the change intervention can be at the second chakra, the emotional level: keeping track of feelings, nurturing the emotional body, keeping a journal, talking about feelings with a friend or therapist, finding ways to allow the emotional energy to flow, seeking to understand the language of emotion and what the deeper levels of the mind are communicating through emotional responses.

Cognitive therapy seeks to overcome difficulties and meet life goals by identifying and changing unhelpful or distorted thinking patterns and beliefs, which then modifies feelings and behaviors.

Yet the power of thought can go way beyond this. Here at the sixth chakra we could command energy to become matter, we could create on the physical level through the power of thought, but the chaos most of us find in our minds when we first try to meditate shows us how much more discipline we need before we will be ready to use the power of thought to create things. We refine the intellect and discipline the mind in order to learn to control our thoughts, to be fully focused as we use the power of our minds to create matter from energy.

Many of us believe, theoretically, that we can heal ourselves with the power of thought, but not many of us can actually do it yet because, Caroline Myss believes, the power of the group belief still dominates in the area of healing. We certainly have the potential to heal ourselves with the power of the mind; I work with hypnosis and imagery and I see miracles all the time. I know that adult survivors of childhood incest can release those painful memories in one session of hypnotherapy because I have seen it happen many times, but for the most part our culture believes that emotional healing takes months or even years of psychotherapy. As long as we continue to believe that, says Myss, we will continue to give the group mind power over our lives instead of exercising personal power, and we will continue to heal at group time. (Of course, insurance companies are trying to change our perceptions of how long it takes to heal, but because they are coming from a second chakra perspective of maximizing profits, rather than a heart chakra perspective of love and compassion, we feel manipulated rather than empowered.)

Before we can use the power of the mind to create—to create healing, or to create physical matter—we have not only to discipline the mind and release old belief patterns, but also to become fully conscious.

We create subconsciously all the time. You have probably had the experience of getting out of bed and, say, stubbing your toe. And you have probably noticed that if you stay in the vibration of irritation over that you continue to attract a succession of experiences throughout the day that make you angrier and angrier. You are, quite literally, attracting experiences that match your vibration of irritation.

You could make a conscious choice to focus your thoughts elsewhere, to rub your toe and then forget about it and enjoy your coffee instead, and look out of the window at the beginning of a perfect day, consciously creating feelings of well-being that will attract experiences to match and subsequently enhance the well-being.

Many of us, though, expend vast amounts of energy justifying our anger, finding all the reasons why we deserve to be angry, and fail to notice that the anger is impacting us negatively on all levels of being. Physically, anger contributes to high blood pressure, headaches, digestive problems, and is the primary risk factor in heart disease. Emotionally anger is uncomfortable, and it has a negative impact on relationships. Mentally, anger keeps our energy locked up so that we cannot focus or concentrate on thoughts of anything else, it intrudes on our attempts to think about other things. Spiritually anger cuts us off from Source Energy.

This is not to say that anger in and of itself is negative. Anger can be the catalyst for positive change. Probably all of our social advances have come about because someone was angry with the status quo. What is damaging is chronic anger, anger that is not used to energize a change in direction but anger that becomes a way of being. All the energy that is locked up in feeling angry is energy lost to positive creative thought, thought that is inspired by the Collective Unconscious, the realm of symbols and archetypes.

At the sixth chakra we recognize that we cannot divide our lives and our reality into neat little compartments. We know better, and once we know it is impossible to return to a state of ignorance. We cannot put the lid back on Pandora's Box or the genie back in the bottle or hide our awareness behind a curtain of ignorance. Just as we know that if we put poison in water and then drink it we will poison ourselves—even if we cannot see it or smell it or if we pretend it is not there—the wisdom of the sixth chakra lets us know that the power of our thought influences our reality. Positive thoughts create the inner peace that we seek, and contribute to a peaceful world. Toxic thoughts have toxic effects, not only on our own physical strength, as we can prove with muscle testing, but also on our world.

It has long been a basic tenet of various systems of justice that we have to take responsibility for our actions. Now, as we approach the threshold of sixth chakra consciousness where we will be able to create through the power of thought, we have to take responsibility for our thoughts as well as our actions. The universal energy field is not fooled by sweet smiles and pleasant observations. It responds to the truth of our thoughts. So if we are smiling sweetly and saying pleasant things but we are thinking: "What a jerk this person is, how boring, how badly dressed," those thoughts have a negative impact not only on our own physical and emotional health but also on the collective energy field.

The sixth chakra, then, is the chakra of wisdom. The challenge here is to learn to trust our internal direction and discriminate between thoughts that are motivated by strength and divine inspiration, and those motivated by fear and illusion. This is where we recognize that creation begins with the energy of thought, not the other way around, and where we can learn consciously to create our own reality, the reality that we want, instead of allowing unconscious creation to attract what we do not want.

A basic tenet of both the Orthodox Jewish tradition and Christian dogma is that Spirit is different from and separate from the material world. Not by any inner quality but only by the grace of God can mankind be forgiven the original sin of Adam and Eve, of disobedience to God, and be saved from our essentially sinful nature. To affirm that Spirit is inherent in nature, according to these teachings, is to affirm that both materiality and divinity emerge from sheer material. It is to sublimate Spirit to materiality.

Why not the other way around? To believe that Spirit is within everything is to affirm that *Spirit* is the first cause, the guiding principle? That Spirit informs, shapes, and gives meaning and purpose to all that is? There are those who believe that this was in fact the message of Jesus, a message that has somehow been lost over the centuries as Christianity developed an orthodox creed that did not encourage direct mystical experience.

And that is not the only distortion. Jesus in his life and his ministry was inclusive; he did not differentiate between classes, creeds and genders. He consorted with prostitutes and tax collectors and gentiles (heathens). His message was one of love, of forgiveness, of acceptance of all beings, regardless of their belief or their lifestyle or their worthiness. However, Christian dogma as it has developed is not inclusive. How did that happen?

There used to be a popular party game where guests sat in a circle and one whispered a short sentence to his or her neighbor. The neighbor passed on what he heard and so on around the circle. The last person would repeat out loud what she heard, and the first would repeat out loud what he had said. Rarely did the two versions match.

If a simple sentence repeated ten or twenty times within a few minutes can become distorted, we can imagine what might happen over several generations of oral transmission, which is what happened with the facts of Jesus' life and the spirit of his teachings. By the time they began to be written down as sacred texts, there were many and often contradictory accounts, as we have learned from the discovery of the Nag Hammadi texts, without even considering the many distortions inherent in multiple translations and errors of copying.

By the beginning of the fourth century several Christian sects were competing over which one had exclusive rights to ultimate truth. At the Council of Nicaea in 325AD the early church fathers examined the various texts and decided which ones would belong in the Bible and which were to be excluded. Constantine had declared Christianity the official religion of the Roman Empire—possibly as a result of a vision of Mary who he believed had led him to victory in a battle, possibly a marriage of convenience that gave the faltering empire a new lease of life and the fledgling church a strong political foundation—and so it came about that the original teachings of equality and unconditional acceptance of and love for all beings became turned on its head. The Church adopted the patriarchal and hierarchical structure of the Roman Empire, a structure that endured after the fall of the Roman Empire in the Holy Roman Empire that lasted for another thousand years and continues today in the Roman Catholic Church and in somewhat diluted form in the Protestant church.

Just how different from one another the early Christian factions were became clear after the discovery of the Nag Hammadi texts in 1945. It was to be many decades before those texts were deciphered and translated and made available, but when they were they told a story of early Christian communities that believed in direct mystical experience. The orthodox church denounced those communities as heretical and destroyed their sacred texts, but some of those texts were buried in earthenware jars in the Egyptian desert and were discovered some sixteen hundred years later.

The Nag Hammadi texts are known as the Gnostic Gospels. "Gnostic" comes from the Greek *gnosis*, or knowledge. But *gnosis*, Elaine Pagels tells us, is not knowledge gathered from facts via the intellect. It is knowledge that comes through direct experience. The meaning is closer to insight. The Gnostics believed that to know the self is to know human nature and human destiny. They did not accept the authority of the orthodox church hierarchy, because they believed that those who had received *gnosis* had gone beyond the church's teaching.

In terms of chakra development, the guidance of religious leaders is helpful, perhaps necessary, at the first, second and third chakras. Then, as we pass through the doorway of the heart and into the inner world, we may find that our subjective experience of the mysteries does not exactly conform to religious teachings. The words of Jesus contained in the Gnostic Gospels indicate that his mission was to open the door of the heart (a mission embraced some five hundred years later by the mythological Arthur of Britain); that he taught that self-knowledge is knowledge of God, and that the self and the divine are identical. The Jesus of the Gnostic Gospels, says Elaine Pagels, "speaks of illusion and enlightenment, not of sin and repentance, like the Jesus of the New Testament. Instead of coming to save us from sin, he comes as a guide who opens access to spiritual understanding. But when the disciple attains enlightenment, Jesus no longer serves as his spiritual master; the two have become equal—even identical." The gnostic *Gospel of Thomas* makes this teaching explicit:

> Jesus said, "I am not your master. Because you have drunk, you have become drunk from the bubbling stream which I have measured out … He who will drink from my mouth will become as I am; I myself shall become he, and the things that are hidden will be revealed to him."

Quoted in Elaine Pagels, *The Gnostic Gospels*

In the same way, Arthur by his example opened the doorway for his Companions to seek the Holy Grail, the opening of the fifth, sixth and seventh chakras.

If we believe that Spirit is transcendent and of a fundamentally different nature from the inner essence of humanity, it is easy and logical to assume that evil too is some kind of outside force rather than inherent in our nature. It gives us a way of not taking responsibility for thoughts, feelings and actions that are contrary to what we want to believe ourselves to be. It is so much easier to say, "The devil made me do it," than to confront the shadow areas within the self that lead to unacceptable thoughts, feelings or behaviors.

So while the idea of demons or Satan is an acceptable explanation for the existence of evil when the focus of development is on the lower chakras, at the higher chakras, John Nelson explains, "Satan" is viewed as an undeveloped and unevolved part of the self that resists higher strivings, an inner negativity that must be acknowledged and overcome through self-knowledge.

Carl Jung too believed that the duality is within us, not only masculine and feminine energy, but also light and shadow. In shadow are the repressed aspects of our consciousness, and we can choose to bring them forth into the light of day, or the light of reason, or the light of spiritual development. We can choose to empower the "shadow" aspects that are undeveloped aspects of ourselves— masculine or feminine, extrovert or introvert, intuitive or sensate, thinker or feeler, judge or perceiver—in order to create balance and emotional health. When it comes to "shadows" of developmental wounds, those repressed toxic memories of hurt, we can defuse their power over us by facing them with courage and honesty, and by learning what they need in order to heal.

"Speaking" to the undeveloped or wounded parts of ourselves is much like speaking to children who are behaving in unacceptable ways. Imagine a child who is acting out at school, disrupting classes, bullying his fellow students. The disciplinary tools of the past—punishment, exclusion, ridicule, shame—did not create any fundamental change in a positive direction; in all probability they made matters worse most of the time. On the other hand, a teacher or friend or school counselor who takes the time to look beyond the disruptive behavior may find that the child is being molested or beaten at home, or that he is being neglected or abandoned, and that his behavior is only a misguided attempt to be noticed; that his disruptive behavior is the universal cry of the heart for love, expressed in dysfunctional ways. If that concerned outsider finds ways to satisfy the child's need for love, there will no longer be any need for acting out behaviors and the child will be freed to express his inner light instead of his inner shadows.

We can be that concerned teacher for our own inner children, the parts of the psyche stuck in the pain of past trauma. We can "talk" lovingly and kindly to images of those parts of ourselves, learn what they need and find appropriate ways of satisfying those needs.

If that child acting out in school does not receive any help, the inner conflict will be repressed, the causes perhaps even forgotten by the conscious mind, but they will continue to influence thoughts, feelings and behaviors. He may find in his adult years that he can't keep a job, has no friends, doesn't know how to relate to women and is unable to create a stable relationship. Possibly he may continue, for the rest of his life, to act as if he doesn't care, or perhaps the yawning void in his soul will at some point demand a better solution, want to stop the merry-go-round, want to stop blaming the world for everything wrong in his life and wonder what he can do to change direction. He can learn how to heal the wounded inner child who has continued to direct his life. It is by bringing light into our places of darkness that we grow, that we reach towards enlightenment and self-realization, towards the ultimate that we are capable of being.

Meditation to heal the inner wounded child

Bring to mind a behavior, or a reaction, or a feeling, that manifests itself in your life and that is uncomfortable, or detrimental to your happiness, or your ability to form stable relationships, or perhaps to hold a job. Perhaps you find yourself thinking such things as: "Why do I do that? I know better." Or even "when I react that way it doesn't even feel like me, I don't recognize myself." Perhaps there is an area of your life that seems out of synch with the rest of it. Allow yourself to remember at least three occasions when that has happened to you, and simply observe the behavior, or the feeling, or the thoughts, without judgment.

Fill and surround yourself with the Triple Shield of Light, and invoke an image that symbolizes for you love, compassion and wisdom: a spiritual teacher, a guardian angel, a beloved ancestor. It could be Merlin, or the Lady of the Lake, or some other archetypal image from the Arthurian myth. Or perhaps an animal that represents those qualities for you.

With that image beside you, imagine that you are walking along a path, perhaps through a forest, or through the countryside, or along the beach. And imagine that the path is the Pathway of Time, and you with your Inner Guide are walking back through the events of your life, searching for the part of yourself that drives the behaviors, thoughts or feelings that you identified before you began this journey.

As you pass by the events of your life perhaps you will recognize people or events that you would like to investigate further, but they are not your destination today; you can consider them at some later time if you so choose. Right now, your focus is on finding an image of the part of yourself, some younger part of you, that reacts in dysfunctional ways, that perhaps becomes angry or afraid for no understandable reason, or is unable to trust.

It may be that this first time it is enough to establish the Triple Shield, invoke your Inner Guide and begin the journey along the Pathway of Time. If that is the case, be patient and gentle with yourself.

The Pathway of Time will always be there when you choose to do this again.

At some point in this journey you will find an image of a younger part of yourself, and you will know that somehow or other this part of yourself holds the key to that dysfunctional response. You can talk to the image, reassure the child or teenager or young adult that you come in love, that you want to hear whatever they choose to tell you, or ask of you. Sometimes the child will be reassured by your words and will tell you what he or she needs in order to heal and to be reintegrated into the whole; and sometimes if the child suffered serious trauma you may choose to work with a therapist or minister to bring healing. It may be that this image of yourself has been neglected for a long time, perhaps even forgotten completely at the conscious level, and it may take some time for the image to trust you. Continue to be loving, accepting, and patient. The image will speak when it feels safe to do so.

It may take several journeys back in time to complete this process. Whatever you learn, each time you communicate with this forgotten part of yourself, must be integrated into your daily life as you find opportunities to put into practice whatever the image has shared with you.

When you are ready, return with your Inner Guide along the Pathway of Time, gently returning your consciousness to present time and place, and when you reach the place where you began open your eyes. Record your experiences in your Quest Journal.

The truth that we seek at the sixth chakra is a different kind of truth from that which can be empirically proven. Empirical truth tells us to trust the evidence of our senses. When an experiment can be repeated over and over again and always leads to the same result we say that an hypothesis is proven. Yet every scientist knows that it is proven, it is truth, only as long as new evidence is not uncovered that proves something different.

The history of science is the unfolding story of countless examples of an accepted "truth" that was later proven to be untrue or incomplete. Empirical evidence seemed to indicate that the earth was flat and for thousands of years we believed it was so. Those intrepid adventurers who ventured beyond the known limits of the world and failed to return were supposed to have fallen off the edge. The notion that the earth was round, and that if you journeyed long enough in any direction you would return to where you started, was a revolutionary concept that defied the evidence of our senses.

Visual evidence likewise indicated that the sun rotated around the earth. Every morning the sun rose in the east, traveled across the sky, and set in the west. It was believed that some divine hand made that happen, and that without the intervention of that beneficent supernatural being the sun would not rise. We believed that we had to propitiate the god, offer sacrifices to keep him or her happy so that he would continue to make the sun rise, or she would continue to make the rain fall. Over time we gathered more information, we developed more sophisticated watching devices, and we discovered that contrary to common sense and the evidence of our eyes it was indeed the other way around and our world rotated around the sun.

Through scientific exploration we search for the truth of our world, of its myriad life forms, and of the physical laws that govern our universe. Sixth chakra truth is metaphysical, and the instruments of science do not serve us here. We are not seeking the truth out there in the world, but the truth within, the inner and transcendent truth. By going deeply within and seeking the fundamental truth of who we are, we trust we can ultimately dissolve all boundaries and discover the truth of all that is.

In our quest for self-understanding it is after the opening of the heart chakra that we meet subtler challenges to our sense of self. It is no longer the approval of others that we seek but the deep knowing of who we really are. At the first, second or even third chakras we may follow right action through fear of punishment or social censure, and give little attention to thinking right thoughts or feeling right feelings. At the upper chakras we seek right action, thoughts and feelings because that is the contribution we choose to make to the flow of Source Energy, regardless of whether anyone else knows about it.

Evidence of a deficient sixth chakra will be thought and belief that there is only one true right way. Accepting that there are many right ways is a challenge to our natural tendency to think in polarities that has been the root of all our wars about religion. If I know that my way is right, and your way is different from mine, then you must be wrong. Because if you are not wrong then I must be, and I know I am not. Ergo you are wrong and if you don't admit it I'm going to cut your head off, or burn you at the stake, or drown you. A healthy sixth chakra can accept the truth in paradox, both/and rather than either/or. We may all be going to the same place but there are many different ways of getting there, and they are all right.

Or deficiency may manifest in a lack of imagination. When we shut down the sixth chakra we find it difficult to visualize or imagine alternatives. We do not remember dreams and have poor memories generally. Physically we may have poor vision, or headaches. Emotionally we tend to be in denial and not "see" what is going on.

Excess energy at the sixth chakra can manifest in hallucinations, obsessions or delusions, nightmares or difficulty concentrating.

A healthy and balanced sixth chakra is intuitive, perceptive and imaginative. The memory is dependable, and there is an ability to remember and interpret the inner wisdom that is communicated through dreams and reveries. We are able to think symbolically, and fully use the power of the imagination and the language of symbol and imagery.

> [T]he serious part of prayer begins when we have got
> our begging over with and listen for the Voice of what
> I would call the Holy Spirit, though if others prefer to
> say the Voice of Oz, or the Dreamer or Conscience, I
> shan't quarrel, so long as they don't call it the Voice of
> the Super-Ego, for that 'entity' can only tell us what we

> *know already, whereas the Voice I am talking about*
> *always says something new and unpredictable—an*
> *unexpected demand, obedience to which involves a*
> *change of self, however painful.*

W. H. Auden

We can empower the sixth chakra by learning to listen to the inner voice. We listen, and evaluate it, and act upon it when we decide it is true. One of the ways we can evaluate the source of a "gut feeling" is to consider whether it inspires fear. The inner voice does not operate on fear; its messages may be challenging but they are empowering and uplifting.

There are many peripheral challenges that accompany a sixth chakra focus. Acting upon the inner voice can create conflict with those in our environment who are used to having us think and behave in conventional ways, or who want us to think and behave in conventional ways. The sixth chakra demands a high degree of courage and conviction.

There was once a young man who lived in the Italian hill town of Assisi. His father was a successful cloth merchant who expected his son to follow in his footsteps, but the son's inner voice told him otherwise. The father tried to coerce him by hauling him before the civil authorities and the bishop and threatening him with destitution. The son's response was to take off his clothes and hand them to his father. Clad only in his breeches he walked out of the hall and into his destiny.

Not many of us are called upon to make such a radical statement as St Francis, but we may well suffer ridicule, or pressure to conform, or perhaps ostracism. It is part of the sixth chakra challenge to stay true to our beliefs and at the same time open to new information and alternative ways of being; to hold strong convictions but renounce judgment.

Many of the Companions' adventures in their quest for the Holy Grail are uncomplicated stories of battles against cruelty and evil, while others, such as Gawain and the Green Knight, seem at first sight to be like the dangerous games of adolescents, risking life and limb for no good reason. When we look beneath the surface of the stories we see it is not the beasts, sorcerers, enchantments and evil knights that the Companions are combating so much as the shadow places within themselves. When victorious they emerge not boastful and obnoxious, but chastened and more wise.

Gawain and the Green Knight

It was the Midwinter Solstice. At dawn they had gathered within the sacred circle of standing stones to watch as the sun rose and cast its light on the symbols of the altar stone, symbols that reminded them of the eternal circle of life and of the seasons. They had welcomed the Mabon, the Child of Light, the youngest member of the community who this year was the child of Gareth and Lionors whose clear childish voice vibrating throughout the circle had reminded them of their promise to the children of the world and to the future: to protect the earth. Merlin had used his sacred golden sickle to gather sprigs of the mistleberry, symbol of life in the moment, from its place of growth on the Oak of Eternity, and had asked the child to distribute them to all those gathered in the circle. Merlin's beautiful bard's voice had rung out strongly as he raised his arms in blessing: "Let the Mabon, our seed and our hope for the future, bear this blessing to each of us. May the Child of Light be reborn forever!"

And now it was evening and they were gathered in the great hall for feasting and celebration. Great platters of food had already disappeared along with quantities of wine, and it was time for the Companions to tell the stories of their adventures during the past year. But before they could choose the first storyteller there was a commotion at the door and an enormous knight strode into the hall. He was bigger than any mortal man, *but the strangest thing about him was that he was bright green. Not only his clothes, but his skin and hair and beard were all green, and he carried a massive battle-axe with a green steel blade more than a yard wide.*

In spite of his rude entrance King Arthur greeted him courteously and invited him to join the feast. The Green Knight refused. He had not come to dine, he scoffed, but to offer sport to the Companions who were supposed to be the bravest and the best. He challenged any one of them to be brave enough to exchange one blow for another. He would receive the first blow and would then have the right to strike a blow in return.

Gawain jumped to his feet and begged the King's permission to accept the challenge. The Green Knight gave Gawain his ax and bowed his head, and Gawain severed his head with a mighty blow. It fell to the ground and rolled away, but the knight did not fall. He strode over to his head and picked it up, and from under his arm the head cried to Gawain: "See to it that you keep your promise! You have one year to find your way to the Green Chapel and make good your pledge to receive a blow just like the one you have given me, as you have sworn to do in the hearing of everyone here!"

The Green Knight strode out of the hall and all thought of celebration left with him. The following day Gawain took his leave of the king and his Companions—he did not expect to see them again—and set forth in search of the Green Knight. It was a painful and difficult journey. In the cold of winter he slept in his armor and almost froze to death; he had to fight dragons, wild men, wolves, bulls and boars and great shaggy bears, even giants. At length, just a few days before the winter solstice, he came to a castle, and asked the lord of the castle if he knew of the Green Chapel.

"Indeed!" cried the lord, "It is only two miles away. Stay you and celebrate the solstice with us, and then you can keep your appointment."

Gawain was happy to agree, and to accept the hospitality of the lord and his lady. The lord suggested that he rest on the morrow, and offered the company of his wife to entertain him while the lord himself went hunting. "Let us make a bargain," he said, "to tell each other in the evening whatever we have won during the day." Gawain agreed.

The next morning the lord of the castle was up early and off with his huntsmen, horses and hounds, while Gawain dozed in his comfortable bed enclosed in curtains. Suddenly, to his great surprise, the lady of the castle pulled the curtain aside and sat down on the bed. She showered him with compliments and told him that she was commanded to please him in any way that he desired, and furthermore that she intended to enjoy herself in the process. Her meaning was very clear, and it took all Gawain's ingenuity both to avoid offending her and to keep his promise to her husband to tell him about his day's winnings.

On succeeding days the lady grew ever more bold, but Gawain managed to keep true to his word and to his sworn duty as a Companion of the King. But on the third day, after having cleverly parried all the lady's declarations of affection, Gawain did accept her gift of a green silk girdle that had the special power to protect the life of the one wearing it. He was to meet the Green Knight on the following day, and with the protection of the girdle he was able to believe, for the first time in a year, that he might escape the encounter with his life. However, when the lady begged him to conceal the gift from her husband, Gawain agreed.

The next day Gawain rode out in search of the Green Chapel. Following the lord's directions he came to a mound beside a stream, overgrown with clumps of grass, with a cave running through it. It was a bleak and ugly place.

"Where is the master of this place?" he cried. "Gawain has arrived to keep his assignation!"

From behind him appeared the Green Knight, brandishing his huge axe with a newly-honed blade. He welcomed Gawain and praised him for keeping his promise.

"And now get that helmet off your head and take your just desserts. Offer me no more argument than I gave you when you sliced off my head with a single blow."

Gawain stood ready to receive the blow, but at the last moment he shrank a little from the sharp edge. The Green Knight checked the blade and taunted him with flinching before he felt any hurt, reminding him that he had not flinched when Gawain had struck him. Gawain told him to proceed and that he would flinch no more, and also reminded him that if his head fell to the floor he would not be able to restore it to his shoulders.

The Green Knight struck again, and this time Gawain did not flinch, and again the Green Knight checked his blade. He laughed and struck again, this time nicking Gawain's neck and drawing a drop of blood. And then he laughed again. He told Gawain that he was in fact the lord of the castle, and he knew all about his wife's attempted seduction for he had himself devised it as a test. And Gawain had passed with flying colors except for failing a little in loyalty in keeping the gift of the green girdle secret in violation of his agreement with the lord. "And for this I gave you the small wound."

Gawain was mortified. He took off the girdle and flung it at the Green Knight, crying that he was false and forsworn. In future he would sin less, he declared. "But but for now tell me what is your will." The Green Knight only laughed and told Gawain that he had been amply repaid by Gawain's confession and his penance, and he made him a present of the green girdle as a token of his adventure at the Green Chapel.

Upon his return to court Gawain told King Arthur and his Companions everything that had happened. He wore the green girdle across his shoulder as a reminder of his cowardice and untruth, but the king comforted him, and the Companions agreed that they would all wear a green baldrick over their breasts. Ever afterwards to wear such a badge was a sign of great honor.

The story of Gawain and the Green Knight is the story of a good and honest man striving to live by the standards he has set himself in following the example of his king. He confronts within himself the temptation to be false to those values; he is humbled by his weakness and emerges the stronger for it. The many adventures experienced by the Companions suggest the manifold ways in which the soul is honed and tempered in its journey towards reunion with the Source. Many of the trials of the Grail seekers are terrifying, and agonizing. Holding on to faith is everything and it is tested to the limit.

Many of us, trained by two thousand years of conditioning, believe that if we are to follow truth, light, love, honor, that we must also suffer. For many, suffering is an integral and necessary part of spiritual development. We have been taught that to be Christ-like we must suffer as Christ suffered.

But what if we have got it backwards? What if Christ suffered for us so that we do not need to suffer; that he freed us to focus on the joy of resurrection and never intended that we feel guilty about his suffering; that his sacrifice was a gift, freely given, in a time when belief in sacrifice was an integral part of religious observance? The focus on the torture and execution of Jesus and the martyrdom of countless early Christians during the Roman persecution has eclipsed the message of joy. Western religious art has tended to pay much more attention to suffering than to joy, yet mystical experiences from the Buddha to Teresa of Avila are described in terms of joy. The Dalai Lama teaches that the purpose of life is joy.

Galahad looked upon the Holy Grail and passed over to the next dimension in ecstasy. Bors chose to bring the message back home. Jesus offered his life in atonement for the sins of humanity. Siddhartha Gautama sat under a Bodhi tree and vowed never to arise until he had found the truth. When he did, he became known as the Buddha, The Enlightened One, and instead of passing over in ecstasy chose to stay and teach those of us who came after him.

It is a choice: spirituality as sacrifice; spirituality as selfless service; spirituality as the expression of joy.

PART V

The Fall of Camelot

What are we to make of the destruction of Arthur's dream? Of the images of the king alone and despairing in his castle? Of the Companions murdered, their disemboweled and limbless corpses hanging from blasted trees in a wasted landscape? Of Merlin, helpless and imprisoned? Of the Grail, symbol of light and hope, disappearing like Avalon into the impenetrable mists?

The challenges of the lower chakras are relatively simple and straightforward, if not always easy. To survive. To create stable and loving relationships. To earn a sense of self-respect. Though opening the heart can feel risky it is at least a simple concept.

The challenges of the upper chakras are subtle, and it is here that in times past we have fallen back on the explanation of some evil force that is bent on our destruction. There was little room for subtleties in a spiritual and religious heritage that simplistically labeled all human experiences either good or evil, and perceived forces of light and forces of darkness engaged in an eternal struggle for the human soul. Within the parameters of such a world-view there could have been no other explanation for the failure of Camelot than some evil force loosed upon Arthur's Britain.

And, of course, like the evil force responsible for the expulsion from the Garden of Eden, it is female. It takes the form of a wicked

227

sorceress, drunk with power, feasting on despair. She commands foul dragons and other grotesque and evil-smelling beasts, created by her and dedicated to her will. She battles Merlin, and bests him. The fruit of her incestuous coupling with the unsuspecting Arthur is the instrument of his destruction. The forces of darkness win. Legend confronts historical fact. The bright flame that was the ideal of Arthur's reign was snuffed out and Britain suffered dark centuries of invasion, plunder and destruction.

In a black and white world, Arthur could have failed only because of some failing within him. He committed incest. Or we see him accused of pride. And yet, the hope persisted. Books were destroyed in the barbarian orgy but the stories lived on, whispered to children over the dying embers. Carried over generations they were a reminder of glories past and—the hope refused to die—of glories yet to come.

Rex Quondam, Rexque Futurus. For Arthur was the once *and future* king. He became the symbol of Welsh resistance to the Norman conqueror, and was then usurped by the descendants of that very conqueror to become the defining myth of England. The myth was adapted and distorted, molded and crafted to suit the needs of succeeding ages, and of tyrants and narrow-minded churchmen. Side by side, some versions of the stories are so different they are hardly recognizable, and yet the core elements are always there. Arthur: strong, charismatic, a brilliant leader, an inspiration to his followers by the light of his character as much as by the might of his sword in an age when the sword's might was usually the only valid criterion; a just king, in an age when justice was perhaps the last thing to be expected of a ruler; a king who loved and honored his queen, no matter what; a king who inspired his followers to reach for the best in themselves, who honored their free will instead of insisting upon mindless obedience; a king whose reign was guided by the belief in and the search for the spiritual connection.

We can imagine a child, in a windowless hovel choked with smoke, listening to the stories by the hearth on a long winter evening. His life is circumscribed by want, relentless misery and injustice. He hears about a golden age: a strong and compassionate king; the wise Merlin; the brave Companions; stories of battles won over overwhelming odds; the cleverness, training, artistry and resourcefulness of the incomparable King Arthur, and saying finally: "Why? What happened? What went wrong?" And what is a beleaguered parent to do but resort to forces of evil, a sorceress, winds of darkness?

If we accept that explanation, in whatever sophisticated guise it is offered, we are accepting that the forces of darkness have more power than Light. And that cannot be.

Mordred

The great hall at Camelot. Long tables laden with food, rush lights in wall sconces, candles on the table casting flattering shadows over the women, noise and laughter all around. King Arthur and his queen, in the company of the king's Companions and their families, were basking in the relaxed ambience of leisure that was the gift of peace.

And beside the king, Mordred.

Mordred gazed around him, holding himself apart from the energy that swirled around the room, the camaraderie and shared history here, the bonds of love that created a cocoon enveloping everyone but him. He was at Camelot, he was sitting at the right hand of the king, yet he was tense and alert. Could not the eddies of fate that had swept him here just as easily and just as unpredictably sweep him away? He watched the laughing faces, some of them turned his way with raised goblets. He nodded in acknowledgment but did not trust in the apparent goodwill, and he kept himself sober as all those around him surrendered to an alcoholic miasma. At length the king and queen left the hall, walking more or less steadily, and the others followed, each one coupled and already groping, until Mordred was left alone.

229

He too left the hall that was by now littered with debris and servants sleeping where they fell and walked to the room he shared with his foster brothers, but the air was close and the amorous noises overpowering. He went outside and walked the battlements, taking in deep breaths of night air. The moon was full and the silver light bathed his surroundings. Camelot glowed, as if it were indeed some magical land blessed by God.

Mordred thought of King Lot's castle in the Orkneys. He had thought it grand, having no measure of comparison, as it rose out of the living rock to dominate the landscape. He had spent his whole life there, dreaming of the world beyond its borders, dreaming in vain he had thought, because he believed he could not expect the life of a warrior that awaited his foster brothers. He had no name, no recognition. His mother was a priestess of Avalon, sworn to the goddess, and had given him to her sister to raise: Queen Morgause. Her four sons were his foster brothers. He had trained with them, hunted with them, fished with them, slept with them. But he was not one of them. They were legitimate princes and he ... he was their bastard cousin.

And now he was here, invited by the king to come and live at court like his foster brothers, to train and to become—one day, if he was worthy—one of the king's Companions. The king who was generous and kind to everyone had decided to be especially kind to the son of his half-sister Morgan. But why now? And for how long? Mordred, against all expectation, suddenly had his every desire fulfilled. The Orkneys were as far from Camelot as they could be and still be within the land of Britain, but he discovered as he breathed the night air of Camelot that he missed the smell of the sea.

Something big, perhaps terrible, was going on. Pages ran thither and yon, summoning important people to the king's presence. Mordred watched, wondering as always if there would be some consequence for him. All morning the rumors flew and then, as the sun reached its zenith, one of the pages came for him.

Mordred hid his anxieties and schooled his face to impassivity as he entered the king's chamber. He noted the details of the tableau in front of him: King Arthur, holding himself still and straight but with anger lighting his eyes; Queen Guinevere, shock and dismay disfiguring the perfect lines of her face; his foster mother Queen Morgause, looking as if she were enjoying the discomfort of the others, her hands folded placidly in her lap and her mouth curved in a mysterious smile.

And a woman he had not seen before but whom he knew instantly. She bore the mark of a priestess on her brow and wore a simple blue robe, and she radiated a power that stopped Mordred cold as if he had run into an invisible wall. Their eyes met in mutual appraisal: years, a lifetime on his part, of questions and wonderings, hopes and desires, resentments and guilt hovered in the air between them. But she was priestess-trained and he could not read her thoughts or feelings as she looked on the son she had not seen since his birth.

She turned to the King. "By your leave, Arthur, I would speak with my son alone."

King Arthur nodded and she led Mordred outside. They walked together across the courtyard and through the massive oak gates, down the steep hill to a small stream. She sat on a fallen log and invited Mordred to sit beside her. She was silent for a long time, as if there were so much to say she did not know where to begin, but at length she began to speak. As the sun made its way across the sky Mordred listened in silence as she told him of his conception during the early days of the Saxon wars, of her decision to give him to her sister to raise, of all the years when she had followed his progress in the sacred pool, believing he was better off not knowing her.

And as the sun began to set and the sky glowed scarlet and gold she came to the heart of her story: the identity of his father. But Mordred realized that he had known it long before the words were formed, as the pieces of his life at last fit together.

"So that is why he brought me to Camelot."

Morgan had been speaking softly, looking into the stream. At his words she seemed to awaken from a trance and turned to look into his face.

"No, Mordred. He brought you to Camelot because he is a wise and generous man. He offered you the same opportunity he offered to your cousins, Gawain and his brothers. He did not know until today that he was your father."

"Why not?"

"I never told him. I would never have told him. Arthur is my half-brother. When we lay together we did not know each other, we sinned in innocence, but sin it was nonetheless. There are those who would have used it against him. I could not allow that to happen."

"And now?"

"And now Arthur knows because Morgause told him. She thought she could use the knowledge to further her own power. And because he knows, you deserved to know." She took his face between her hands and looked into his eyes. "But others must not. You must promise me, Mordred." Her eyes at last filled with tears. "Believe me, my son; I know how unjust this is. You are a son any man would be proud of, but we live in an imperfect world. We have to accept things the way they are."

Mordred could not summon his voice to answer her. He kept his churning emotions to himself as they walked back up the hill to Camelot and he met King Arthur for the first time, not as his sovereign and benefactor, but as his father. He could see that Arthur too was containing his emotions only by a great effort of will, and he felt the currents of energy between them shift as each of them adjusted to this new awareness. Yet outwardly, they both knew, there could be no change.

In time, the awkwardness they both felt began to ease. As they stood side by side on the battlements watching the sun set Arthur tentatively rested his hand on his son's shoulder:

"I know what it is to grow up a bastard, Mordred. But even though I didn't know who my parents were I had foster parents who loved me and treated me as their own. And I had Merlin. But for you, there was only Morgause. I should respect her as the mother of four of my warriors but ... god's truth, Mordred, she's not an easy person to love! In all honesty she makes my flesh crawl." He drew in his breath sharply.

"Forgive me, lad. She's the only mother you've known. If I've wounded you I ask your pardon."

"Indeed not. She dazzles her sons, or used to. She kept them all dancing to her tune, competing for her attention. But I felt always her eyes on me, green and sly, and I knew somehow that she was only superficially kind because she thought she could use me in some way. Back then, those feelings made no sense to me. I thought I was no one, and I could not imagine what use I could be to her."

"You were right, though. She thought to use you to have power over me." The king fell quiet, looking out over the countryside. When he turned back to face Mordred his voice was low and serious.

"I count myself the most blessed of men that your heart is true, Mordred. You are a son to be proud of lad, and I wish with all my heart that I could shout from the battlements that here is my son. But you know as well as I that that cannot be. But I want you at my side; I want you to learn."

He touched Mordred's shoulder in farewell and smiled. Mordred's returning smile faded as soon as Arthur turned away.

Mordred maintained the fiction that he was no more than the king's nephew. Arthur treated him with all honor, and in spite of himself Mordred was drawn to the king's warmth and charisma. He could well believe the stories of battle that were told and retold during the evening hours. Men talked of Arthur as of some being greater than life, riding his white stallion into the thick of combat, controlling the beast with his thighs while leaving his hands free to wield sword and shield. At the Battle of Badon Hill, they said, he had slain nine hundred and sixty Saxons single-handed. The sun seemed to seek him out, reflecting off the blade of Excalibur and the white shield, back-lighting the black hair haloed around the leather helmet. He needed no banner to signal his presence. It was as if he were six feet taller, or somehow hovering above the ground, clearly visible to his men and evoking the best in them. In Arthur's presence they were more courageous, more dedicated, more confident of victory.

The young warriors drank in the glorious battle stories of the past, while the older generation and the young mothers gave their love unreservedly to the King Arthur they knew in the here and now, the king who had created peace and safety, who dispensed justice with an even hand, who recognized even the humblest contribution. For them, the sun rose and set on their beloved king, he was the very spirit of the land, and they revered him with a devotion close to worship.

Mordred, too, felt that quality in Arthur, and was irresistibly drawn to it. But at the same time there was a part of him that hated Arthur, that resented the secrecy, most of all resented the unspoken awareness that if Guinevere even now were to bear Arthur a legitimate son Mordred's legacy would be lost and he would be cast once more into the limbo of the unrecognized.

The barge deposited Mordred on the shore of Avalon where Morgan awaited him.

"Welcome to Avalon, Mordred. I had hoped you would come.'

"Indeed. I thought it was time to see where you live, and what goes on here."

Morgan ignored both his flippancy and the anxiety it was hiding and led him to her dwelling where they shared a breakfast of fresh fish, bread, fruit and water. Mordred ate in silence, stealing surreptitious glances at Morgan from time to time as she ate calmly, as if unaware of the underlying tension. Later she led him around the orchards and along the lake shore, pointed out the House of Maidens and the Druid Center, and at last led him up the processional way to the circle of standing stones on top of the tor.

"Here is the most sacred spot in all of Britain. It is at the intersection of two lines of power. The ceremonies we hold here are offerings to the Goddess for the safety and prosperity of Britain. Look, you can see Camelot from here, and the sea far over that way."

The stone circles of the ancient ones were familiar to Mordred—there were many of them in the Orkneys—but as he entered this circle he felt something he had never felt before. He turned away from

Morgan and slowly walked around the perimeter until he could bring his emotions under control, then walked over to where she waited in front of the altar stone.

"When I came here I was angry. I wanted to be angry: with you for abandoning me to Morgause; and with my ... my father for not telling the world who I am. But here ... here it is not possible to be angry."

Morgan nodded. "I can only beg your forgiveness for entrusting you to Morgause. I felt I had little choice at the time. And at the very least there you found training in the warrior arts which I could not have offered you."

"True. My training is my vocation and has been ... my salvation. And yet ... and yet there is such peace here."

"Are you thinking of following the call of spirit, my son? Is the warrior life perhaps not the one for you?"

Mordred laughed. "Oh no, m ... mother. Mother." He repeated it as if trying out the sound on his tongue. "No. I am a warrior. And I will be a good leader, I can feel it. I always did, even when I believed I was an unnamed bastard and that leadership would always be denied me. But now ... now that I know who I am ..."

"I am sorry, Mordred. Arthur cannot acknowledge you his heir; that has not changed."

"No. I don't suppose it has." His voice had a dreamlike tone, and he was looking beyond her, at the altar stone. Then he looked directly into her face: "But I should like to visit this place from time to time."

As for Guinevere, she lavished on Mordred all her unrequited maternal love. It was clear to the whole court that he was her favorite, and that he had taken the place of the son she had never borne. But Mordred's love for Guinevere was not of the filial kind. He thought her the most beautiful woman he had ever seen, even though the beauty of his foster mother—his aunt, Queen Morgause—was legendary and made her seemingly irresistible. Mordred, perhaps, had been the only one at the court of King Lot to see beyond her beauty to the darkness within. She could bewitch her sons, as well as her legions of lovers, with a smile, or a caress, that wiped their memories clean of her fickleness and cruelty. But Mordred's flesh crawled at her touch, and her languid heavy-lidded smile made him want to run and hide, or scrub his flesh clean.

Queen Guinevere's beauty was pure, and Mordred offered her his uncomplicated devotion. He followed her everywhere, abandoning the company of warriors in training to tag along with the queen's guardians as she took her morning ride, lurking in the corners hoping for a breath of her perfume as she walked in the gardens, drinking in the sight of her at table. His passion for Guinevere gnawed at his entrails, made him toss restlessly at night and drove him from his bed to pace the battlements. And it fed his sense of grievance and injustice. It was not enough that Arthur was beloved of the whole kingdom; he also had Guinevere.

But not exclusively. Mordred was a watcher, and he had something of the Sight bequeathed by his mother. He saw the deep love that Guinevere felt for Arthur, and he also felt the passionate energy that bound her to Lancelot, even though their behavior was at all times above reproach. And he savored his secret knowledge against the day when he could put it to use.

Morgause seemed to materialize out of thin air at Mordred's side as he stood gazing out over the ramparts. He did not acknowledge her arrival.

"I have seen little of you since we came to Camelot, Mordred. And look how you are grown! A man indeed. It is time for us to talk about our plans."

"Our *plans, madam?*"

"Yes, Mordred. Our plans. The plans I have been nurturing since the moment Morgan entrusted you to me." She put her hands on his shoulders and turned him to face her. "The plan for you to rule at my side as king of Camelot."

Mordred looked at her in disbelief, then laughed harshly and shrugged her hands off his shoulders. "You are mad, madam." He turned and began to walk away but she grabbed his arm.

"*All these years I have waited, Mordred. I loved you; I took care of you. Arthur was not there, no nor Morgan either, to care for you as I did. You owe me.*"

Mordred shook her hand loose with a savage gesture. "*I owe you nothing! Your 'care' of me was nothing more than the protection of your investment! Do not talk to me of love; you know not what it means. My father loves me. I am always at his side ...*"

"*Loves you? You are a fool, Mordred. Does he admit that you are his son? Does he declare to the world who you really are?*"

"*You know why he cannot.*"

"*Oh aye, the scandal of it! Are you sure, Mordred, that that is the only reason? Does he not perhaps favor Galahad? He has chosen him his heir, has he not, over both you and my sons, who are his nephews and of his blood.*"

"*Only until I am initiated.*"

"*I repeat, you are a fool. If you do not seize your destiny, Mordred, it will escape you. And you are nothing without me. I molded you, I crafted you, you are mine Mordred. Mine!*" *She grasped his shoulders.* "*You and I together, we can rule this land ...*"

Mordred grabbed her hands off his shoulders and held them in an iron grip. He brought his face close to hers and all but growled:

"*Should I ever become king, you can be sure I will have you nowhere near me.*" *He pushed her away from him; she stumbled and fell against the parapet, grazing her forehead, and Mordred turned his back and strode away.*

Like Arthur, Mordred was raised a foster child, and ignorant of his royal blood. Though he lived exactly as his foster brothers did he was aware, always, of the difference between them. They knew who they were and what life held in store for them, and he did not. Like Arthur, Mordred was charismatic and talented, blessed with natural gifts, and yet he followed a very different path.

It is one of the great mysteries of existence why—with similar beginnings—the outcome is often so very different. Siblings who resemble each other physically, and who may have comparable natural gifts, often develop into adults with very different attitudes to life and enjoy different levels of success, both material and psychological. Psychologists will point to subtle differences in the emotional climate that perhaps favored one child over another. Metaphysicians will think of karmic burdens or accumulated wisdom. Both Arthur and Mordred grew up believing themselves illegitimate, facing a future—they thought—severely circumscribed by the limitations of their birth. Arthur's inner light shone forth regardless, while Mordred succumbed to the darkness.

The differences between Arthur and Mordred can be traced to the developmental wounds suffered by Mordred at the first and second chakras, where the differences, rather than the similarities, of his and Arthur's experience were manifest. Though Arthur did not know who his biological parents were, his physical and emotional development was nurtured within a stable and loving environment. And most important, Arthur's moral and intellectual development was supervised by Merlin.

Mordred was raised in a household characterized by its instability and unpredictability. He and his foster brothers came to their mother's notice when she was bored and wished for distraction or entertainment. They were there to serve her needs, but their own needs received no priority from her. Their tutors and trainers were indifferent, and their education spotty, but while Gawain and his brothers at least knew who they were and could look forward to an inheritance and some status, Mordred had no stable foundation at all. And where Arthur enjoyed the guidance of Merlin, wise Avatar, Mordred had only Morgause, who used her natural psychic ability to manipulate people and situations for her own power and ego.

Merlin symbolizes the Right use of psychic abilities. Merlin may have been born with natural psychic sensitivity, but he was trained in the use of that ability, and was highly educated, not only in healing and herbal lore but in the sciences, mathematics, astronomy and philosophy. He was a poet and a musician and an engineer, he spoke several languages, and was something of a Renaissance man in his talents and abilities. Most of all, his life was dedicated to spirit, and he lavished on Arthur the benefit of his learning and wisdom, as well as a deep love. (This view of Merlin is best seen in Mary Stewart's *Merlin Trilogy.*)

Morgause symbolizes the shadow side or misuse of psychic ability. She is usually portrayed as very beautiful—and much of her power over men is no more magical than that—but she was also a practitioner of the dark side of magick, the manipulation and abuse of psychic gifts to increase her personal power over others.

Mordred maintained a healthy skepticism in his evaluation of his foster mother yet she was the only mother he knew, and the only example of psychic power available to him. The foundations of his character were already laid when he was called to Camelot, and though he consciously rejected the control or guidance of Morgause he was at a deep level influenced by her and her approach to reality. Where Arthur was loved and respected at the court of Ector and Flavilla, even though the fiction of his secondary status was maintained, we can only speculate at the psychological and emotional climate prevailing within the orbit of Morgause's energy field.

As humans we are social beings. We find ourselves within communities. We establish the foundation of our being and sense of who we are through the support of our primary group at the first chakra, and through the reflections that we see of ourselves in others at the second chakra. Arthur and Mordred began their life journeys with similar resources and similar challenges, but while Arthur was loved in his foster home, and was molded and guided by an enlightened being, Mordred knew only a kind of benign neglect and a climate of emotional unpredictability in his foster home. And his only experiences of spiritual power were the distorted and manipulative magical practices of Morgause.

The myth, therefore, offers us two opposite examples of ways of being. But unlike Mordred, those of us not fortunate enough to be cocooned in love and bombarded with healthy, positive energy in our formative years now have enormous resources at our disposal to heal the wounds to the lower chakras. At any time, we can choose to follow Merlin or Morgause, to feed the light, or drift into the darkness that can manifest in destructive tendencies towards others or towards the self. Darkness is only absence of light, and there are now numerous flints available to kindle the flames that will bring light into the dark spaces of the psyche.

Mordred lacked a healthy first and second chakra foundation that would have allowed him to feel safe and to trust, and would have given him the ability to bend with the winds of fortune. He found himself on the threshold of third chakra dominance with only the talent for manipulation and belief in power over—the distorted shadow side of Manipura chakra—that he had learned at Morgause's knee. Much as he loved Arthur—as much as he was capable of loving—he never found the inner strength to risk trust.

The Battle of Camlann

The August moon hovered just above the treetops, surrounding the silhouettes of the trees in a silver halo. On the ground the air was still, but high in the sky the wind tossed fragments of cloud across the heavens. Mordred could hear the night sounds of an army preparing for battle, some warriors sleeping restlessly, others talking softly or passing the time with dice. All around him were the glowing embers of countless fires, and far in the distance the pin pricks of light that signaled the fires of the other army, the enemy.

How had it ever come to this? That Mordred was to face in battle the king he loved and revered above all others? That the "enemy" should be his father?

Arthur had appointed Mordred regent during his campaign in Gaul, and Mordred had been faithful in his execution of Arthur's orders. But then had come the battle with the pretender Lucius, and the news of Arthur's death. And suddenly Mordred was no longer the agent of power but power itself. And he discovered in himself what he had always known, that he had the ability to rule and to lead. And he found that he had become the beacon that attracted the allegiance of a vast army of those who had no love for Arthur: the treaty Saxons, as well as those disaffected noblemen at court who for their own reasons felt slighted by Arthur; those who envied him; the generation of warriors who had been too young to participate in the twelve battles, and who were spoiling for a fight because they saw no honor or excitement in keeping the peace.

Then had come the news that Arthur was still alive and on his way home to reclaim his kingdom. Only then, after having known power, Mordred found he could not put it aside, not even for Arthur. He had considered countless options—shared power, Arthur's abdication or honored retirement—but the option of stepping aside and awaiting the uncertain return of power he was not willing to choose. It was uncertain only because Mordred had never learned to trust in anyone but himself. Not even the years at Arthur's side—honored and cherished and ultimately, after the death of Galahad on the quest, the declared heir—had managed to overcome his early conditioning.

The sun rose on the "wicked day" of reckoning. The battle was joined soon after dawn and continued throughout the day as the two armies well matched in numbers and strength hacked each other to pieces. And with the dying sun, Arthur and Mordred found themselves facing each other, surrounded by the fallen bodies of their friends and comrades. They were both exhausted. They circled each other with barely the strength to move their feet and to hold their swords, until in one final burst of energy they flung themselves on each other. Excalibur struck home, and Mordred fell, but in his fall his sword too inflicted a mortal—perhaps—wound on Arthur.

Arthur was dying. And he was alone. He tried to raise Excalibur but had not the strength to honor his promise to the Lady of the Lake and he sank back into the mud at the edge of the lake. Against his will his eyes closed and his world became dark and silent. Silent, and ever more dark. Nothingness.

"Arthur!" It was a voice he knew, not the voice of angels as yet. He forced his leaden lids to open and looked into the weathered and blood-smeared face of Bedivere, his Companion from the earliest days. Arthur grasped Bedivere's hand and in a voice that was little more than a croaking whisper told him to take Excalibur and throw it into the lake. Bedivere thought he was delirious. He took the sword and hid it under a tree, and returned to tell Arthur that he had thrown the sword into the water.

"And what did you see?" Arthur asked.

"Nothing but waves and winds," Bedivere replied.

Arthur sank back on the ground. A tear escaped and trickled down his face. "Do not lie to me, old friend. This is not a request. It is my final order as your High King: throw the sword into the lake."

Bedivere retrieved the sword. Arthur gazed over the water as Bedivere swung back his arm and threw the mighty sword over the lake. It flashed as it tumbled point over hilt, reflecting the dying sun, until it fell hilt first towards the water. Arthur saw a lady's hand appear out of the water; the hand grasped the sword and held it aloft for a moment before drawing it down beneath the surface.

Arthur lost consciousness. He was not aware of the barge approaching, nor of the four priestesses who lifted him into it and sailed with him back to Avalon.

Mordred's desperate bid for power cost him everything. It was focused on the second chakra, where we identify power with externals: social or political status, money, physical appearance. Second chakra wars are fought for territory, resources and ego. It is at the second chakra, Caroline Myss points out, that we typically store our weapons: guns, knives, and swords are worn on the belt.

But while Mordred's frantic gamble cost him everything, it cost Arthur nothing. Nothing. Arthur had already fulfilled his purpose as a beacon of light and an example of right action. It was a beacon that continued to shine through the dark centuries to follow until the time was ripe for Arthur's return.

With no unifying leader the tribes of Britain succumbed to the forces of invasion. Saxons, Angles and Jutes, fleeing floods in their low-lying homelands in what are now Germany and Denmark, had already colonized the eastern shores of Britain. After the "brief shining moment" of Arthur's reign they continued their inexorable expansion westward, and new arrivals continued to swell the population of those already settled. They would in time establish Angle-land, England, that was a collection of independent Anglo Saxon kingdoms. And once established, like the Celts before them, they would suffer plundering raids, by the Danes and the Vikings this time, and then conquest by the Normans.

The surviving Celts were pushed into the farthest western reaches of Wales and Cornwall. Many left the shores of Great Britain for Less Britain, what became Brittany in northwestern France. There, for hundreds of years, they felt themselves in exile, nourished with their mother's milk on bardic songs and stories of the legendary King Arthur. In 1066 they returned to Britain at the side of the Norman king William the Conqueror to "liberate" their homeland and establish, for the first time since Arthur, a unified nation within the shores of Britain. They brought with them the elaborated myth of Arthur, a most Christian king by now, who became the ideal for the age of chivalry.

Whether or not the grave in Glastonbury Abbey is that of King Arthur, in legend he is the once and future king: the king who reigned in a past golden age and the king who will return at some future time. Arthur, or the seed that Arthur planted, the seed of honor and justice and kindness, will come to fruition when the time is right.

Mankind had to wait more than a thousand years before it was again ready to consider building a society based on Arthurian ideals. After the fall of the Roman Empire and the end of King Arthur's reign night descended on Europe. In the period known as the Dark Ages hordes of barbarian tribes swept over the continent: libraries were burned; learning and art and culture were lost; the great cities of the Roman Empire were sacked; sheep and goats grazed in the ruins of the Roman Colosseum.

Then we began slowly to crawl out of the pit of darkness. There was the great architectural flowering of the Gothic era; the rise of city-states and nation states; the artistic blossoming of the Renaissance; and finally we began to flirt again with some of the concepts introduced by the legends of King Arthur. Changes in the power structure gradually evolved in Britain, while in France and the United States they were introduced by revolution. France fought its revolution for liberty, equality and fraternity and almost lost them again in the blood of the revolution's excesses. The United States fought its revolutionary war to claim the inalienable rights of life, liberty and the pursuit of happiness, though those rights, when won, were afforded only to some. The architect of the Declaration of Independence was himself an owner of slaves, and the female half of the population as well as those without property were excluded. Jefferson articulated the ideal, but those truths that he claimed were self-evident were slow to manifest for certain sectors of the population. Only in the past few generations has political and legal equality been extended to African Americans and to women, and we still have a way to go before those legal concepts become ingrained and accepted in our social and emotional attitudes.

In the Age of Enlightenment there was a belief that man was evolving towards perfection. There was even a belief that that perfection was close at hand, a belief that fueled the various idealistic movements of the nineteenth century. Idealism in the political arena took the form of various movements to bring about the ideal social structure, based on this conviction of the basic goodness of man and the innate drive towards the expression of that goodness. A tenet of Marxism—"from each according to his ability, to each according to his need"—is a fourth chakra concept, one of unconditional love towards our fellows. It transcends the selfish acquisitive drive of the shadow second chakra, and the selfish power drive of the shadow third, to envision a society—not of equally bestowed natural gifts, which is obviously not the case and over which we have no control—but of equally shared responsibility and reward, based on ability and need.

Obviously, we were not yet anywhere near perfection and the fate of the socialist movement is all too familiar. In the first country to proclaim itself a socialist state Lenin introduced the shadow first chakra concept of the violent overthrow of the existing power structure and paved the way for Stalin's pitiless totalitarianism, with which communism is now identified. In the West, the late nineteenth century saw the triumph of the shadow second chakra qualities of materialism and greed in the robber barons and the Gilded Age. Society valued and respected the power of money above all else, a situation that still persists for the most part more than a century later.

Nineteenth century anarchism, too, had its roots in an idealistic view of man. Whereas socialism blamed corrupt institutions for social injustice, anarchism blamed corrupt individuals and set out to eliminate them via assassination. They thus attempted to realize a fourth chakra ideal through shadow first chakra means, and the movement self-destructed on its internal contradictions. The word "anarchism" itself is now synonymous with chaos and senseless violence, and all vestiges of its idealistic beginnings have been forgotten.

Is it true, then, as the cynics among us will have it, that our "basic nature" is selfish and greedy, and that all political structures not based on this premise are doomed to fail? It would seem, as we look at the historical record, to be so. But then we remember that most of our history has been written by and to the advantage of the winners in the myriad win/lose scenarios of our collective past. Until recently we have accepted their accounts and interpretations as "fact," but in recent years we have begun to take another look at the historical record through a different lens.

Riane Eisler in *The Chalice and the Blade* introduces us to a mid-European partnership culture that predated the cultures based on the dominator model that has been the model for all of our recorded history. We are challenged by this work to open our minds to the possibility that a fully functional society can be based on equality and partnership rather than domination by one sector of society over another, whether it be based on gender, birth, color, or economic status. Eisler is telling us that this notion does not belong only to the various utopian theorists whose ideas have been judged unworkable because they contradicted "basic human nature"; it belongs in our history. And it is a society exemplified by the golden age of King Arthur.

On the world stage in the last century, the bloodiest in all human history, we had examples of both traditional second chakra and revolutionary fourth chakra responses to injustice. We experienced two World Wars and innumerable local wars; wars of liberation; wars of terrorism; wars of ideology and of religion; and a terrifying "Cold War" that shadowed more than two generations. In the Middle East, cradle of our civilization and of our religious traditions, nations continue to respond to violence and force with greater violence and force, a second chakra perception of power.

In India, on the other hand, Mahatma Gandhi's tactics of non-violent non-cooperation with the British, and his own sacrifice in carrying out hunger strikes, led to the liberation of his country. The Dalai Lama continues to respond with love and compassion to the violent takeover of his country by the Chinese. Martin Luther King pioneered the drive for racial equality through non-violent action.

These tactics take time in order to achieve results, more than a lifetime in some cases, and demand a degree of patience that we in the West do not yet possess. (A woman who attended a lecture I gave on the chakras asked me: "How long does all this take?") A perspective that not only takes the long view, but a multi-lifetime view, of human destiny is one as yet foreign to most of us and certainly to the leaders of Western democracy who look no further than the next election. Perhaps we could say that the Dalai Lama's tactics have not worked against the Chinese, because more than half a century later Tibet still is not free. But in the long term we may find that the Dalai Lama's example and the teachings of Tibetan Buddhism—out in the world now, no longer locked within the borders of a small mountain theocracy—will have a greater lasting impact on the world stage than the brutality of a few generations.

In German there is a wonderful word *Zeitgeist*, which means more or less "the spirit of the times." The spirit of our times may be the recognition that not only our growth, but our survival, depend upon recognizing that we are part of a greater whole. Each of us, according to a Native American tradition, is a strand in the basket of life, of a unique color and texture. Without each individual strand the basket is not complete. Each of us not only takes from the whole, being nourished and supported by it, but we each give our own unique contribution. We choose whether to create a healthy, balanced and beautiful basket, or one that is a frayed, weak and leaky container of the life force.

Here is a provocative thought, offered by Guy Murchie. The average breath contains about 10 sextillion atoms, or 10 to the 22nd power. The entire atmosphere contains about the same number of breaths. So every time you inhale you breathe in an average of one atom from each of the breaths contained in the whole sky. And every time you exhale you are sending back into the atmosphere the same average of one atom to each of the breaths inhaled by every other living person. This exchange is repeated about twenty thousand times a day by some seven billion people, and it means that every breath that each of us takes must contain a quadrillion (ten to the 15th power) atoms breathed by the rest of mankind within the past few weeks, and more than a million atoms breathed at some time by every person who ever lived. Every time you breathe, you breathe in more than a million atoms breathed by Jesus, by Buddha, by

Socrates, by Mahatma Gandhi and the Dalai Lama. And by Hitler and Stalin and Idi Amin and Genghis Khan and Osama bin Laden.

Even at the physical level, therefore, we are not separate beings. We are constantly exchanging atoms and molecules. The field of quantum physics has taught us that matter and energy are interchangeable. When we break matter down to the subatomic level, whether we find a particle or an energy wave depends on what we are looking for. In other words, the energy of the scientist's mind affects the outcome of the experiment. We are all part of a Whole, and Spirit is the unifying and animating force or energy that binds us all together. Different religions represent the many ways in which people have tried to understand and communicate about that force, and they have had to use the languages of symbolism, myth, and parable, because it cannot be reduced to logical analysis. At the most basic level they are all saying the same thing, and what they have in common is more important than what separates them.

The early Christian church understood that its success depended in large measure on grafting the new belief system onto the old, and one of the ways of making Christianity more easily acceptable was to subsume the already existing festivals and rituals. Easter, for example, is the Christian version of the pagan fertility festival Oestre, hence its inclusion of the egg and the rabbit which have nothing to do with the Passion. The timing of Christmas has nothing to do with the actual date of Jesus' birth and everything to do with its proximity to the Winter Solstice.

The early church wanted to be *catholic*, which means universal, and sought to bring all Christianity under one roof. Then for several centuries we went in the opposite direction; the Roman Catholic Church split off from the Eastern Orthodox Church, and the Protestants split off into numerous sects that are still subdividing themselves. Several years ago the Dalai Lama organized a series of concerts around the world to celebrate the music of the world's religions: the sacred music of pre-Columbian America, Jewish and Catholic sacred music, the various flavors of Protestantism, Native

American. One church in Dresden, Germany, would not participate, because they did not want foreign religions in their church.

That kind of thinking appears, finally, to be on the wane, and more and more of us are turning to the commonalities of our experience and recognizing that what unites us is the spiritual context in which we live and move and have our being. Everything that we say and do and think and feel is spiritual. We cannot separate the spiritual from any of the ways in which we express who we are. Everything is spiritual: every act, every thought, every relationship, every experience. And the way in which spiritual energy works, at each stage of our physical, emotional, cognitive and psychological development, can be understood within the conceptual framework of the chakras.

The work of the lower chakras is to bring light into our places of shadow as we confront our tests: survival issues; challenges in relationships; fears of vulnerability and betrayal; the seduction of earthly power and wealth; threats to self-esteem and our sense of self; temptations to dominate and manipulate in order to create a comforting illusion of safety and power. As each of these shadows is brought into the light we strengthen our individual will, until we discover, after we pass through the doorway of the heart, that at the fifth chakra there is no longer any conflict between individual will and divine will, and that surrender to "thy will not mine" means only that we are finally in alignment with our divine purpose.

We have lived through millennia of dualism, of separation into east and west, masculine and feminine, science and religion, sacred and profane. Perhaps that separation was necessary in order for us to understand the component parts, and perhaps now is the time for integration, for putting it all back together into a new understanding of the wondrous whole. It is a time of renewed interest not only in the spirituality of eastern countries but also the spirituality of our own pagan past, when we understood that there was no separation between heaven and earth, and that the divine was in all things.

We stand on the threshold of a new age of integration, and that is one of the reasons why the Arthurian myth is particularly relevant right now. It is time for the return of "the once and future king," not only as war duke to lead in battle (balancing and cleansing the lower chakras) but also to send us within, to the inner light and truth of the upper chakras. That is why the legends hold such fascination for us. It is the return of the inner Arthur, the best that we each individually can be. We have finally evolved to the point where we can begin to realize, to manifest in our own beings, the ideals of King Arthur's reign.

As we each heed the Merlin within we will reach towards an understanding of Oneness, a recognition that we are all part of the same whole. We are the king that was and the king that will be. "What was" is the spiritual dimension that we came from, the Oneness that breathed us forth in order to learn and grow through the experience of being in physical form. "What will be" looks forward to when we recognize why we are here, when we learn what this physical dimension has to teach us, and when we integrate the knowing that is the gift of this specific experience in time and place and return to the full awareness of spiritual oneness.

In the legends, then, after the Battle of Camlann, a woman—Morgan, or the Lady of the Lake, or a Priestess of the Holy Grail—washed Arthur's wounds in the healing waters and bore him to the sacred isle of Avalon, there to rest until it would be time to be born again. Avalon itself disappeared into the mist. It was believed that only by being removed into another dimension would Avalon be safe from the [lower chakra] threats of the physical world.

Spiritual communities—mystery schools, and monasteries—serve the earth by withdrawing from physical and emotional concerns and entanglements, building and channeling spiritual power through ritual prayer and meditation and offering that power to the world. The world, by and large, has respected those communities, partly under threat—in the Christian tradition—of damnation and eternal hellfire. But in Britain the Romans had destroyed the Druid isle of Mona, and Roman Christianity was imposing its patriarchal structure on the Christian world. Avalon had to withdraw beyond the mists, in fact or in belief, because those believers who remained needed to know that somewhere their gods were being revered and their spiritual power was still a force for the good.

According to legend, then, King Arthur did not die. He sleeps on the Isle of Avalon, and will awaken and return again to lead his people in time of need. And so we journey to the Avalon of the heart to awaken the sleeping Arthur, the archetype that has been sleeping in the depths of our psyche, the archetype that is the blueprint for the expression of our inner light. The Child of Light, the Mabon, the spark that was ignited at our conception at the Spring Solstice and came into the world at Midwinter, has been quietly maturing along with us, and has been "sleeping," waiting for this moment when in full consciousness we awaken him and bring him out into the world.

Night fell on the fair isle of Britain. Arthur slept. But his name and the golden age of his reign lived on in song and story and the dreams of Britons. In the way of myth they traveled the pathways of the global mind until the name of King Arthur and the human potential that he exemplified became an inspiration in countries far from the cool green land of his life, under tropical palms and beneath volcanic mountains and alongside oriental rivers.

Arthur slept. Until it was time to awaken. The time is now.

Avalon of the Heart meditation: quest for the Holy Grail

In your sacred place, free of interruptions, take some deep cleansing breaths and invoke the Triple Shield of Light.

We have followed the story of King Arthur from his mystical conception at Spring Equinox and birth at midwinter, through his early life and education when he was unaware of who he was, to finding his sword and claiming his rightful place as king. We have seen him fight his battles and establish peace and safety in the land, and administer that peace according to principles of justice and respect and equality. And now it is time to turn to nurturing the spirit, and the quest for the Holy Grail.

Imagine, then, that you are a Companion of the Round Table. You have fought beside Arthur during the twelve battles; you have helped him to maintain the peace and learned from him the principles of a conscious life. And now you are riding forth from Camelot on the quest for the Holy Grail. You know that spiritual teachings are to be found all around you: in nature, in the animals and birds; in the fellow travelers you will meet on your journey; in your memories. They are to be found in the colors of the sunset and the configurations of clouds, and in rainbows and in the smiles or tears of a child. As you ride your mind and heart are open to the messages and guidance all around you, as you release any need for maps and plans and guarantees, and trust in your intuition to recognize the way.

Following your intuition, you find yourself on the shores of a lake. It is autumn, and the leaves are gold, orange and scarlet. The sun is setting into the water, sinking into its brilliant gold reflection. The sky is a dazzling palette, echoing the colors of the leaves. Gold, scarlet, purple: the entire western sky is brilliant color. Far away, through the mists that hover over the water, you can see a barge coming across the water. It has come to take you to the island that is hidden in the mists. The boatman expertly brings the barge ashore at your feet, and there is a scraping sound as it comes to a stop with its prow on the shore. The boatman helps you aboard and pushes off, and as you sail across the water the sun disappears over the western horizon, and the evening takes on the mystical quality of twilight. As the barge glides into the mist, the world seems to disappear. There is no sound but the gentle slap of the oars on the water. The mist is cool and damp on your face. You lose all sense of direction and have to place your trust totally in the boatman.

The barge is taking you to your own personal Avalon of the heart. You emerge from the mist and as you approach the island you begin to notice details. Only you can describe this island that you know is a sacred place. Here you will find and awaken the sleeping Arthur within you, the Arthur who will send you forth on your quest for the Holy Grail. What kind of an island is it? Is it low and green, covered with trees or grasses? Or is it rocky, thrusting up out of the water? The details become clearer as you approach, and now the barge deposits you on the shore and you find that, awaiting you there, is someone who will guide you to the sleeping Arthur. Perhaps it is Merlin, or Morgan, or the Lady of the Lake.

Follow your guide. Perhaps you will find Arthur in a circle of standing stones. Or in a cave. Or maybe there is a Grail Castle here. … When you find him, look upon the sleeping Arthur and listen to your intuition. Is it time to awaken him? When you decide that it is time, he will send you on your quest for the Holy Grail, for your personal symbol of the quest for enlightenment. Perhaps it will be one of the traditional symbols: a cup, or a bowl, a sword, spear, book, stone, jewel. Or perhaps it will be a symbol unique and specific to you. Whatever it is, you will take it into your heart. Full understanding and integration will come when the time is right. …

When you are ready, begin to bring your focus back into the outer world, and take some time to write or draw about your Avalon and your inner Arthur in your Quest Journal.

Selected Bibliography

As mentioned elsewhere, there is an immense body of work on the Arthurian legends, greater than on the Bible. These are only the works quoted or referred to in the text. For the many more that I have read and loved and been influenced by, I can only say thanks.

Alcock, L. (1971, 2001). *Arthur's Britain.* London: Penguin Group.
Ashe, G. (1987). *The Landscape of King Arthur.* (A delightful tour of the British Isles to visit all the sites that claim a connection with King Arthur. Photographs.)
(1985) *The Discovery of King Arthur.* A historical context of King Arthur, an examination in layman's terms of the historical evidence, and the development of King Arthur's myth.
Bargent, M, Leigh R., and Lincoln, H. *Holy Blood, Holy Grail.*
Brown, D. (2004). *The Da Vinci Code*
Cahill, T. (1995). *How the Irish Saved Civilization.*
Campbell, J. (1988). *The Power of Myth*
- (1974). *The Mythic Image*
Carr-Gomm, P. (1993). *The Druid Way.*
- (1996). *The Druid Renaissance.*
Chefitz, M. (2001). *The Seventh Telling*
Crowley, V. (1998). *Celtic Wisdom.*
Durant, G. M. (1969). *Britain. Rome's Most Northerly Province. A History of Roman*
Britain AD 43-450.

Eisler, R. (1987) *The Chalice and the Blade.*

Gardner, L. (2000). *Bloodline of the Holy Grail*

Geoffrey of Monmouth. (1136, 1966). *The History of the Kings of Britain.*

Goodrich, N. L. (1986) *King Arthur.*

- (1988) *Merlin*

- (1992) *The Holy Grail*

Graves, R. (1948, 1975). *The White Goddess*

Hopkins, A. (1993). *Chronicles of King Arthur.* A collection of original sources, with commentary, color reproductions of Arthurian paintings and black and white etchings, and photographs of Arthurian sites.

Judith, A. (1996). *Eastern Body Western Mind*

Khalsa, S. K. (2001). *Kundalini Yoga.*

Malory, T. (1485, 1975). *Le Morte d'Arthur.*

Markale, J.1995). *Merlin. Priest of Nature.*

Murchie, G. (1978, 1999). *The Seven Mysteries of Life.*

Myss. C. 1996). *Anatomy of the Spirit*

- (2001) *Sacred Contracts*

Nelson, J. (1994). *Healing the Split. Integrating Spirit Into Our Understanding of the Mentally Ill.*

Pagels, E. (1989). *The Gnostic Gospels.*

Pascal, E. (1992). *Jung to Live By.*

Sharkey, J. (1975, 1987). *Celtic Mysteries.*

Shlain, L. (1998). *The Alphabet Versus the Goddess*

Snyder, C. (2000). *The World of King Arthur.*

Starbird, M. (1993). *The Woman with the Alabaster Jar. Mary Magdalen and the Holy Grail.*

Stewart, M. (1980). *Merlin Trilogy.*

- (1983). *The Wicked Day*

Teresa of Avila. *The Interior Castle.*

White, T. H. (1939, 1965). *The Once and Future King.*

- (1939, 1977). *The Book of Merlyn.*

Zimmer Bradley, M. *The Mists of Avalon*

Printed and bound by PG in the USA